KEATS'S MAJOR ODES

KEATS'S MAJOR ODES

*An Annotated Bibliography
of the Criticism*

Jack Wright Rhodes

Greenwood Press
Westport, Connecticut • London, England

Library of Congress Cataloging in Publication Data

Rhodes, Jack Wright.
  Keats's major odes.

  Includes indexes.
  1. Keats, John, 1795-1821—Bibliography. 2. Odes—
History and criticism—Bibliography. I. Title.
Z8461.R48 1984 [PR4836]   016.821'7   83-16634
ISBN 0-313-23809-X (lib. bdg.)

Library of Congress Catalog Card Number: 83-16634
ISBN: 0-313-23809-X

First published in 1984

Greenwood Press
A division of Congressional Information Service, Inc.
88 Post Road West
Westport, Connecticut 06881

Printed in the United States of America

10 9 8 7 6 5 4 3 2 1

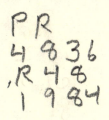
For Jean and Evan, with love

For ever Jung, and still to be enjoyed—
At least till the return of Dr. Freud.

Richard Harter Fogle

CONTENTS

ACKNOWLEDGEMENTS

First of all, I want to thank Jean Rucks Rhodes for her forbearance in times of tempestuousness or neglect which may have come in part, I would like to be allowed to believe, from the rigors of this undertaking. Thanks, too, for helpfulness in many intelligent ways when help has been wanted.

This book has been in part made possible by The Citadel Development Foundation, for whose support I am grateful. Thanks are also due to all my colleagues here at The Citadel for the time, advice, and encouragement which they contributed so generously. I am particularly indebted to Philip Leon for his experienced guidance and to David Allen for his untiring and cheerful aid in the wearisome task of reading proof.

Though it would be impossible to repay Morse Peckham the fullness of his contribution to this project, I would like to thank him here for his free-flowing intellectual stimulation and exemplary scholarly guidance. I am also grateful to George Geckle and Ashley Brown for their unselfish donations of time, support, and advice, to Eugene Long for his careful judgments, and to G. Ross Roy for his interest, encouragement, and counsel.

Various library staff members of the Thomas Cooper Library of the University of South Carolina have also laid claim to gratitude and appreciation: Jean Rhyne by her wonderful resourcefulness and unfailing helpfulness; Virginia Ashley, Harriet Oglesbee, and Michelle Yarus by their painstaking tenacity; and Caroline Lundy by her good-humored patience. Thanks, too, to the generous people of the Louis Round Wilson Library at the University of North Carolina and the William R. Perkins Library at Duke University. And, finally, I want to thank Herb Nath and the rest of the faculty and staff of the Daniel Library at The Citadel. To all of the people mentioned above, and to many more, I will remain truly grateful.

INTRODUCTION

John Keats's odes are among the most famous poems in English litera-
ture. The list of people who have felt a need to make a written reaction to
them is impressive. Here is a sample of the artists who have had some-
thing to say about them: Robert Bridges, Edward Burne-Jones, Algernon
Charles Swinburne, Oscar Wilde, Matthew Arnold, Coventry Patmore,
Gerard Manly Hopkins, Vincent Van Gogh, James Russell Lowell, John
Ruskin, George Meredith, T. S. Eliot, André Gide, William Faulkner, D.
H. Lawrence, Conrad Aiken, Amy Lowell, W. B. Yeats, Allen Tate,
Aldous Huxley, W. H. Auden, Archibald MacLeish, Jorge Luis Borges, F.
Scott Fitzgerald, Wilfred Owen, Stanley Kunitz, and Stephen Spender.
Among recent scholars and critics, the odes have moved men of such
stature as Gilbert Highet, Harold Bloom, Geoffrey Tillotson, Harry
Levin, F. R. Leavis, E. M. W. Tillyard, Kenneth Burke, Marshall
McLuhan, William Empson, and A. C. Bradley. Nineteenth century
figures for whom the odes demanded response include Clarence
Stedman, Jonathan Gilmer Speed, Edmund Gosse, Mrs. Oliphant,
Sidney Lanier, W. J. Courthope, Walter Bagehot, George Gilfillan, and
Sir Sidney Colvin. Whenever basic questions have arisen concerning
literature and its functions, the odes have been a part of the attempt to
answer them. The odes are so germinal to English literature that they
have been used as a standard by which to determine its nature. One
critic, in fact, went so far as to use them as his very definition of poetry: a
poem is any piece of writing which succeeds in the way the odes have.
Because of the fame and influence of these poems, a study of the trends
in the responses to them can reveal with particular clarity something of
the nature of the development of literary culture from 1820 to the
present.

For the first forty years after the publication of Keats's odes in 1819-20,
readers' reactions to them were largely evaluative. However, Keats
criticism in the early years was first tainted and later warped by political
considerations. John Gibson Lockhart's unfortunate essay in *Blackwood's*

associating Keats with the "Cockney School of Poetry" was, as is generally acknowledged today, more of an attack on the politics of Leigh Hunt than on the poetry of John Keats. It is regrettable that Keats was not in a position to interpret it that way. And even though this essay, as well as the equally damning one by Croker in the *Quarterly Review,* was directed at the admittedly diffuse and "immature" "Endymion," the epithet "cockney" continued to frequent Keats criticism up to the time of his death, when Shelley's "Adonais" replaced it with an equally misleading account of Keats. However, this whole matter of Keats's personal reputation is somewhat incidental to the issue of the trends in the responses to the odes—"somewhat," but not "entirely" incidental, for, as will be shown later, Keats's life became an important means of responding to his poetry for many readers. However, neither Keats's cockneyism nor his alleged death-by-review influenced directly the way people responded to the odes. When critics discussed Keats's Whig association or his treatment by the Tory reviewers, they did not often at the same time consider the odes as poetry, and vice versa.

Critics' first reactions to the odes had as their purpose the determination of whether or not the poems should be recommended to the general reading public and the quotation of such lines as would give the reader an idea of the kind of poetry to be found in them. It is fair to say that the odes were widely and well received in 1820, especially when one takes into consideration that they amounted to what Keats labeled in the title "Other Poems." There is no evidence that Keats himself valued the odes over his other works. Although his letters recorded his ambitions for "Lamia" and "The Eve of St. Agnes," the odes received no mention at all. "To Autumn" almost surfaced in the letter to Reynolds of September 1819, but Keats was more interested there in the weather than in the poem.[1] The reviewers of the 1820 volume, as might be expected, reflected the author's attitude. They gave greater consideration to the title works than to the shorter lyrics which fleshed out the book.[2]

In spite of the fact that the odes were considered minor works by Keats's contemporaries, however, they did receive a considerable amount of comment, most of it favorable. Of seventeen essays concerning Keats published in 1820, there were only seven which contained no mention of the odes. It ought to be remembered at this point, too, that, human nature being what it is, we should not necessarily assume that every reviewer of this work had read every poem in it. The only one of the odes treated harshly was "Urn." It was criticized for striking a trite conceit in the phrase "ditties of no tone"[3] and attacked as an example of Keats's unfortunate obsession with mythology and his tendency to ignore the problems of real life.[4] On the other hand, "Urn" was also highly praised; it was, in the opinion of one critic, the best of the minor poems, "many of which possess considerable merit."[5] The pattern of reception thus established for "Urn"—extreme praise and extreme censure—was one that was to last for many decades. "Nightingale" was awarded the most consistent praise of all the odes; "Autumn" also was quoted and lauded often. Neither "Psyche" nor "Melancholy" received any public notice at all that first year.

II

One of the main problems the romantics struggled with was the concept of self. The collapse of Enlightenment thinking, resulting from the debacle of the French Revolution among other things, made it no longer possible for man to consider himself a part of Nature and a member of a vast scheme. He lost his well-established place along with the order of things and was forced to create one for himself. Whereas in the Enlightenment mode he had defined himself in relation to the forces he saw in operation in the world, now he turned inside within himself to discover a sense of identity. This concern for the self resulted in the intense personal element in romantic poetry. Examples of it abound; Wordsworth's "Prelude," supreme among them, traces a stage in the author's psychological development. It is by title "An Autobiographical Poem." The nineteenth century poet, impelled by the need to establish an identity from within, often wrote this kind of highly personal poetry. The critic, working under the same assumption as the poet, was naturally led to discover in a poem those parts of it which might have been derived from the author's personal experience. It was not until the twentieth century, however, that the act of criticism was to become fully romanticized and critics began to find in poems reflections, not of the authors' personal experiences, but of their own: the "what this poem means to me" approach.

Perhaps because of the dramatic quality of Keats's life and the pathos arising from its brevity, Keats has been the subject of a large amount of biographical criticism. "Adonais" was not instigatory but reflective of this trend. Biographical criticism of the odes began, logically enough, with Keats's close friends, those in a position to know something of his life before sketches began to be published. For example, Leigh Hunt, who had a greater effect on Keats's life than on his poetry, discussed "Nightingale" biographically in three separate publications. In his review of the 1820 volume, Hunt attempted to render the poem more "striking" to the reader by informing him that Keats had for some time been forced to contend with critical malignity while under the continuous strain of physical infirmity.[6] Hunt's assumption, unstated and perhaps unrealized, was that poetry ought to reflect an actual emotional response of the poet. By grounding the feelings expressed in "Nightingale" in Keats's life, he was validifying the poem, helping the reader to appreciate it by showing that it did what he conceived poetry ought to do. Hunt had good reason for insisting that "Nightingale" was a personal poem—something that seems obvious to us today. It was a needful task in the early nineteenth century to instruct readers of the poem that it ought not to be approached with the same expectations as "Alexander's Feast" should. Dryden's famous poem and others like it exerted a predisposition in readers to find in an ode the formal working-out of a principle operating in the universe at large. Hunt wanted to make sure that the reader saw that Keats's was a different kind of ode.

There is good reason for the popularity of biographical criticism in the nineteenth century: it was a source of redemptive value. During this period, art replaced religion as the medium for the exercise of ascription of value. Unless man is capable of esteeming something other than himself, he will be unable to maintain a sense of self-worth, since the only difference in the two acts is the object; the mechanism is the same in each. When Enlightenment Christianity collapsed, art took its place in this operation. The primary function of art, after all, is to be appreciated. One is reminded of man's purpose in the Christian system: to glorify God. Art, then, stood as a source of value or value-creation, and what biographical criticism did was to reveal the artist's method of attaining that value. The implicit injunction to the reader was, "Go, thou, and do likewise." That was the relevance of it. Through it, the ideology of the self as a source for identity and value was spread.

Other romantic ideologies can be found in the early reactions to the odes as well. One of these is what has been called the "cult of the imagination." The religious applied to the secular involved here is more than just that of an *ex post facto* label; that label is descriptive in a comprehensive way of the itensity with which the imagination was revered. Since the nature of reality was no longer decreed by Christian dogma, but since man had to develop some notion of the nature of things in order to act, the role of the imagination was elevated to fill the need to interpret experience. The imagination is related to the concept of the self in this regard because it is an individual means of knowledge. Thus, along with the personal, it was one of the qualities that readers of the early nineteen hundreds found exciting in poetry.

Closely connected with imagination at this time was the concept of fancy. Although fancy was sometimes used interchangeably with imagination, it more often took the meaning Coleridge assigned to it in the *Biographia Literaria*. While he found imagination to be an "Agent of all human Perception," fancy was merely, ". . . a mode of Memory emancipated from the order of time and space."[7] The fancy, then, operated by joining things together in unusual and delightful combinations, but it was only a surface manipulation and redistribution of existence, not a penetrating or revealing insight into it. It may come as a surprise to the twentieth century reader of Keats that the ode which was most often criticized for excessive fancy was not "Nightingale," with its flight on the song of the imagination, or "Psyche," with its temple of the mind built to an unworshipped goddess, or "Melancholy," with its contrary doting upon sadness, but "Urn," a work which to many "modern" readers has embodied the essence of classical serenity and repose.

III

The decade of the 1870's was pivotal in the history of the reactions to the odes. The paucity of recorded thought about the odes in the 1860's— they were less written about in that decade than in any other—indicates that a trend in their interpretation was drawing to a close at this time. In the 1870's the number of written responses to them began to increase. It still was not large; there were only about half as many essays which discussed the odes in this decade as there had been in the 1840's. This was due in part, no doubt, to the publication of Milnes' influential and popular biography in 1848, but growth of population along with the increased concern for public literacy shown by the Education Act of 1870 more than compensates for that factor. Still, interest in the odes had been low in the sixties, and the seventies marked a change. The 1880's was to see the reactions to the odes more than double, and in the nineties they were to increase even more. The reason for the decline in the 1860's can perhaps be attributed to the second romantic generation's need to struggle for its own set of values instead of tamely accepting those of its predecessors. And along with rejecting their values, the new generation also rejected the vehicles for those values. For the succeeding group of readers, however, the odes offered no such associations, and their validity as value-sources was re-established, although on different grounds.

When the popularity of the odes began to increase again in the 1870's, most of the reactions to them were much the same as they had been previously. There were only a few hints that the odes were being considered in a new light. There are two main reasons that this should be so. First, cultural development is non-linear. Communication on a high cultural level is such a relatively rare thing that new ideas are communicated rather spasmodically. Thus, at any time in history there will be both people whose actions are governed by ideologies which have not yet been grasped by most and those whose actions are governed by ideologies long since abandoned by many. At no point will culture be homogeneous or coherent. From this point of view, the fact that the responses to the odes in the 1870's were for the most part characteristically similar to those of the preceding years and that there were a few novel responses merely indicates that the 1870's was an ordinary time in history. It is the fact that those few novel responses were adumbrations of a growing mode of response which makes this decade pivotal.

Second, writing involves a relatively high degree of consciousness, but response does not. In fact, writing is one process of bringing intuitions into consciousness and making them ideas. Perhaps the only difference between a feeling and an idea is that the one is articulated and the other is not. Response is non-rational; it cannot be controlled totally. One either likes paisley, for example, or one does not. This gap between reaction and writing sometimes engenders a situation in which a critic, aware of a stimulating response to a piece of literature, remains unaware of the precise nature of his own response. Nonetheless driven by his response and his occupation to discuss his source of stimulation in writing, however, the best he can do is discuss the work according to the scheme of values he has heard it discussed by before. His essay will be inadequate, then, to be sure, but it serves to express the sense of importance of its subject, if nothing else. And that sense of importance is all, at this juncture, that the critic is conscious of in his reaction to the work of literature. Such was the situation of many critics of Keats's odes in the 1870's. They were finding them exciting, yet they were not sure why. Unable to address them in a new way, yet driven by a new-found sense of their importance, they dealt with them the only way they knew how: with the language of the past.

For instance, earlier critics had frequently ascribed to the odes the classical qualities of tranquillity and simplicity under the adjective "Greek." No doubt these observations were spurred in part by Keats's having written about a Grecian urn. "On First Looking Into Chapman's Homer" may have served as an ancillary stimulus as well. In addition to Matthew Arnold's argument concerning the Greek-ness of "Urn" in *On the Study of Celtic Literature* (1867), the eighth edition of the *Encyclopaedia Britannica* (1857) also attributed those qualities to the poem.[8] Likewise, in 1843 a *Dublin University Magazine* critic wrote that "Urn" reminded him of "the scenic poets of Greece."[9] Then in 1873 Joseph Devey classified Keats as an Alexandrine poet and discussed "Psyche" and "Urn" in terms of their Greek qualities.[10] Again, in 1875, "Urn" was ascribed with "the tranquillity of Sophocles or of Phidias."[11]

Biographical criticism of the odes, which we have seen to have been popular from the first, also continued in the 1870's. William Cullen Bryant's two volume anthology edited in 1874 printed "Nightingale" with a headnote explaining that Keats had written the poem while "suffering from physical depression."[12] Joseph Severn, who lived to be eighty-five, was still offering biographical comments in the 1870's. William Graham reported a conversation with Severn which took place in 1879 in which Severn claimed credit for "Urn" on the basis of having been the one to show Keats the original vase.[13] His reference here is probably to the Townley Vase, which was housed in the British Museum, a place Keats and Severn frequently visited together.

Although there was much about the 1870's that was the same as in previous decades, there seems to be general agreement that these years also mark a turning point in British history. Many factors made this so. In politics, the second Reform Bill of 1867 extended the vote to parts of the working classes and gave the labor force a foothold in government. Economically, the nation began to experience a general drop in prices and a slowdown in the growth of the economy. This resulted in the beginnings of an erosion of faith in *laissez-faire* economics which led to increased government regulation of trade. Foreign influences also affected Britain's previously undisputed economic superiority, and Bismarck's defeat of France put Germany in a position to rival seriously British manufacturing and trade. The re-united States of America presented a threat now, as well. Japan was beginning to make itself felt economically, too. All these forces, coming as they did directly upon a period of blunt, idealistic optimism, supported an attitude of skepticism which became an analytical temper under the control of scientific methods.

It is not the purpose of this discourse to argue that the scientific method, which consists primarily of applied logic, originated in the 1870's. Indeed, such a *modus operandi* has likely existed enthymemically since the beginnings of thought, and it has been applied to literature since the time of medieval hermeneutics. However, the history of the criticism of Keats's odes suggests that an analytical approach to criticism began to appear in the 1870's after having been relatively little used since 1820 and possibly before. That analysis rather than synthesis may have been the direction in other facets of English culture may be hinted at by Samuel Butler's *The Way of All Flesh*, much of which was written in the 1870's, whose purpose was to dissect un-lovingly rather than to embellish Victorian society.

In 1877 there appeared the first source study for the odes. J. L. Warren submitted a query to *Notes and Queries* asking for the possible allusion in the last three lines of stanza seven of "Nightingale" ("The same that oft-times hath/Charm'd magic casements, opening on the foam/Of perilous seas, in faery lands forlorn").[14] Two weeks later Jonathan Bouchier published a reply, citing Leigh Hunt as his authority for saying that the scene came from some fairy tale.[15] This was not much help, of course; later source studies were to argue the same lines with greater particularity in the same journal. The real significance of this exchange is as a phenomenon, the dawning of the analytical approach to the odes. The assumption which underlies the study of the source behind a literary passage is presumably that such a knowledge will benefit an understanding of the work in question. When one reads the lines from "Nightingale" considered by Warren and Bouchier, for example, one can be guided in his interpretation of them by a knowedge of what Keats may have had in mind or may have expected his readers to have in mind when he described the fairy scene with window and sea. Knowing the context of previous such scenes can offer that guidance. However, Warren and Bouchier seem to have been unconcerned with interpreting these lines. The poem as a whole seems to have interested them even less. Their function was that of data gatherers in the tradition of Tycho Brahe, with the assumption that a literary Kepler would be along after them to draw conclusions. The nineteenth-century middle class virtue of postponing gratification fostered these data-gathering responses to literature. They did not prove to be an inchoative stage in the development of criticism, however; pure source studies continued to be made for the rest of the nineteenth century and into the twentieth, and without doubt someone, somewhere is preparing one at this moment.

Textual criticism of the odes began with Swinburne's dispute with the author of an *Athenaeum* article over a line in "Nightingale." When it was averred that Keats did not actually intend that the word "away" appear in line twenty ("And with thee fade away into the forest dim"),[16] Swinburne wrote a letter to the editor arguing that when Milnes had included it he had been correct.[17] Textual studies are similar to source investigations in that they do not necessarily have interpretation of literature as an immediate purpose. Since textual criticism deals with symbols in relative isolation from response, it cannot actually be a form of interpretation of the odes. It does constitute an interpretation of literature in general, however, for the act of textual criticism itself implies a judgment about how literature may appropriately be studied. The textual response to literature is implicitly scientific in that it argues disinterestedly for the use of a given symbol regardless of its implications for interpretation. Similarly, a scientist is not immediately concerned with the implications of his experiment; his role as scientist is to see that the results are accurate.

The decade of the 1880's was, in part, a continuation of the analytical temper born in the seventies; the force of this approach has continued to be felt right up to the present day. What took root in the seventies began to grow in the eighties. For the first time, the odes became more than poems to be read; they became subjects to be studied, and at length. There were, for example, three book-length studies of Keats published during this decade.[18] The analytic and experimental variety of approaches to literature displayed in these three longer works was also reflected in the growing number of periodical publications in the 1880's. The method of hypostatization, which involves "proving" a concept to be true by reference to empirical data, worked its influence on the vocabulary of literary criticism. Thus, John Mackinnon Robertson spoke in 1884 of the superiority of "Melancholy" over the other odes in terms one might rather expect to find in a technical journal: "I say that the last has a much higher average of felicitous phrase and cadence and a less percentage of the alloy of commonplace term and prosaic association than the others."[19] Robertson showed his concern for data, but many others were more interested in the concept. What we are discussing here is the concept of concept, which proves that we are still under some control of this ideology today. In the 1880's, many critics used the odes to help form a notion of Keats's poetry in general. To unify somehow the various ideas, sentiments, and directions of Keats's poetry became an increasingly important aim. In the eighteenth century, harmony was a value sign for creative artists, but in the 1880's, it became one for critics. In a lecture delivered on January 9, 1882, Oscar Wilde used "Urn" as an example of the poetic virtue of including nothing harsh, painful, or debatable in a poem.[20] As an outspoken advocate of aestheticism, Wilde certainly must have been aware of the controversy and debate over the last lines of this ode. It was his control by the ideology of order, harmony, and unity which led him to ignore these qualities. Other critics, however, have not been so generous; lines 49-50 have frequently been charged with being out of keeping with the rest of the poem and sometimes with the universe at large. Both kinds of treatment of the lines depend upon the ideology of coherent unity; in the one, the critic agrees with Keats's statement, and in the other he does not.

In this decade the interest in harmony and order developed into a corollary concern to formulate a set of beliefs for Keats which would subsume the ideas and feelings expressed in his poetry. Readers sought to form a hypothesis about Keats by using his poetry as data. As a result, we find in the criticism a great deal of talk about Keats's creed. The specific subject of this talk was usually the last two lines of "Urn."

To value order and unity means also to value the rationality it takes to perceive and produce them. For this reason, the sensuous qualities of Keats's poetry became a real issue in this decade. His ecstatic indulgence in sound, color, and taste countered the flow of analytical, methodical process. It was this conflict which kept Matthew Arnold from giving his entire approbation to Keats's poetry. He saw in "Urn" a yearning for the principle of beauty which was not sensuous but "an intellectual and spiritual passion," yet he could not help deploring the occasional outbursts of pure sensuousness.[21] Likewise, T. Hall Caine found cause in "Urn" to regret that Keats valued the senses too highly, though his overall evaluation of his poetry was favorable.[22] Not all readers objected to sensuousness, however. C. E. Tyrer, in his 1888 essay on the subject, argued that the odes were indeed highly sensuous, but that they were not sensual.[23] He felt that Keats used sensuousness, not for its own sake, but as an aid in demonstrating a higher moral lesson. Tyrer discriminated Keats's sensuous ideality, in this way, from Shelley's pure idealism. John Shairp also praised Keats's sensuousness for its transcendent qualities. Chapter Three of his book was entitled "The Spiritual Side Of Poetry," and it is here that we find the sensuousness of the odes extolled. Shairp especially praised "Autumn" for its record of the sensuous response of a human soul to the sights and sounds of fall.[24] So whether readers enjoyed or deplored Keats's sensuousness, it became an issue during this decade and has remained one through modern times. Yeats's picture of Keats in "Ego Dominus Tuus" as a schoolboy, "With face and nose pressed to a sweet-shop window," has remained one way of viewing his poetry up to the present day.

During the 1880's another interesting phenomenon began to emerge in people's reactions to the odes. The rhetoric employed began to be more consciously turned toward emotional effect. E. C. Stedman described "Nightingale" as "a strain that has a dying fall; music wedded to ethereal passion, to the yearning that floods all nature."[25] And Sidney Lanier remarked about "Melancholy":

> ... if one may say a word *obiter,* out of the fullness of one's heart—I am often inclined to think for all-in-all,—that is, for thoughts most mortally compacted, for words which come forth, each trembling and giving off light like a morning-star, and for the pure beauty of the spirit and strength and height of the spirit,— which, I say, for all-in-all, I am often inclined to think, reaches the highest height yet touched in the lyric line.[26]

The emotional lushness here and the aridity of John Mackinnon Robertson when he spoke of the percentages of commonplace terms in Keats's poetry are both secondary symptoms of each other. Each in its extremity reveals the shortcoming of the other, yet both were just being born in this decade and were to have further years of growth before them.

By the middle of the 1890's it had been a hundred years since Keats's birth. The kinds of responses given to the odes in this decade bear traits of the direction of the 1870's and 1880's toward objective, analytical, and experimental approaches, but the distance implied by those approaches between the reader and the poetry was augmented and reinforced by the distance of time. Less and less the odes were read for simple delight; more and more were they studies as documents of some kind, valuable perhaps because of their importance for literary history, perhaps because of their importance for the study of poetics, and perhaps for the "truth" to be found in them. This is not to say that the odes were incapable of receiving a spontaneous reaction; however, that kind of non-contingent, direct relationship between reader and ode had to be achieved; it did not come naturally. The reader was obliged first to disengage himself from his academic orientation to the poems, divest himself of his original reason for reading them, and then read them for no reason at all beyond curiosity and respond in a more immanent way. It should be remembered at this point, though, that no response is possible without a value field. Even if a poem is read purely for curiosity, the spontaneous reaction it effects determines reflexively and retroactively the value field upon which the poem is placed. The quality about Keats's odes which has kept them alive and actively discussed for over a hundred and fifty years has been their ability to disarm the reader of one value system through their beauty and vitality, and to vault him into a realm of reacting which he had not supposed existed. It is in this way that the odes have excited readers to offer such a multitude of varying interpretations. The door to this multitudinousness had been unlocked by the analytical nature of the 1870's, the handle had been turned in the 1880's, and now in the 1890's the door began to open.

One factor in the diversification of interest in Keats's poetry in the 1890's is the particularization which Keats studies underwent at that time. Excepting an isolated pair of items in *Notes and Queries* in 1877, this decade produced the first studies of Keats which concentrated solely on the odes. Heretofore, reactions to the odes had always been only a part of a larger study; often they had come in reviews of editions of Keats, often in general essays about Keats's life and work. In fact, there was a book-length study of Keats's odes published in 1897, one of the few works of that size which have been done on the subject, Arthur Downer's *The Odes Of Keats*.[27] This book serves as a good example of the character of this decade's reactions to the odes because of the diversity of approaches it contains. Within its covers can be found a chapter on Keats's life, one on his poetry in general, ones on each of the odes, including the fragmentary "Ode to Maia" and the inferior "Ode on Indolence," a chapter on the pre-Keatsian ode, and a brief bibliography. The format in the chapters covering the individual odes is remarkably consistent. Downer opened with a consideration of the background of the ode, including its publication data, details of composition, possible sources or influences, and general critical comments. Then he printed a text of the ode in question, followed by a metrical and, in some cases, formal discussion and an accounting of textual variations. In this part of the chapter he was wont to include charts illustrating the rhyme scheme of the ode and tracing with transversal lines the minor rhyme shifts from stanza to stanza. He also traced alliterative sounds through the ode in some detail. Finally, in a section labeled "Analysis," he gave a stanza-by-stanza reading of the ode in which he mixed paraphrase with comment, sometimes considering the opinions of previous critics. Throughout the analyses, Downer subjected the odes to biographical criticism which at times seems to have had as its purpose the use of the poetry to shed light on the life, rather than the other way around. Speculations on Keats's likes and dislikes, events in his life, and feelings he must have had, abound.

One indication that the odes were becoming in the 1890's subjects of study in addition to objects of appreciation is the growth of textual studies during this period. Textual scholarship has never been a dominant field in terms of the number of books and articles written, and the resulting small size of the body of evidence in this area makes it difficult to reach firm conclusions. However, when viewed in the perspective of what had gone before and what was to come after, the 1890's can be seen clearly as a time when textual study of the odes underwent its first real growth. It had begun in a brief and minor way in 1877 when Algernon Charles Swinburne noticed a textual comment in a review of an edition of Keats and sent in a brief article to refute it. Seventeen years elapsed before the next textual essay on any of the odes was published. In 1894 an article appeared in the *Athenaeum* describing the British Museum Egerton Manuscript #2780, which contains holograph copies of "Nightingale," "Urn," "Melancholy," and "Autumn." The author collated the texts of the poems with Forman's 1883 edition and printed the variants.[28] Two years later Thomas Wentworth Higginson published in *Forum* a reproduction of the manuscript of the first two stanzas of "Melancholy," then owned by R. S. Chilton and now housed in the Robert H. Taylor Collection of the Princeton University library. He discussed textual variants, also.[29] When Swinburne wrote the first textual consideration on one of the odes back in the 1870's, he was writing in objection to a specific point in a review of an edition of Keats. The two articles above, however, are textual in their own design, not just by response. From this time on, textual studies were to have a small but steady and important role in the way people responded to the odes.

For the 1890's, the growth of textual studies marks a trend toward the artifactualization of the odes. Although on the surface neither of the articles above seems to have offered an interpretation of any of the odes, in actuality both of them did so, although only insofar as Keats's odes belong to that class of communication known as literature. Since the interpretation of any phenomenon is implicit in the response given to that phenomenon, we may judge that the authors of both of the textual essays on the odes in the 1890's interpreted the poems as artifacts. For the purposes of their essays, at least, these men operated under the belief that the poem was the manuscript. To respond to the poem, in this way, was to respond to the manuscript, and this is what both authors did by reproducing the manuscript or by comparing it to other artifacts, or printed manuscripts if you will. An artifact is an object which has no immediate, active function for the perceiver, and it is in this regard that the textual studies of the odes were artifactual.

An artifact is capable of being put to the use for which it was originally intended, but the main response which it elicits is study. The tendency to study the odes rather than just to read them developed in the 1890's from the same spirit of artifactualization which fostered textual studies. If something is appropriate to be studied, then it must be appropriate to be taught. It was mainly during the 1890's that Lafcadio Hearn delivered his lectures at the University of Tokyo. In his talk on Keats, he tried to render the Western experience of "Nightingale," "Urn," and "Autumn" into Eastern terms.[30] The self-consciousness of study had entered into the reading of Keats to such a great extent by 1895 that the study of the study of his works became the subject of an article.[32] Jonathan Gilmer Speed's essay on the history of Keats criticism indicates that by this time Keats's poetry was already beginning to develop the potential for securing man's fame as well as his poetic pleasure. But, of course, the agency is misplaced here; Keats's poetry itself secured nothing. The critics secured the fame themselves, using the poetry and the reading public as vehicles. To suggest that the love of fame may have motivated some of the critics of Keats's odes in the 1890's, however, should not obscure the more significant observation that this period saw the odes begin to be responded to as objects to be scrutinized, examined, and inspected with a view to being "learned." Thus began their entrance into the field of phenomena popularly called knowledge, whose mastery is every educated man's need to obtain. The odes, along with Keats's poetry as a whole, took a larger place in formal education. A master's thesis, for example, was written at the University of Chicago in 1893 on the use of color in Keats's poetry.[32] Outside of secondary and post-secondary educational institutions, in the journals of a relatively high cultural level, Keats was treated with a tone of didacticism, not discovery. That is, the articles appearing about Keats assumed his poetry to be a cultural *fait accompli*, and the authors acted as agents of transmitting his wonders to an audience presumed capable of appreciating and desirous of being better acquainted with them. The reader was supposed to have some awareness of Keats, but of such a desultory, fragmented, and casual kind as to want instruction. The 1890's saw a slew of these general, almost popular essays on Keats published in such journals as *Scribner's Monthly*, *Belgravia*, *Mid-Continent*, and *Chautauquan*.[33] Of a similar nature were essays appearing in collections of the time, such as those by Hamilton Wright Mabie and James Henry Hallard.[34]

Further evidence of Keats's institution into the syllabus of English literature can be found in the various commemorative essays published in the nineties which mention the odes. By the 1890's it was growing impossible for any reader of Keats to approach the odes as if they had been written that morning. He was aware that they were seventy years old, and it made a difference.

When a reader approaches a poem which he believes to have been recently written, his assumed function is to evaluate the poem after coming to some understanding of its purport. But when he approaches a poem he believes to be old, his task is compounded in his mind. He must, he feels, not only appreciate the substance of the work but also account for it in a historical way by noting elements in the poem which differ from the contemporary or by defining elements in the poem in terms of intellectual, cultural, literary, or social history. In the 1890's, when the shift was being made to viewing Keats's poetry as a part of a history, a new and corresponding way of treating the odes sprang up. Critics began to employ a method of ideological veneer. They interpreted the odes as exemplifying an ideology whose source lay clearly outside the original thoughts of John Keats. Furthermore, this was done without particular attention to whether or not Keats himself was an avowed adherent to the ideology in question and whether he intended his poem to be an expression of it. Rather, the poems were often considered to be reflective of the operation of the ideology throughout the non-cognizant universe. In 1892, for example, we find the first Christian interpretation of the odes. Oblivious to the fact that Keats referred to Christianity in terms of its "pious frauds," Hamilton Wright Mabie explained that the last lines of "Urn" point to the dual roles of God as moralist and artist. He extolled the service Keats performed by revealing to men the beauty in God's world which is the "breathing soul" of righteousness.[35] Then in 1893 the Canadian poet Archibald Lampman wrote an essay on Keats in which he made a Platonic interpretation of the last lines of "Urn." He argued that the beauty/truth equation was a part of Plato's Beauty-Truth-Goodness trichotomy.[36] However, Alice Groff found still a different ideological interpretation of these lines. She read them as an embodiment of the principles of the art-for-art's sake movement.[37] The trend here established has enjoyed an unhindered growth up to the present day, when it is popular still.

The first decade of the twentieth century was a relatively calm one for the odes. No new trends developed in the way people responded to them. Though modern literature has been said to have begun around this time, marked by the death of Queen Victoria, for Keats criticism modernity started in the 1870's, and in the early 1900's it was producing nothing startlingly different. Ways of responding to the odes developed corollary and associated approaches from what had begun in the seventies, but the basic analytical direction criticism had taken thirty years earlier remained the same. In fact, the currents of present day criticism have their source in the 1870's as well. The reason for this phenomenon arises out of the relationship between romantic poetry and criticism of romantic poetry. The criticism of Keats's odes was, for the first fifty years, not romantic at all in the sense that it did not address itself to the same problems as the poetry. The original task of romanticism was to de-bunk, as it were, the Enlightenment ways of thinking and to find a source of value to take their place. To a large extent the search for value and the investigation of the nature of value itself became its primary occupation. The methods which the romantic critics developed later may be misleading in their resemblance to what has been called the scientific method, for science has often been associated with rationalism, a cornerstone of Enlightenment thinking. While eighteenth-century rationalists lay their major emphasis on the general laws of nature and on the deduction of order and harmony from those laws, the romantics, for whom the absolutism of previous laws no longer held validity, employed an inductive method in order to build a new and coherent way of viewing the universe. But romantic criticism lagged fifty years behind romantic poetry. There were, of course, those early romantics such as Hazlitt or De Quincey who wrote criticism, but they were rather the exception than the rule. For Keats's odes, at least, the readership did not respond romantically for a full fifty years. It took that long for readers to develop an analytical attitude toward them, and this approach is romantic in its methods.

Textual criticism, source studies, and the breaking up of poetry into smaller and smaller segments to be studied, all are romantic responses to the odes in the alienation they imply. Each of these operations is a kind of separation from the whole act of reading a poem. The poetic analogue to these acts is the wanderer, as found in works such as the "Prelude," "Alastor," "Endymion," "The Rime Of the Ancient Mariner," and even "Don Juan," in which the romantic hero separates himself from his society in order to establish a sense of identity and, simultaneously, a source of value. The tendency toward particularization in response to Keats's odes indicates a dissatisfaction with a more synthetic approach to the poetry of Keats. The presumption is often made that textual studies or source studies of limited scope have value because of the benefit they will have for later readers. It is assumed that someone will eventually come along who will reveal the significance of the information so assiduously collected, and the concept of the communal advance of scholarship and knowledge which guides this assumption is indeed a noble one and deserving of praise. However, so seldom does the reality approach the dream that one is justified in concluding that these virtuoso acts of criticism operate themselves as a source of value for their performers outside of the altruistic one so often supposed. Insofar as the particular, analytical kind of criticism puts the reader into areas of knowledge unknown by anyone but himself, or at most known by only a few, it gives the reader a sense of adeptness and identity which cannot be found by one striving to say, "What oft was thought, but ne'er so well expressed." Like the romantic poets, the romantic critics created a *locus obscurus* to wander in, only theirs was scholarly or academic instead of imaginary and natural.

What began in the 1870's, then, continued through the first decade of the twentieth century and beyond, with such modulations and variations as to prevent the same ideas from being repeated too often. Textual studies, for example, maintained its effort to determine precisely what words Keats meant his poems to include, in what order, and with what punctuation.

From 1900 to 1910 the odes came under scrutiny as a group of poems separate from the other works in Keats's canon. This was in the analytic trend of dividing literature into parts to be studied. The smallest segment is the individual word which receives textual or perhaps glossary attention. The odes as a group fall into the middle size of segments. The largest segments are such things as genres or traditions among poems which are read together and associated in thought, which are likely to span centuries and embrace elements of several cultures. Because treating the odes as a group involves bringing together poems which are often studied separately, it may easily escape observation as a particularizing act. However, when considered in the perspective of the overall hierarchy of divisions of literary study, it can be seen to belong to the same area of critical behavior as textual studies. Both narrow their focus to a limited area and analyze within those boundaries. When Keats's odes have been grouped together for study, it has often been on the basis of an assumption of thematic congruity, the pitfalls of which were demonstrated by Robert Gleckner in 1965.[38] Formal grouping of the odes had been done by Dowden and others in the 1890's, but thematic grouping did not develop popularity until the next decade. Paul Elmer More, for example, treated the odes as a group in his essay on Keats based on their common theme of sadness at the passing of beauty.[39] A. E. Hancock found the odes united by their intellectual sense,[40] and Hamilton Wright Mabie recognized the unity of them so strongly that he felt free to dwell on some of their differences, pointing out "Urn"'s restrained and chiselled qualities as opposed to the effusiveness of the other odes.[41]

At the same time that the odes were being compared with each other, the trend which had been established in the 1890's of interpreting them in terms of an outside ideology enjoyed extended application and led to the odes' being compared with and connected to a wider and wider range of phenomena. All these kinds of reactions to the odes had as their tentative and unspoken purpose to determine what the odes properly stood in relation to. They were efforts to supply a context for the odes, and the diversity to be found in the contexts which readers discovered indicates a randomness in their procedure. As we have seen, in their attempts to find analogs or parallels which would help them respond to the odes, readers seem to have ruled out almost no ideological settings. The odes were not felt to be limited by either the author's intentions or his knowledge. They might be Christian or Platonic, personal or traditional, Shelleyan, Rossettian, or pictorial. The experimentalism with which this decade approached the odes marks its reading as romantic.

One final quality of this decade's reaction to the odes ought to be mentioned before it is abandoned for the next ten years. That is the continuation of the aesthetic view of the odes which arose so strongly in the 1890's. The evaluation of the odes based on their beauty outside of any moral context colored criticism throughout this period. Thus, the pure beauty of "Urn" was assigned as the reason for its enduring fame.

A basic incongruity may seem to exist between the popularity of the aesthetic response to the odes and the persistence of the more academic analytical response. However, the incongruousness of the co-existence of these two reactions is based on an over-simplified approach to literary criticism in which too much attention is paid to what the critic has to say and not enough to how he came to know it. Although the results were quite different, the critics who studied the odes to find aspects of beauty in them and those who studied them to learn more about their details and arcana were alike in this way: they both were engaged to at least some extent in a process of self-satisfaction. The "scientific," analytical critic pursued his area of specialization, as has been argued above, as a means of alienating himself from other readers and arriving at results which would give him a personal sense of value. The aesthete responded to poetry in a different way to produce similar results. In seeking an aesthetic experience from poetry, he was undertaking a process which cannot be shared because it depends entirely on the eye of the beholder, hence the alienation and the sense of value. Thus, both aesthetic and analytical responses to the odes were, at least in part, redemptive acts.

The importance that criticism was coming to have during this period is reflected in the degree of emphasis put on what other critics had said. Edwin Chubb, for example, in his Keats entry in *Masters of English Litera-*

ture, spent much of his space quoting and paraphrasing other critics on Keats.[42] Edward Shanks displayed a similar concern for evaluating contemporary criticism in his review of Colvin's 1917 biography. Shanks noticed the distance which criticism had drifted away from a direct reaction to the odes.[43] The reason for the remoteness and lack of enthusiasm with which some readers responded to the odes was the fact that the study of the odes, and not the odes themselves, was the real focus of attention and source of value. Even such enthusiasm as was generated by the odes in this period cannot be said to have been generated purely for the odes. When it was announced that Mr. E. S. Willard would recite "Urn" at the Haymarket Theater dressed as an ancient Greek, "amid scenery that has been arranged by Sir Lawrence Alma-Tadema and painted by Mr. Joseph Harker," the event was clearly understood to be a theatrical, not a literary one.[44]

The decade of the 1920's has a few more publications about the odes than the decades surrounding it, a fact which is probably due to the occurrence of the centenary of Keats's death in 1921. The most notable centenary event was the appearance of the *John Keats Memorial Volume,* issued by the Keats House Committee, Hampstead. The effects of the centenary can be felt for several years beyond 1921. The opening of the Keats House in Hampstead in 1925 undoubtedly was made possible in large part by the publicity which the centenary attracted. Furthermore, it may be assumed that much of the Keats criticism in the early 1920's (and perhaps beyond, through the process of chain reaction) was stimulated by the impetus toward reconsideration which the centenary generated. The essays resulting from the Keats centenary constitute a novelty in the history of the odes' criticism, as does the phenomenon of the fame of so many of the critics. However, the main course of reactions to the odes remained analytical in the 1920's. The scale of operations had broadened by this time, though. The books published on Keats in this decade which dealt with the odes reveal this tendency toward a larger scale. The most striking example is Bernard Massey's book length study entitled *The Compound Epithets Of Shelley and Keats Considered From the Structural, the Historical, and the Literary Standpoints, With Some Comparisons, From the Greek, the Old English and the German.*[45] Massey devoted two hundred and fifty-six pages to the study of a topic which thirty years earlier would have taken up no more than a long article. The concept of extended consideration of relatively narrow subjects (relative, that is, to a subject such as the life and works of Keats, which formed the material for most previous books concerning the poet) was put to use by other writers of this decade as well.

The increase in length of the written analytical responses to the odes indicates that it was becoming more and more difficult to achieve an act of critical virtuosity. Methods of analysis had become so widely adopted that in order for someone to stand alone and in undisputed control over an area of Keats studies it became necessary to add length to particularization. Others, however, did not yet feel such extreme measures necessary. For them, the alienation and sense of value could still be achieved through narrow analytical studies that were fairly brief. Although it is true in some cases that the length of a work is determined by the subject of it, in many cases this does not hold. Certainly V.R.'s 1925 note arguing that Keats capitalized "Beauty" in "Nightingale" in order to indicate personification is an unlikely prospect to be expanded to book length.[46] However, Bernard Massey's aforementioned book-length consideration of Keats's and Shelley's compound epithets might easily have been reduced to the length of an article, as evidenced by David Rannie's twenty-one page effort covering Keats's epithets, compund and others, which was written in 1912 before length became so much to be desired. The conclusion is that length is almost as much a matter of choice for the writer as subject, within the limits of the writer's information and imagination. Thus, while some writers, such as Spurgeon, Murry, and Massey, felt the need to write at length, others were still being satisfied by briefer analytical penetrations.

In this decade, as in the one before it, the academic environment in which the reading of Keats's odes existed can be demonstrated by their inclusion in books whose intent was clearly pedagogical. Arthur Quiller-Couch's *On the Art of Reading* is the best example of this. The book contained lectures which he had given at Cambridge and included one on "Urn" which presented a reading of it in order to demonstrate the proper method of teaching a poem.[47]

In the 1930's a larger way of dealing with the odes came to prominence which had been gaining strength for the past two decades. It involved viewing the odes in relation to the rest of Keats's poetry or in relation to some other body of literature. Caroline Spurgeon, for example, had mentioned "Urn" in her 1913 study of mysticism in English literature, in which she argued Keats's mysticism was based mainly on "Endymion" (I, 744 ff.) and used "Urn," 49-50, as an expression of his mysticism.[48] Similarly, in 1919 Irving Babbitt had attacked the beauty/truth identification as part of his overall debunking of romanticism.[49] And in 1929 G. R. Elliott had held that Keats's odes were the pinnacle of his work and that his poetry would have been less successful had he lived to write more because he would have tried to express his ethical side, something beyond his poetic powers.[50] Although this kind of approach to the odes is not in itself analytical of them, it is analytical criticism and has interest because it indicates the relationship between the way people were responding to the odes and the way they were responding to other literature. Certainly some responses made to the odes were not made to most other writing. Few poems can, like "Urn," lay claim to having been used as a means of interpreting the motivation of British troops in World War I.[51] Few have had their composition serve as the subject for scenes in performed drama.[52] Few have ever been the subjects of essay contests.[53] However, in other respects, because of their great familiarity to many readers, the manner in which people responded to the odes approached that in which they responded to poetry in general. In this way, the history of the trends in responses to the odes plays a significant part in the history of the role of literature in society.

In *Reason and Beauty in the Poetic Mind*, Charles Williams used a similarly analytical sytem. His subject was the conflict in literature between the forces of the intellect and those of the imagination. He narrowed his study to the works of Milton, Wordsworth, Marlowe, Shakespeare, and Keats. Within the area of the writings of Keats, he further narrowed his specimen to "Urn" and "Nightingale," about which he argued that Keats abandoned the intellect for the imagination of beauty.[54] The telescopic narrowing here corresponds in its purpose to the biological system of classifying with increasing particularity according to kingdom and phylum through genus, species, and scientific name. Of course, the primary reason for such a biological breakdown is to facilitate and organize the naming of animals, but secondarily it allows one to observe minutely a small part of the entire group of living organisms without losing a sense of perspective of its place in the order of things. The hierarchy established defines relationships and stabilizes them so that they can be assumed and ignored temporarily in order that a limited and finite human mind may use its powers on a concentrated examination of a small subject. Thus, Williams, unable to devote the time necessary to cover all of Keats's writing, along with all the writing of the other authors he included, limited himself to certain works within the canon, chosen for their particular relevance. And on a different level, unable to discuss literature at large, Williams confined himself to one particular mood or idea in literature, and further limited that by a time frame. This sounds elementary and obvious to the twentieth-century reader. It seems to be nothing more than the "narrowing the topic" process familiar to all college freshmen. However, it has not always been familiar.

Though traces of it can be found earlier, the first time it emerged as a prominent feature in the criticism of the odes was in the 1930's. And in spite of the scientific affinities, or rather regardless of them, for there are no real mutual exclusions between romanticism and science, Williams' kind of essay, responding to the odes as it does in terms of another body of literature, is romantic in its motive. To devote a chapter of a book to considering a specific element of two of Keats's poems is to narrow the topic so as to guarantee being one of only a few people to have considered the subject so closely. The originality of the study insures its value, not as a piece of criticism, but as an act. The ideas expressed may be flawed, but the undertaking of reaching them is its own reward.

The pedagogical text which represents the most significant development of the decade in ways of responding to the odes is the standard Brooks and Warren *Understanding Poetry*. This book, coupled with William Empson's *Seven Types of Ambiguity*, reflects the beginnings of a way of dealing with the odes which was to spread and grow and which continues to thrive at the present time. Brooks and Warren attempted to approach the poems in their volume as poems rather than as historical documents, biographical documents, sources of inspiration, or sources of ethical judgments. In doing so, they hoped to promote a new way for teachers to present poems to students. "Autumn," "Nightingale," "Psyche," and "Urn" were all included in the book, but only "Nightingale" received treatment beyond the mere printing of the text followed by a list of study questions. "Nightingale" was accorded extra attention as an illustration of poets' methods of using imagery; however, once committed to a discussion of the poem, Brooks and Warren went on to expand upon the various themes of the ode: alienation, death and deathlessness, the ideal and the actual.[55] It is difficult to determine whether Brooks and Warren's book has made the treatment of literature in terms of its themes important or whether public readiness for thematic criticism caused the popularity of the book. Whatever the case, the approach of Brooks and Warren was to be practiced widely in the following decades. William Empson's book detailing seven different kinds of ambiguity in literature harmonized with the Brooks and Warren text. Empson took "Melancholy" as an example of his seventh type of ambiguity, one in which the two meanings inherent in the word are opposite, showing a division in the author's mind. For instance, he explained that the urgency of the opening of the poem ("No, no, go not to Lethe . . .") shows that the author was possessed of a very strong inclination indeed to go Lethe's way.[56] The interest for us here, however, is less in Empson's view of "Melancholy" than in the multiplicity which his method allowed and demanded. In order for a poem to be ambiguous, it must be saying at least two different things at once. Similarly, Brooks and Warren were loathe to oversimplify a poem by claiming the exclusivity of one particular theme; rather, they delighted in revealing the intricacies with which the poet related those themes to one another. The result was that it became possible for one poem to support several different interpretations at the same time. Indeed, Empson's book almost required it. The impact of the development of this attitude will be seen in later decades.

The number of written responses to the odes grew in the 1940's, and it has continued to grow ever since. For the most part this growth has been occasioned not so much by the development of new kinds of responses but by a further development of the analytical means of dealing with them which began in the 1870's. It has been shown that, for the two decades before the 1840's especially, studies which examined relatively small parts of the odes were multiplying, along with essays relating the odes to each other, to the rest of Keats's work, or to some other body of literature. In the 1940's, ideological criticism, which reads the odes in terms of an organized body of thought existing outside of the poet's canon, expanded its scope similarly. Ideological relativism was not yet accepted in the 1940's, however, and most of the responses made to the odes in this decade were bound by better established conventions of literary scholarhip. At base, there is no difference between a tradition and an ideology, and this fact makes the commonly-adopted dichotomy artificial. The seams of it sometimes show. But what is artificial may nonetheless be useful. Moreover, it matters less that a response may be either traditional or ideological than that it is analytical, a form of response subsuming both of these.

Altick and Chew's essay on Keats in Baugh's *Literary History of England* gave brief thematic descriptions of the odes and recommended the study of their background and influences.[57] There was a large group of critics who may or may not have been taking Altick and Chew's advice, but who, at any rate, reflected the same opinion regarding the appropriateness of tracing the influences on the odes. However, as in previous decades, publications revealing the sources of the odes most often neglected to show how that information is helpful in arriving at the meaning of the odes or in responding to them in any way. The reason for this neglect in this decade is the same as it was in decades previous: the study of influences and sources was its own end. The aim was not so much to gain useful information about the odes as to attain a self-ascription of value by becoming adept in a field of knowledge, a feat becoming more and more difficult as time went by and publications on all authors increased in numbers. By this time, the competition had become almost incredibly intense. Two lines of Keats's poetry received an especial amount of attention. The beauty/truth equation at the end of "Urn" is probably the most remembered quotation in all Keats's poetry, but even considering their popularity (or, in some opinions, notoriety), the number of source studies done on them was remarkable. This had been true in previous decades, but it was an even more outstanding phenomenon in the 1940's. The crux of the matter is usefulness. Literary articles were conventionally intended for the benefit of the reader; it began to be noticed, however, that the benefit to the reader of source studies was limited. The resolution of this incoherence, which actually began in the 1940's but was not completed until the 1950's, was achieved in an interesting way, as will be seen in the history of the next decade. Yet, if the critics of this decade were publishing relatively useless essays on the odes, one must be careful not to judge them too harshly. They were, as Lord Gorell realized in 1948, caught up in a dilemma: "To say anything fresh or interesting of poems which have been interminably quoted, read, recited, and dissected in every part of the globe is to tax ingenuity to the uttermost: to say nothing of them is impossible."[58]

IV

In the 1950's publication on the odes increased enormously. There were more things written about them during these years than in the previous two decades together. One reason for this increase in volume was the popularity of the polysemous approach to literature taken earlier by Empson, Brooks, Warren, and others. I. A. Richards ended his Boston television lecture on "Urn" with an injunction to his viewers to remember that there can be no single, correct reading of a poem as complex as Keats's ode.[59] However, there does not seem to have been a growth in readership to parallel the expansion of publication. Both of the studies of journal publishing printed in *PMLA* in the fifties decried the lack of subscription support being given to scholarly periodicals.[60] This indicates a phenomenon whose growth and development has made it a trend in scholarship since the 1950's: more and more books and articles were being written for an audience of fewer and fewer readers. As the first study reported, ". . . we write for each other (and not very many of each other at that)."[61] The degree of specialization with which the odes have been approached has been an effective block against popular readership, and the prolificity of scholarship has sometimes been a barrier to even academic readers. No less a figure than Walter Jackson Bate balked at the voluminousness of criticism on the odes, opting to pass over what seemed to him an unmanageable mass of opinions in his treatment of the odes in his essay on Keats's style.[62] By 1958 there had been so much work done on "Urn" that Harvey Lyon's response became appropriate. In his academic study guide to this ode, Lyon printed all of Keats's major odes, relevant selections from the letters, and the work of eighty-eight different critics on "Urn."[63] In spite of the size of the business of studying Keats's odes that Lyon's book suggests, relatively few people seem to have been reading those studies.

For example, the circulation of *PMLA*, which was twice as large as that of any other journal listed in the 1954 "Facts" survey, totaled eight and a half thousand, while *Saturday Evening Post* in 1950 could boast of a circulation of over four million. The nascent *Keats-Shelley Journal* had a readership of only 193, and *ELH* 574.

Some scholars during this period began to feel disenchanted with the academic mechanism of research and publication. The function of criticism, which was originally directed towards aiding the reader in understanding or appreciating a work or body of literature, was seen to be disintegrating. In the last two stanzas of his poem attacking the over-criticism of "Nightingale," Harry Brown ironically expressed his frustration:

> *In Faery Lands.* Here beauty holds a feast.
> See Colvin's comment on Brown's comment, with,
> Of course, the two new letters just released
> On nightingalism in English myth.
>
> *Forlorn! The very word is like a bell*
> To toll back that fled music. Though we sleep
> Or wake, immortal Truth and Beauty spell
> Their magic over critics buried deep.[64]

One causative force behind the bewildering multiplication of articles and books in this decade was the growth of the romantic motive of alienation and self-ascription of value through achieving original knowledge or insight. By this time the critic was discovering that self-ascription of value was an operation in need of constant renewal. The sense of self-worth which could easily be attained by learning and communicating new facts and ideas was found to be short-lived. For those who had chosen teaching literature as a profession, the real value of publication, it became clear, was not the achievement, but the process of it. It was partly for this reason that critics engaged in increased amounts of research and publication. As is natural in all areas where great gains are to be had, these scholars failed to examine their motives for publication closely. Scholarly publication was adopted as a means of executing a process of continual self-ascription of value. Whereas in the past the press served its readers, it now, more and more, began to serve its writers. This accounts for the increase in publication coupled with the small readership which characterizes the 1950's.

One consequence of the increase was that subjects which had heretofore been the sole province of one scholar were now subjected to the pens of various writers. Originality was still the premium, though, and each essayist tried to be careful not to express views of his subject which had already been voiced. Several writers, for example, wrote articles considering the odes as a sequence. Instead of taking one of the odes to be the key to an understanding of the others, another approach shared by many students of the odes found its touchstone in some other writing of Keats, whether it was from his letters or from his other poetry. Other studies of this decade used the odes to develop supporting material for theses dealing with subjects not essentially Keatsian. Ideological interpretation, like almost all responses to the odes, enjoyed growth in the 1950's, too. Critics took the odes on the one hand and an already-developed ideology on the other and joined the two as an expression of the same phenomenon. There is an assumption of pluralism implicit in ideological criticism unless, as sometimes happens, it can be shown that the artist whose works are being examined was an avowed disciple of the ideological system his works are being shown to embody. The limit to the pluralism, however, is the degree of universality which the ideology is presumed to have. Thus, a Christian and an economic interpretation of the odes might amicably co-exist, whereas a Marxist and a capitalist one would certainly be exclusive of one another. In the 1950's one or more of Keats's odes were argued to operate under the principles of Heidegger, mysticism, Freud, economics, and Christianity.

While these critics secured the isolation necessary for a sense of self-value by arguing minority approaches to the odes, others took more conventional approaches and argued positions within them which were minority because they were original. One way of doing this was to pursue the route of high analytical particularity which was popular in previous decades. An almost inexhaustible source of novelty could still be found in influence studies, whose only limit lay in the finite number of written documents in existence before the odes were published. Truly, if Keats had been influenced by all the authors who have been ascribed sway over him, his short life would have been taken up with an amount of reading which would have precluded any time for his own composition. During this decade alone, Keats's odes were demonstrated to have owed something to Poussin, Marlowe, Shakespeare, Coleridge, Pliny the Elder, Spenser, Homer, Camoens, Wordsworth, Hazlitt, Webster, William Kirby and William Spence, Mary Robinson, William Browne, and Mark Akenside, along with Wieland, Chaucer, Sandys' Ovid, Longus, John Potter, Sidney, Shaftesbury, and Theocritus.

Comparison studies presented an even wider field of study. For one thing, they could include authors who came after Keats. For another, they required no definite proof that the author had read the other. To be sure, not all writers of source studies were scrupulous to show such acquaintance by an author with the person who supposedly influenced him, but it was generally understood that such proof was desirable. Nonetheless, in the pure comparison study, influence is not an issue.

The purpose, rather, is to provide a perspective for the understanding of one work by examining it in the light of another. The goal is to establish some kind of pattern in the methods of the two artists which will reinforce an appreciation of the efforts of each. During this decade, one or more of the odes were compared to Wordsworth's "To the Cuckoo," Wallace Stevens' "Le Monocle de Mon Oncle," Anne Bradstreet's "Contemplations," Pai Chu Yi's "Song of a Guitar," Hardy's "The Darkling Thrush," Yeats's "Sailing to Byzantium," and Rilke's "Sonnet to Orpheus" and "Auf eine Lampe." Closely related to this kind of comparison study is the influence study which traced, not the impact of various authors on Keats but his effect on later writers. These first began to appear in numbers in the 1950's, like the comparison studies, and they often are highly comparative in nature.

Neither comparison studies, nor influence searches, nor ideological essays were developed in this decade at the expense of the first form of romantic criticism, the analytical essay which broke the subject down into small segments for minute examination. Expertise, that quality which enables a person to see things as no one else can, was still obtainable in the field of textual studies. Scholars more than ever sought to become experts, and they did so in order to enable themselves to say what had never been said before. This valuation of originality had its source in the collapse of Enlightenment ideology in the early nineteenth century, but by this time the emphasis had shifted from the original work produced to the process of creativity. In a sense, this is related to the concept of the progress of civilization. The individual steps of progress all lose their value as soon as the next step is taken; thus, the steps have a merely ephemeral importance. The real value belongs to the process of progression. Since almost any idea expressed in regard to Keats's odes was bound to be contradicted by someone eventually, the important thing was to be responding to the poems, not to deliver the immutable truth about them. This contentious quality is illustrated clearly by Newell Ford's 1952 textual study of the word "ruthless" in line 70 of "Nightingale." In asserting that Keats had originally written "keelless" instead of "ruthless," Ford was responding directly to adversary positions already taken by Woodhouse, Garrod, and Ridley.[65]

In addition to all these avenues of investigation of the odes, the pluralism resulting from the New Criticism which had begun in the thirties produced many new essays. William Empson himself wrote an essay on "Urn" in which he reacted against Cleanth Brooks's treatment in "History Without Footnotes." Empson believed that in trying so hard to keep biographical concerns from entering into his reading of the poem Brooks had done it the injustice of over-objectivity. While he appreciated the dramatic qualities of the poem which Brooks emphasized so heavily,

Empson still insisted that the poem should be viewed primarily as an expression of the poet's feeling.[66]

Robert Langbaum used the same idea to form the basis for a theory of one kind of modern poetry. In his book he explained what he called "the poetry of experience," characteristic of modern poetry, in which an observer imaginatively penetrates an object to arrive at its meaning.[67] The search for the feelings expressed in a poem, however, is as multi-faceted and divergent as the attempt to determine a person's motivation. The idea of poetry of experience added fuel to the flames of pluralism and helped them blaze. A holocaust ensued. The graduate schools were singed with Lester Wolfson's dissertation offering new critical readings of the odes.[68] The scholarly journals, too, were affected.

In the 1960's the number of publications on the odes continued to grow. Almost the entire scholarly publishing industry, for it was in this medium that most written responses to the odes were made, was enjoying proliferation. In 1954, when William Riley Parker put out the first "Facts of Journal Publishing" in *PMLA*, he ended it with a plaintive appeal for subscribers to support scholarly journals.[69] However, in 1966, when John Lavelle published the fourth "Facts," none of the periodicals listed in the 1954 survey had disappeared; in fact, the expansion of academia necessitated adding nineteen titles to the new study.[70] One cause of the increase in academic writing was the growth in college enrollments (though not in the way which might be first supposed; the evidence does not support the conclusion that the larger numbers of highly educated readers formed the audience for the larger number of essays being written). In 1930, the number of students enrolled for degree credit in American colleges and universities was 1,101,000. By 1960, that number was 3,583,000. The rate of growth was increasing each decade. Between 1930 and 1940, the enrollment had gained 393,000, but between 1950 and 1960, 1,302,000 more students were matriculating.[71] A greater number of students requires more instructors to teach them, but during this period a sufficient quantity of qualified instructors was not available.

Ironically, it was out of this need for competent teachers that the "publish or perish" policy grew. Since teaching positions were too easy to find, instructors were in a position to demand earlier decisions on tenure. Before World War II, most tenure decisions had been made when the candidate was in his forties and had already had ten or fifteen years in which to prove his abilities. After the war, however, tenure decisions tended increasingly to be made while the candidate was in his thirties. With less time to judge, tenure committees began to rely more heavily upon publication as a guide to teaching excellence.[72]

No doubt the "publish or perish" phenomenon began in the fifties when college enrollments almost doubled their previous size, but it did not gain really widespread attention until the 1960's and the Richard Bernstein tenure decision case. Bernstein was a thirty-two year old associate professor of philosophy whose teaching was valued highly by the Yale student body. When his tenure was denied, a three-day, round-the-clock demonstration was staged which gained national publicity. The main issue of the protest was said to be the "publish or perish" policy; however, the number of Bernstein's publications seems to have been appropriate for the success of a person his age. Perhaps their quality was felt to be wanting. Although this may have been the case, Norman Care felt instead that Bernstein was a victim of the "celebrity" system in faculty hiring. Care pointed out that few junior faculty ever succeed in working their way up into tenured positions; administrations prefer to add to the prestige of their schools by bringing in someone from outside with an established reputation to fill the tenured slot.[73] In fact, that is what eventually happened to Bernstein. Celebritized by his tenure denial at Yale, he became a sought-after figure.

Care ended his article differentiating between "publish or perish" and the "celebrity" system by deploring the results of both on teaching and on publishing. When making a written response to Keats became connected with the criteria for promoting or hiring a professor specializing in the British Romantic Period, the nature of the responses to the odes changed. What had been entered into since the 1870's as a romantic act of maintaining alienation from society developed into a means of becoming securely integrated with it. The number of written responses to the odes increased dramatically, but the enthusiasm in these publications was for professional status as much as for John Keats. The rhapsodic quality of the prose used in essays of the nineteenth century disappeared. This is not to say that many of the writers were incapable of being deeply or genuinely moved by the odes, but that rather too infrequently was that emotion unalloyed with professional ambition. Furthermore, while the large numbers of publications testify to the great vigor with which aspiring professors pursued Keats studies, the lack of vitality and wit in the content of many of these publications indicates no real love of the pursuit.

The "publish or perish" policy flooded the market with many more essays and books than the educated public was willing to read. Part of the reason for the neglect of this scholarship had to do with its quality. Of the 166 journals surveyed by John Lavelle in 1966, only three editors could complain of having to reject worthy articles for lack of space.[74] The same situation had existed five years earlier when "Facts, III" was published. At that time it was concluded that there was no need for additional journals in the field of language and literature.[75] The need which demanded the addition of nineteen new periodicals to the 1966 study, then, did not arise from the subject of literature and language; rather, it was the need of the writers for professional advancement. The readership for these scholarly journals was the very people who wrote for them.[76] Professors read essays by other professors too often merely to help discover ideas for the articles they were planning to write and to avoid the charge of critical naivete. The fact that journal subscriptions remained relatively low at the same time that the number of journals was expanding supports this incestuous concept of academic publication. Since it was in the economic interest of college instructors to address their colleagues in print, the student analog to the professor, the graduate student, gained desirability as a pupil. As Andrew Hacker noticed in his essay "Who Wants To Teach Undergraduates Anymore?" graduate students, as apprentice professors themselves, were naturally more interested in what their professors had learned through scholarly research and thus were more attractive as students than the undergraduates who were less willing to feel the importance of what they were being taught.[77]

The 1960's produced so much material, both good and bad, dealing with the odes that the student of Keats almost does not know where to begin. The decade produced three important biographies: Walter Jackson Bate's *John Keats*, Aileen Ward's *John Keats: the Making of a Poet*, and Robert Gittings' *John Keats*. Three major biographies, such as these are, in one decade is rather many, but in this case they announce a prophesy of multitude which the period fulfilled with a vengeance.

The area of largest growth in criticism of the odes in the sixties was that of ideological criticism. One or more of the odes was responded to in the terms of Freud, Aquinas, Hegel, Kierkegaard, Camus, Jung, Plato, and Nietzsche. Of these ideologies, the most frequently invoked was the Freudian. Obviously, the variety of all these interpretations does not represent an attempt to home in on a circumscribed locus of meaning for the odes. The nature of pluralism lies in the centrifugality with which it operates. Under its orientation, a single work of literature can support as many interpretations as can be argued coherently. When truth became relative, point of view became all, and the sophistication with which relativity was accepted was rewarded financially in the academic world, for greater opportunities for publication meant greater opportunities for advancement.

At least partially for this reason, New Criticism, the act of responding to the words on the page in isolation from all other information, continued to grow in importance in the 1960's. Inevitably, some critics' opinions were more intelligently thought out and more impressive than others', and the view of these people received the kind of scholarly attention which had previously been reserved for more factual information. Brian Lee, for instance, devoted over a fourth of his essay on New Criticism to the views of "Urn" of Wasserman, Spitzer, Burke, and others.[78]

The popularity of New Criticism, however, did not grow at the expense of other kinds of reactions to the odes. Those studies which treated the odes as a part of a larger topic continued to increase in number as well. For example, the odes were used to help demonstrate Keats's tendency to use the negative in his poetry, to trace the progression of Keats's symbols, to illustrate the thesis that Keats's frustration with social issues caused his poetry to lean toward escapism, and to exemplify the theory that the romantic ode combined the emphasis of the eighteenth-century ode on rhetoric and that of the seventeenth-century ode on drama.

Likewise, the kind of study which took a small segment of one of the odes for minute examination also continued to be made. The areas of study which these essays explored were far-reaching and multifarious. On the one hand there was David Green, who found the hitherto overlooked publication of "Urn" and "Psyche" in *Rivington's Annual Register* for 1822.[79] On quite a different hand, Dwight Robinson argued that the phrase "Fair attitude" in "Urn" alluded to Emma Hart, later Lady Hamilton, who made a minor stir in Europe, attracting Goethe among others by her semi-nude *tableaux vivants* simulating ancient Greek statuary of Aphrodite. These posings came to be celebrated as her classical "attitudes."[80] On a third hand still was Cleanth Brooks, who pursued his course of irony and ambiguity study in an article examining the structural significance of the quadrupal repetition of "fade" in "Nightingale."[81] It would be necessary to invent a creature with many more arms than an octopus to give an adequate forum for all the particularized studies made of the odes during this decade.

Also during this period the odes were claimed to have been influenced by Coleridge, Vergil, the Bible, Shakespeare, Thomas Warton, Raphael, Giulio Romano, Luca Giordano, Canova, Thomas Heywood, Charlotte Smith, Josiah Wedgewood, Wordsworth, Pope, Southey's translation of *Palmerin of England,* William Beckford, and Chatterton. And in turn they were claimed to have influenced Faulkner, Eugenio Montale, Wordsworth, Evelyn Waugh, Fitzgerald, and Yeats. In addition, several scholars wrote essays which discussed the odes in terms of Keats's thought as previously expressed in other poetry or in letters.

At the time of the writing of this study, the decade of the 1970's is not long past. Anything that may be said about this period now is likely to prove errant to eyes fifty years hence, uninfluenced as they will be by forces and directions which turned out not to be real trends at all but more ephemeral and exploratory forays. However, several observations may be made in a vein more descriptive than analytical. Scholarly publication and academic promotion had become so intertwined by 1970 that something basic to the nature of the one will be missed if the condition of the other be ignored. From 1960 to 1970, degree credit enrollment in the United States colleges and universities jumped 4,337,000. Between 1950 and 1960, the increase was only 1,302,000. Figures show that up through 1976 enrollments were still climbing strongly.[82] Furthermore, in 1960 the total expenditure of institutions of higher learning in the United States was $5,601,000,000.[83] By 1975, that figure had reached $34,057,563,000.[84] By comparison, in 1940, before the boom had actually begun in education, the expenditure totaled only $675,000,-000.[85] Clearly, in the second half of the twentieth century education was becoming an important business concern, and publication has been an integral part of the system of advancement in the profession. One unavoidable result of requiring teachers, who may be disinclined, to write articles in order to secure promotion has been a lamentable increase in publication of essays really not worth publishing. From the scholar/student's point of view, time is lost both in reading inferior essays and in searching through the morass of scholarship to find the good ones. In this second area, the proliferation of scholarly articles confounds both writers of the essays and editors of the journals which publish them. In March 1975, for example, Barry Gradman had an article published in *English Language Notes* arguing "Nightingale"'s debt to *Measure for Measure* based on the speeches of the Duke and Claudio in III.i. Six months later there was published in *Modern Language Quarterly* an essay by Eamon Grennan which also argued the influence of *Measure for Measure* on "Nightingale," and it likewise used the same two speeches in the play as evidence. The convergence was even verbal. Gradman wrote, ". . . the play apparently 'most read' by Keats, after *The Tempest* and *A Midsummer Night's Dream,* was—somewhat unexpectedly—*Measure for Measure.*"[86] Grennan differed mainly in the area of expectation: ". . . the most read play after *A Midsummer Night's Dream* and *The Tempest,* a pair whose choice seems obvious enough, is *Measure for Measure.*"[87] No blame should be attached to the authors of these pieces. Working separately, they without doubt arrived at the same idea contemporaneously. The problem was that the editor of the later journal to appear was unable to contend successfully with the ever-growing body of published essays. He made the mistake of allowing an article to be published whose substance had already appeared in print. In 1970, the Modern Language Association of America began publishing *Abstracts* as an aid to scholars in their attempt to keep abreast of current learning. When *Abstracts* ceased in 1975, the sole reason was not the rising costs of publication; another factor no doubt was the growing amount of scholarship to be surveyed. The task became too great even for the MLA. However, there are indications that perhaps during this decade the abuse done to scholarly publication by the tenure and promotions committees of colleges and universities across the United States will reach a peak and begin to decline. For one thing, the number of people willing to participate in that system seems to be leveling off. In 1960, the number of Ph.D.'s awarded in the area of English and American language and literature was 386. In 1970, that figure had risen to 1,097.[88] A survey of 1977, however, shows the number of Ph.D.'s produced in English to be 1,094.[89] Furthermore, there seems to be a growing discontent with the present state of scholarly publishing. In 1973, "Facts of Scholarly Publishing" enjoined the academic world to reconsider the publish or perish policy and blamed it for "the proliferation of second-rate material on topics that interest few."[90] Unless college and university administrations change this policy, the report said, it will become necessary for them to provide more money to support scholarly publishing, since it has become a servant of their offices. This shift in the purpose and function of scholarly writing has led some to advocate on-demand publication, in which a summary of an essay along with the full text would be submitted to a central agency such as Dissertation Abstracts now is, and the essay would be printed only upon request. In the long run, it is argued, there will be a savings of the time, money, and effort it would have taken to print so many copies of so many articles left largely unread.[91] Whether the concern over the current state of affairs has reached the level necessary to effect a change in it is a matter difficult to judge, and, if a change is forthcoming, what direction it will take is impossible to predict. But it seems likely that if scholarly publishing is not now changing, it is at least moving toward an alteration.

By the 1970's a modification had taken place within the trend of responding to the odes by pointing out passages in previous works which influenced them. Essays of this kind were now longer than before. Writing shares with any gas the quality of being able to be expanded or compressed according to need without altering the basic elements. Perhaps the need in this decade was for longer articles so that tenure or promotion might be achieved, but perhaps that is being unfair. Equally possible is that the uselessness of merely pointing out influence became apparent. Whatever the case, more interest began to be taken in explaining the thematic importance of the odes' reliance upon previous literature. Overall, however, the criticism of the seventies seems to continue to approach the odes in the same basic ways that of the sixties had. We find in this decade the tendency toward thematic response to the odes which resulted perhaps from the emphasis put on it earlier by

Brooks, Warren, and others. Also, the force of that highly analytical and particular kind of criticism which narrowed study down to a small segment of the work and then subjected it to intense scrutiny still is felt. Similarly, the practice of interpreting the odes in terms of Keats's other writing flourishes. And the vogue of ideological criticism is extended as well.

In retrospect, then, one can trace in the trends of the responses to Keats's odes, from their publication date to the present day, the course of the development of a criticism motivated in nature by a romantic view of life. This kind of criticism, characterized by various strategems for setting its critic apart from the rest of his society, began around the 1870's, after a sufficient time had passed so that Keats's poetry could be considered widely as a proper subject for study rather than mainly as a corpus which might be read for enjoyment and recreation. There were those, of course, who recognized the importance of Keats's work from its early days, but even among them only a few were so convinced of it as to devote serious study to the odes. Rather, those who were aware of the worth of the poems served mainly to keep that estimation alive, to prevent the odes from being buried under the mass of lesser poetry which rivaled it in its own day, until the 1870's when it could be considered as a part of England's canon of poetry. By that time, romanticism had ceased to be a set of new ideas and attitudes heralded by Wordsworth, Hazlitt, and others; it had been absorbed and assumed by the more intellectual individuals. The collapse of Enlightenment thinking had had time to reach those men of secondary but still very competent intelligence who uphold the determining qualities in any culture. Feeling the necessity to find within themselves alone some source of value and meaning, they turned in their literary criticism to areas of study which had been relatively ignored. In this way, individual poems began to receive more minute analysis, textual details developed a high degree of interest, and source studies became more numerous and appealing.

"This grew," as a famous duke once said. The development of pluralism in the middle of the twentieth century was a logical result of the use to which the odes were being put, not to imply that the odes caused in any way the birth of pluralism but merely that they can be connected in an orderly sequence. The evolution of the idea that two differing and even opposing views of the same work may both be held to be valid indicated that a shift had taken place in the function of criticism. What had previously been meant to benefit the odes and their readers by offering information to facilitate understanding them correctly was now shifted so that it served the writer of the criticism. In one aspect, pluralism allowed for the development of alternative readings in cases of genuine ambiguity so that a greater number of readers would be able to find something in the poem meaningful and relevant to their own experience. In another, pluralism gave the critic freedom to use the poem as a justification for his own pre-determined value system. Neither of these aspects should be argued to be either good or bad, for pluralism is the natural consequence of the romantic need to find meaning from within. It rendered poetry subject to this kind of operation with remarkable fecundity. At the same time, it marked an advance in romantic criticism in that it recognized that the value of criticism was in the act of creating it, not in the results it achieved. Pluralism responded to the romantic discovery that it was necessary to continually re-evaluate the odes.

Beginning with the 1950's, however, an added force came into play in the growth of the responses to the odes. When, as a result of the incredible expansion of academia, publication attracted financial as well as metaphysical reward, its nature shifted. In one sense, perhaps a narrow one, this change deserves condemnation, for it led to the proliferation of writing not motivated primarily by a belief in the ideas expressed. When writing about the odes became a stepping-stone to success, it acquired the attribute of conducting the author directly to the place writers fifty years earlier had been trying to avoid—the mainstream of society. Clearly, literary criticism is performing a role different today from the one it had before 1950. Whether it turns out for the better or for the worse, we shall have to wait to see.

NOTES

[1]"To J. H. Reynolds," 21 September 1819, Letter 193, *The Letters of John Keats, 1814-1820,* ed. Hyder E. Rollins (1958; rpt. Cambridge: Harvard University Press, 1972), II, 167.

[2]This view is shared by John O. Hayden in *The Romantic Reviewers: 1802-1824* (Chicago: University of Chicago Press, 1969), p. 196.

[3]Rev. of *Lamia, Isabella, The Eve of St. Agnes, and Other Poems,* by John Keats, *Monthly Review,* 92 (July 1820): 308-309.

[4][Josiah Conder?], Rev. of *Lamia, Isabella, The Eve of St. Agnes, and Other Poems,* by John Keats, *Eclectic Review,* 14 (September 1820): 170.

[5]Rev. of *Lamia, Isabella, The Eve of St. Agnes, and Other Poems,* by John Keats, *Literary Chronicle,* July 29, 1820, p. 484.

[6][Leigh Hunt], "The Stories of 'Lamia,' 'The Pot of Basil,' 'The Eve of St. Agnes,' etc. As Told by Mr. Keats," *Indicator,* August 9, 1820, p. 345.

[7]Samuel Taylor Coleridge, *Biographia Literaria,* in *Prose of the Romantic Period,* ed. Carl R. Woodring (Boston: Riverside Press, 1961), p. 98.

[8]A. S-H., "Keats," in *Encyclopaedia Britannica,* 8th ed., 13 (Boston: Little, Brown, 1857), p. 57.

[9]"Keats and His Poetry," rev. of *The Poetical Works Of John Keats,* ed. William Smith, in *Dublin University Magazine,* 21 (June 1843): 702.

[10]Joseph Devey, *A Comparative Estimate Of Modern English Poets* (London: E. Moxon, 1873), pp. 263-274.

[11]"Keats," *American Bibliopolist,* 7 (April 1875): 95.

[12]William Cullen Bryant, *A New Library Of Poetry and Song* (1874; rpt. New York: Fords, Howard, and Hulbert, 1877), I, 236.

[13]William Graham, "Keats and Severn," *Last Links With Byron, Shelley, and Keats* (London: Leonard Smithers, 1898), p. 120.

[14]J. L. Warren, "Keats's 'Ode to a Nightingale,'" *Notes and Queries,* 5th ser., 8 (October 6, 1877): 267. All quotations from the odes come from John Keats's *Lamia, Isabella, The Eve of St. Agnes, and Other Poems* (London: Taylor and Hessey, 1820).

[15]Jonathan Bouchier, "Keats's 'Ode to a Nightingale,'" *Notes and Queries,* 5th ser., 8 (October 20, 1877): 316.

¹⁶Rev. of *The Poetical Works Of John Keats,* ed. Richard Monckton Milnes, *Athenaeum,* January 13, 1877, p. 45.

¹⁷Algernon Charles Swinburne, "The 'Ode to a Nightingale,'" *Athenaeum,* January 27, 1877, p. 117.

¹⁸Frances Mary Owen, *John Keats: A Study* (London: C. Kegan Paul, 1880); William Michael Rossetti, *Life of John Keats* (London: Walter Scott, 1887); and, Sir Sidney Colvin, *Keats* (1887; rpt. New York: Harper and Brothers, 1901).

¹⁹John Mackinnon Robertson, "The Art Of Keats," in *New Essays Towards A Critical Method* (New York: Bodley Head, 1897), p. 248.

²⁰Oscar Wilde, "The English Renaissance Of Art," in *Essays and Lectures* (1908; rpt. London: Methuen, 1909), pp. 129-130.

²¹Matthew Arnold, *Essays In Criticism: Second Series* (London: Macmillan, 1888), p. 115.

²²T. Hall Caine, "That Keats Was Maturing," *Tinsley's,* 31 (August 1882): 199.

²³C. E. Tyrer, "The Sensuousness Of Keats," *Manchester Literary Club Papers,* 14 (1888): 217-246.

²⁴John Campbell Shairp, *Aspects Of Poetry* (Boston: Houghton, Mifflin, 1882), p. 62.

²⁵Edmund C. Stedman, "Keats," *Century Magazine,* NS 5 (February 1884): 600.

²⁶Sidney Lanier, *The English Novel,* vol. IV of *Centennial Edition,* ed. Clarence Gohdes and Kemp Malone (1883; rpt. Baltimore: Johns Hopkins Press, 1945), pp. 83-84.

²⁷Arthur C. Downer, *The Odes Of Keats, With Notes and Analyses, and a Memoir* (1897; rpt. Folcroft, Pa.: Folcroft Press, 1969).

²⁸F.G.K., "The New Keats Ms.," *Athenaeum,* December 29, 1894, pp. 894-896.

²⁹Thomas Wentworth Higginson, "A Keats Manuscript," *Forum,* 21 (June 1896): 420-424.

³⁰Lafcadio Hearn, "Keats," in *Interpretations Of Literature,* ed. John Erskine (New York: Dodd, Mead, 1924), I, 171-179.

³¹J. G. Speed, "The Critics Of John Keats," *Outlook,* 52 (October 26, 1895): 660-662.

³²Alice Edward Pratt, *The Use Of Color In The Verse Of The English Romantic Poets* (Chicago: University of Chicago Press, 1898). This was originally a doctoral dissertation. The chapter on Keats (pp. 78-88) had been used as an MA thesis.

³³Richard Henry Stoddard, "After Many Days: A Study Of Keats," *Scribner's Monthly,* 15 (1894): 203-213, 402-417; Charlotte A. Price, "Famous Poets: John Keats," *Belgravia,* 87 (1895): 404-428; Thomas C.

Carrington, *Mid-Continent*, 6 (June 1895): 174-178; Kenyon West, "A Study Of Keats," *Chautauquan*, 22 (March 1896): 691-696.

34Hamilton Wright Mabie, "John Keats: Poet and Man," in *Essays In Literary Interpretation* (1892; rpt. New York: Dodd, Mead, 1897), pp. 138-174; James Henry Hallard, "The Poetry Of Keats," in *Gallica and Other Essays* (London: Longman, Green, 1895), pp. 119-127.

35Hamilton Wright Mabie, "John Keats: Poet and Man," pp. 168-169.

36Archibald Lampman, "The Character and Poetry of Keats," (1893), ed. E. K. Brown, *University of Toronto Quarterly*, 15 (July 1946): 356-372.

37Alice Groff, "Ideals Of Beauty In Keats and Browning," *Poet Lore*, 5 (May 1893): 247-253.

38Robert F. Gleckner, "Keats' Odes: The Problems Of The Limited Canon," *Studies In English Literature, 1500-1900*, 5 (Autumn 1965): 577-585.

39Paul Elmer More, "John Keats," in *Shelburne Essays* (1906; rpt. Boston: Houghton Mifflin, 1922), pp. 117-118.

40Albert Elmer Hancock, *John Keats: A Literary Biography* (New York: Houghton Mifflin, 1908), pp. 149-151.

41Hamilton Wright Mabie, "'Ode on a Grecian Urn' by John Keats, the Third Of A Series Of Great Poems With Introductions," *Outlook*, 91 (February 27, 1909): 473-477.

42Edwin Watts Chubb, "Keats," in *Masters Of English Literature* (1914; rpt. Freeport, New York: Books For Libraries Press, 1967), pp. 230-247.

43Edward Shanks, "Keats and His Critics," *New Statesman*, 10 (November 17, 1917): 157.

44"Table-Talk," *The Bookman Keats-Shelley Memorial Souvenir*, June 20, 1912, p. 4.

45Bernard W. A. Massey, *The Compound Epithets Of Shelley and Keats* (Poznan: Poznanskie Towarzystwo Przyjaciol Nauk, 1923).

46V. R., "Keats's Use Of Capitals," *Notes and Queries*, OS 149 (July 4, 1925): 15.

47Arthur C. Quiller-Couch, *On The Art Of Reading: Lectures Delivered In The University Of Cambridge 1916-1918* (Cambridge: Cambridge University Press, 1920), pp. 91-93.

48Caroline F. E. Spurgeon, *Mysticism In English Literature* (1913; rpt. Cambridge: Cambridge University Press, 1922), p. 444.

49Irving Babbitt, *Rousseau and Romanticism* (1919; rpt. Cambridge, Mass.: Houghton Mifflin, 1957), p. 357.

50G. R. Elliott, "The Real Tragedy Of Keats," in *The Cycle Of Modern Poetry* (Princeton: Princeton University Press, 1929), pp. 38-57.

51Sir Ian Hamilton, "John Keats," in *The John Keats Memorial Volume* (New York: John Lane, 1921), p. 85.

52*Aged Twenty-six*, by A. C. Flexner, appeared at the Lyceum. It was based on Keats's life and contained scenes depicting the composition of "Urn" and "Autumn," according to a review by Joseph Wood Krutch, "What Porridge Had John Keats?" *Nation,* 144 (January 2, 1937): 25-26.

[53]Wilbur F. Murra won a prize for the best essay on "Melancholy": "The Prize Winning Letter," *Wilson Bulletin For Librarians,* 5 (September 1930): 64 and 96.

[54]Charles Williams, "The Evasion Of Identity: The 'Nightingale' and the 'Grecian Urn,'" *Reason and Beauty In The Poetic Mind* (Oxford: Clarendon Press, 1933), pp. 63-81.

[55]Cleanth Brooks and Robert Penn Warren, *Understanding Poetry* (1938; rpt. New York: Holt, Rinehart, and Winston, 1960).

[56]William Empson, *Seven Types Of Ambiguity* (1930; rpt. Norfolk, Conn.: New Directions, 1953), pp. 205-206.

[57]Samuel C. Chew and Richard D. Altick, "John Keats," in *A Literary History Of England,* ed. Albert C. Baugh (1948; rpt. New York: Appleton, Century, Crofts, 1968), pp. 1241-1251.

[58]Ronald Gorell Barnes, *John Keats: The Principle Of Beauty* (London: Sylvan Press, 1948), p. 77.

[59]I. A. Richards, "Beauty and Truth," in *Complementarities: Uncollected Essays,* ed. John Paul Russo (Cambridge: Harvard University Press, 1976), pp. 215-225. This was talk number six of the "Sense Of Poetry" series broadcast on WGBH-TV, Boston, in the winter of 1957-58.

[60][William Riley Parker], "Facts Of Journal Publishing," *PMLA,* 69 (December 1954): viii-ix; and, "Facts Of Journal Publishing, II," *PMLA,* 72 (September, Pt. 2., 1957): vii-ix.

[61]Parker, "Facts Of Journal Publishing," p. viii.

[62]Walter Jackson Bate, "Keats's Style: Evolution Toward Qualities Of Permanent Value," in *The Major English Romantic Poets: A Symposuim In Reappraisal,* ed. Clarence D. Thorpe, Carlos Baker, and Bennett Weaver (Carbondale: University of Illinois Press, 1957), pp. 217-230.

[63]Harvey T. Lyon, ed., *Keats' Well-Read Urn: An Introduction To Literary Method* (New York: Henry Holt, 1958).

[64]Harry M. Brown, "Ode On The Restoration Of A Keats Nightingale," *College English,* 19 (March 1958): 251.

[65]Newell F. Ford, "Keats's Romantic Seas: 'Ruthless' or 'Keelless'?" *Keats-Shelley Journal,* 1 (1952): 11-22.

[66]William Empson, *The Structure Of Complex Words* (New York: New Directions, 1951), pp. 368-374.

[67]Robert Langbaum, *The Poetry Of Experience: The Dramatic Monologue In Modern Literary Tradition* (New York: Random House, 1957).

[68]Lester Marvin Wolfson, "A Rereading Of Keats's Odes: The Intrinsic Approach In Literary Criticism," Diss. University of Michigan 1954.

[69]Parker, "Facts Of Journal Publishing," p. viii.

[70]John Lavelle, "Facts Of Journal Publishing, IV," *PMLA,* 81 (November 1966): 3.

[71]U.S. Department of Commerce, *Historical Statistics Of The United States, Colonial Times To 1970,* I (Washington, D.C.: U.S. Bureau of the Census, 1975), p. 383.

[72]Henry M. Wriston, "Publish or Perish," *Saturday Review,* 48 (July 17, 1965): 59.

[73]Norman S. Care, "Yale's Tenure Trouble," *New Republic,* 152 (March 27, 1965): 13-14.

[74]Lavelle, p. 7.

[75]"Facts Of Journal Publishing, III," *PMLA,* 76 (December 1961): v.

[76]Norman Wagner confirms the continuation of this situation in his essay, "Scholars As Publishers: A New Paradigm," *Scholarly Publishing,* 7 (January 1976): 103: "Let us be clear about one thing: when we speak about scholarly publishing, we scholars are speaking about ourselves, for we are both the authors and the readers."

[77]Andrew Hacker, "Who Wants To Teach Undergraduates Anymore?" *Saturday Review,* 49 (December 17, 1966): 80-81.

[78]Brian Lee, "The New Criticism and the Language Of Poetry," in *Essays On Style and Language: Linguistic and Critical Approaches To Literary Style* (London: Routledge and Kegan Paul, 1966), pp. 29-52.

[79]David B. Green, "An Early Reprinting Of Three Poems From Keats's 1820 Volume," *Papers of the Bibliographical Society of America,* 60 (1966): 363.

[80]Dwight E. Robinson, "Ode on a 'New Etrurian' Urn: A Reflection Of Wedgwood Ware In the Poetic Imagery Of John Keats," *Keats-Shelley Journal,* 12 (1963): 11-35.

[81]Cleanth Brooks, "The Language Of Poetry: Some Problem Cases," *Archiv fur das Studium der neueren Sprachen und Literaturen,* 203, (April 1967): 401-414.

[82]U.S. Department of Commerce, *Historical Statistics Of The United States, Colonial Times To 1970,* I (Washington, D.C.: U.S. Bureau of the Census, 1975), p. 383; and, W. Vance Grant and C. George Lind, *Digest Of Education Statistics* (Washington, D.C.: Department of Health, Education, and Welfare, 1976), p. 85.

[83]*Historical Statistics Of The U.S.,* Vol. 1, p. 384.

[84]Grant and Lind, p. 142.

[85]*Historical Statistics Of The U.S.,* Vol. 1, p. 384.

[86]Barry Gradman, "*Measure For Measure* and Keats's 'Nightingale' Ode," *English Language Notes,* 12 (March 1975): 177.

[87]Eamon Grennan, "Keats's *Contemptus Mundi:* A Shakespearean Influence On The 'Ode to a Nightingale,'" *Modern Language Quarterly,* 36 (September 1975): 273.

[88]*Historical Statistics Of The U.S.,* Vol. 1, p. 388.

[89]"1977 Ph.D. Survey," *MLA Newsletter*, 10 (spring 1978): 1.

[90]William Pell, "Facts Of Scholarly Publishing," *PMLA*, 88 (September 1973): 643.

[91]Datus C. Smith, Jr., "A Case For On-Demand Publishing," *Scholarly Publishing*, 7 (January 1976): 169-178.

BIBLIOGRAPHY

The following bibliography is arranged by year of publication, and, within the year, by alphabetical order. When an essay has been printed in more than one place, an effort has been made to list it at the earliest date of appearance. The annotations do not, in all cases, give a comprehensive account of the entire book or article they derive from. Rather, the aim has been throughout to garner only such information as is pertinent to Keats's odes.

Also, the orientation of this bibliography is historical. Thus, in an attempt to preserve an accurate chronology, letters are entered at the date of their writing rather than at the date of their publication, since oftentimes many years pass before a person's letters are collected and published. The anthology reprints of the odes included here by no means represent a complete list. Only those which were so broadly popular as to have had a real part in the history of the odes' fame and reputation were included. And, finally, no attempt has been made to trace reprintings, except for items which are not generally accessible in their originally published form.

1820

[Condor, Josiah?]. *Eclectic Review,* Second Series 14 (September 1820): 158-171.

> Attacks Keats for an over-enthusiastic imagination and for a lack of religious values. Quotes "Autumn" in its entirety without comment except that it is a favorable specimen of Keats's shorter lyrics. Attacks "Urn" as an example of Keats's unfortunate obsession with mythology.

[Hunt, Leigh]. "The Stories of Lamia, the Pot of Basil, the Eve of St. Agnes, etc. As Told by Mr. Keats." *The Indicator,* August 2, 1820, pp. 337-344 and August 9, 1820, pp. 345-352.

Champions Keats against the attackers of "Endymion." Treats mainly the narrative poems in the volume, but quotes all of "Nightingale" and praises it highly.

[Jeffrey, Francis]. *Edinburgh Review,* 34 (August 1820): 203-213.

Reviews the 1820 volume and, belatedly, "Endymion." Spends most of its words defending "Endymion"'s "pure poetry." Also praises "Nightingale" for harmony and feeling.

Literary Chronicle, July 29, 1820, pp. 484-485.

Blasts the longer poems and praises the shorter lyrics in the 1820 volume. Beginning with an admonition to renounce the Cockney School, it goes on to quote all of "Urn" as the best of the shorter poems, "many of which possess considerable merit."

Literary Gazette, July 1, 1820, pp. 423-424.

The author says that he received his copy of the 1820 volume too late for a regular review. As a result, he merely gives a sampling from the "minor productions": "Nightingale," "Lines on the Mermaid Tavern," and "Autumn."

"The Mohock Magazine." *Baldwin's London Magazine,* 2 (December 1820): 666-685.

Compares the journalistic activities of *Blackwood's Magazine* to the eighteenth-century gang of hoodlums known as the Mohocks. Discusses *Blackwood's* mistreatment of Keats and mentions "Nightingale," along with "Hyperion," as an excellent poem.

Monthly Review, Second Series 92 (July 1820): 305-310. Seen in Donald H. Reiman (ed.). *The Romantics Reviewed: Contemporary Reviews of British Romantic Writers.* 9 vols. New York: Garland Publishing, 1972.

Defends Keats against the attacks on "Endymion." Praises "Hyperion" most highly, censures "Urn," ll. 11-14, for the use of a trite conceit, and admires the imaginativeness of "Autumn," which is reprinted.

"Remarks on Keats's Poems." *The Edinburgh (Scots) Magazine,* NS 7 (October 1820): 313-316.

Likes "Nightingale" best of all the poems in the 1820 volume. Quotes the last six stanzas, praises "Autumn" briefly, and discusses the major poems.

[Scott, John]. *London Magazine*, 2 (September 1820): 315-321. Seen in Donald H. Reiman (ed.). *The Romantics Reviewed: Contemporary Reviews of British Romantic Writers*. 9 vols. New York: Garland Publishing, 1972.

Feels that Keats is too narrow in his depictions of the qualities of social class, especially in "Isabella." However, quotes two stanzas of "Nightingale" as evidence that Keats is capable of dealing with essential human problems in an intelligent and understanding way.

Woodhouse, Richard. "From a Correspondent." *Sun*, July 10, 1820. Seen in Lewis M. Schwartz. *Keats Reviewed By His Contemporaries: A Collection of Notices for the Years 1816-1821*. Metuchen, N.J.: Scarecrow Press, 1973, pp. 207-210.

Concerns himself mainly with "Hyperion," though he does say that he regrets being unable to print "Urn" and "Nightingale" because of lack of space. Those works, he says, "deserve high praise."

1821

G.V.D. "On Reading Lamia, and Other Poems, by John Keats." *The Gossip* (Kentish Town), May 19, 1821, p. 96.

This is a three-stanza eulogy to Keats. It echoes "Nightingale" heavily and uses Keats's ode stanza.

Haydon, Benjamin Robert. *The Diary of Benjamin Robert Haydon*. Ed. Willard Bissell Pope. Cambridge: Harvard University Press, 1960. Vol. II, p. 318.

In the March 29, 1821, entry in his diary, Haydon reports that Keats once recited "Nightingale" to him while walking in the Kilburn meadows.

M.M. "On the Neglect of Genius." *Imperial Magazine*, 3 (December 1821): 1076-1080.

This letter to the editor laments the neglect that genius so

often suffers. It brings up Keats as a case in point and quotes
ll. 19-30 of "Nightingale."

1827

Hone, William. *The Table Book*. 1827; rpt. Detroit: Gale Research, 1966.
Vol. I, p. 410.

Quotes the first three stanzas of "Nightingale" in the course
of a treatment of Hampstead Heath as one of England's
popular groves.

1828

Hunt, Leigh. "Mr. Keats, With a Criticism on His Writings." In *Lord Byron
and Some of His Contemporaries*. Philadelphia: Carey, Lea, and Carey, 1828,
pp. 213-231.

Relates Byron's confusion over the concept of a beaker "full
of the warm south." Quotes all of "Nightingale" and the
second stanza of "Urn," which is especially praised.

1836

Brown, Charles Armitage. "Life of John Keats." In *The Keats Circle*. Ed.
Hyder Edward Rollins. Cambridge: Harvard University Press, 1969.
Vol. II, pp. 52-96.

In an 1836 speech, Brown presents his famous account of
Keats's composition of "Nightingale." According to him, Keats
wrote the poem sitting in his breakfast chair under a plum tree
in the Hampstead Heath garden one spring morning in 1819.
Brown later found him inside, thrusting behind some books
four or five scraps of paper which, when they had with difficulty been arranged in their proper sequence, turned out to
contain the "Ode to a Nightingale."

1838

Hall, S. C., ed. *The Book of Gems*. London: Whittaker, 1838. Vol. III, p. 120.

This anthology of "modern poets and artists of Great
Britain" includes printings of "Nightingale," "Urn," and

"Autumn." The one-page comment on Keats, attributed to Hunt, praises "Nightingale" and "Urn" for feeling and music.

1841

"Chapters on English Poetry: Moore, Keats, Crabbe, Campbell, and Rogers." *Edinburgh Magazine,* NS 8 (October 1841): 648-653.

Quotes almost five stanzas of "Nightingale" and discusses them in terms of Keats's love of beauty and the spell he was under when writing descriptive poetry.

1843

"The Genius of John Keats." *Christian Remembrancer,* 6 (September 1843): 251-263.

Condemns Keats for his pagan indulgence in mere sensuality but admits the compelling beauty of "Urn" and "Nightingale."

"Keats and His Poetry." *Dublin University Magazine,* 21 (June 1843): 690-703.

Apologizes for not printing sections of "Nightingale" and "Urn" on the basis of their general familiarity.

1844

Horne, Richard Hengist. *A New Spirit of the Age.* 1844; rpt. London: Oxford University Press, 1907.

Uses the odes, among other of Keats's works, as evidence that Keats can justly be considered "Divine."

1845

Coleridge, Sara. *Memoir and Letters of Sara Coleridge, Edited By Her Daughter.* New York: Harper and Brothers, 1874, pp. 236-239.

In a letter concerning Keats to Aubrey DeVere in September 1845, Sara Coleridge criticizes the third stanza of "Urn" for being mere fancy, not imagination.

Craik, George L. "Keats." In *Sketches of the History of Literature and Learning in England.* London: Charles Knight, 1845. Vol. II, pp. 193-196.

This brief account of Keats's poetry criticizes the lack of discipline in most of Keats's work, but praises "Nightingale" as a poem of "great beauty" and reprints it in its entirety, comparing it to Shelley's "Skylark."

Gilfillan, George. "John Keats." In *A Gallery of Literary Portraits.* Edinburgh: William Tait, 1845, pp. 372-385.

Finds Keats's creed in the ending to "Urn": aversity to speculative thought. Praises "Nightingale," "Urn," and "Autumn" as among the best of Keats's shorter pieces.

1847

Howitt, William. *Homes and Haunts of the Most Eminent British Poets.* London: Richard Bentley, 1847.

Compares Keats's longing for death in Rome with the similar longing in "Nightingale," which he praises as full of the "soul of poetry."

1848

Dilke, Charles Wentworth. Rev. of *Life, Letters, and Literary Remains of John Keats,* ed. Richard Monckton Milnes. *Athenaeum,* August 12, 1848, pp. 789-791.

Argues that "Indolence" can be viewed as a study for "Urn" in tone and spirit, though much inferior in execution.

"John Keats." *Eclectic Magazine,* 14 (July 1848): 409-415.

This general essay on Keats's life and works prints "Urn" as a specimen of the odes and comments that Keats's odes, like his sonnets, successfully restrain Keats's sometimes-excessive fancy because of their shortness.

Milnes, Richard Monckton, ed. *Life, Letters, and Literary Remains of John Keats.* London: Edward Moxon, 1848.

Quotes the cancelled first stanza of "Melancholy," claiming that Keats omitted it from the final version because it clashed with the "luxurious tenderness" of the rest of the poem. Prints the letters containing "Psyche" and "Autumn," but leaves out the texts of the poems. Mentions "Nightingale" and "Urn" in biographical anecdotes.

1849

Rev. of *Life, Letters, and Literary Remains of John Keats*, ed. Richard Monckton Milnes. *Dublin University Magazine*, 33 (January 1849): 28-35.

This anti-utilitarian reviewer praises enthusiastically the beauty and imaginativeness of "Nightingale."

Rev. of *Life, Letters, and Literary Remains of John Keats*, ed. Richard Monckton Milnes. *Edinburgh Review*, 90 (October 1849): 424-430.

Contends that Keats and Shelley used sometimes to argue over the relative merits of beauty and truth, and that the conviction that beauty is the embodiment of truth can be found throughout Keats's thought.

Rev. of *Life, Letters, and Literary Remains of John Keats*, ed. Richard Monckton Milnes. *Sharpe's London Magazine*, 8 (1849): 56-60.

Feels that "Nightingale," "Urn," and "Melancholy" rival in quality any poems of the kind in English literature.

"The Poetry of Keats." *Massachusetts Quarterly Review*, 2 (September 1849): 414-428.

Praises "Nightingale" and "Urn" for their perfectness of detail and general completeness. Interprets the ending of "Urn" as expressing a sense of one force acting in different circumstances.

1851

Moir, D. M. *Sketches of the Poetical Literature of the Past Half-Century*. London: William Blackwood, 1851.

Quotes from "Nightingale" and praises it, along with "Urn," "Melancholy," and "Autumn," as being deep in thought, picturesque, and suggestive.

1852

Chichester, Frederick William. *Poets and Poetry of the Nineteenth Century.* London: Longman, Brown, Green, and Longmans, 1852.

The hasty composition of "Nightingale" and Keats's neglect of its preservation, according to Brown's account, are used as an example of Keats's trait of writing poetry only to satisfy his own need to write it.

Mitford, Mary Russell. *Recollections of a Literary Life.* London: Richard Bentley, 1852.

A conversational book introducing the reader to works the author loves by way of comment and quotation. "Nightingale" is quoted and discussed briefly in Volume 3, Chapter IX, "Poetry that Poets Love."

1856

Bagehot, Walter. "Percy Bysshe Shelley." *National Review,* 3 (October 1856): 342-379. Seen in *Literary Essays.* Vol. I of *The Collected Works of Walter Bagehot.* Ed. Norman St. John-Stevas. Cambridge: Harvard University Press, 1965.

Uses "Urn" to distinguish between the fanciful quality of modern literature as opposed to the imaginativeness of classical writing. Also compares "Nightingale" to Shelley's "Skylark."

1857

A. S-H. "Keats." In *Encyclopaedia Britannica.* 8th ed. Boston: Little, Brown, 1857. Vol. XIII, pp. 55-57.

Cites "Urn" as the best of Keats's poetry, noting its "spirit of antiquity—eternal beauty and eternal repose."

1860

Ruskin, John. *Modern Painters.* Vol. V of *The Works of John Ruskin.* Ed. E. T. Cook and Alexander Wedderburn. New York: Longmans, Green, 1903-1912.

Ruskin shows a familiarity with the odes by quoting from

"Psyche," "Nightingale," "Urn," and "Melancholy." He discusses in particular the image of the pine tree in line 55 of "Psyche."

1861

Masson, David. "The Life and Poetry of Keats." *Macmillan's Magazine*, 3 (1861): 1-16.

Quotes portions of "Nightingale" as examples of Keats's sensuousness. Labels Keats one of the "Hampstead Heathens."

Meredith, George. *The Letters of George Meredith.* Ed. C. L. Cline. Oxford: Clarendon, 1970.

Meredith quotes part of "Nightingale" in a letter to Frederick A. Maxse of December 13, 1861, accepting his wedding invitation.

Palgrave, Francis Turner. *The Golden Treasury.* 1861; rpt. London: Macmillan, 1888.

A very popular anthology of lyrical poetry in the nineteenth century, enjoying nineteen printings between 1861 and 1888. The Keats selections include "Nightingale" and "Autumn," among other poems.

1864

Hopkins, Gerard Manley. *The Journals and Papers of Gerard Manley Hopkins.* Ed. Humphry House. London: Oxford University Press, 1959.

In his diary entry for September 9, 1864, Hopkins copies out the first six lines of the last stanza of "Psyche."

1867

Arnold, Matthew. *On the Study of Celtic Literature.* London: Smith, Elder, 1867.

Quotes from "Nightingale" and "Urn" in his discussion of Keats's Greek and Celtic qualities. His Greek poetry is com-

posed with a descriptive radiance, while his Celtic is characterized by natural magic, charm, and spirituality.

1869

Howitt, William. *The Northern Heights of London.* London: Longmans, Green,
1869.

A book describing local London geography. Associates
Hampstead Heath with "Nightingale."

1870

Allibone, S. Austin. "John Keats." *A Critical Dictionary of English Literature.*
Philadelphia: Lippincott, 1870. Vol. I, pp. 1009-1011.

The Keats entry of this encyclopedia of English authors
mentions "Autumn," "Urn," and "Nightingale," along with
"On First Looking Into Chapman's Homer," as the most
famous of Keats's minor poems.

Swinburne, Algernon Charles. *The Swinburne Letters.* Ed. Cecil Y. Lang.
New Haven: Yale University Press, 1959-1962.

Swinburne complains in a letter to William Michael Rossetti
of May 23, 1870, that Moxon's editions of Keats made it impossible for him to read "Nightingale" without finding "some
schoolboy nonsense" a few pages away.

1873

Devey, Joseph. "Keats." In *A Comparative Estimate of Modern English Poets.*
London: Moxon, 1873, pp. 263-274.

Ranks Keats as an Alexandrine poet and mentions briefly
the Greek qualities of "Psyche" and "Urn" as compared to
those of Collins' poetry.

1874

Bryant, William Cullen. *A New Library of Poetry and Song.* 1874; rpt. New
York: Fords, Howard, and Hulbert, 1877.

"Nightingale" is printed in this anthology with a biographical headnote. "Urn" is included also, but with no comment.

Coleridge, Sara. *Memoir and Letters of Sara Coleridge, Edited By Her Daughter.* New York: Harper and Brothers, 1874, pp. 236-239.

See 1845.

1875

"Keats." *American Bibliopolist,* 7 (April 1875): 94-95.

Praises "Urn," as opposed to the "spasmodic" "Endymion," for its Sophoclean tranquility infused with a new sentiment and sadness.

Van Gogh, Vincent. *The Complete Letters of Vincent Van Gogh.* Trans. C. de Dood. Greenwich, Conn.: New York Graphic Society, [1958].

In a letter of August 7, 1875, Van Gogh says Keats is the favorite of London painters and copies out ten lines from "Autumn."

1876

Lowell, James Russell. "Keats." In *Among My Books, Second Series.* 1876; rpt. Boston: Houghton, Mifflin, 1892, pp. 303-327.

Praises the odes briefly for their sense of form and proportion.

1877

Bouchier, Jonathan. "Keats's 'Ode to a Nightingale.'" *Notes and Queries,* 5th Ser., 8 (October 20, 1877): 316.

In answer to J. L. Warren's query as to Keats's allusion in the last three lines of stanza seven of "Nightingale" (*Notes and Queries,* 8 [October 6, 1877]: 267), Bouchier quotes Leigh Hunt's explanation in *Imagination and Fancy* suggesting that the scene comes from some fairy tale.

Rev. of *The Poetical Works of John Keats.* Ed. Lord Houghton. *Athenaeum,* January 13, 1877, p. 45.

Avers that Keats did not include the word "away" in line twenty of "Nightingale."

Swinburne, Algernon Charles. "The 'Ode to a Nightingale.'" *Athenaeum,* January 27, 1877, p. 117.

In this letter to the editor of the *Athenaeum,* Swinburne defends Lord Houghton's inclusion of the word "away" in line twenty of "Nightingale."

Warren, J. L. "Keats's 'Ode to a Nightingale.'" *Notes and Queries,* 5th Ser., 8 (October 6, 1877): 267.

A query as to the allusion in the last three lines in stanza seven of "Nightingale."

1879

Allen, Grant. "A Fragment from Keats." *Gentleman's Magazine,* 246 (June 1879): 676-686.

Uses a detailed analysis of the description of the food Porphyro brought forth from the closet in "The Eve of St. Agnes" as a springboard for a discussion of aesthetic concerns in poetry. Praises the "dreamy golden haze" of the second stanza of "Nightingale" and touts that stanza as the only equal in Keats's poetry to the lines from "Eve."

Dowling, Richard. "My Copy of Keats." *Tinsley's Magazine,* 25 (November 1879): 427-436.

A memoir recording many affectively valuable times the author spent reading his volume of Keats's collected poetry. The author gives a detailed account of an oral reading of "Urn" a friend of his once made and describes another friend's reaction to some lines from "Nightingale."

Graham, William. "Keats and Severn." In *Last Links with Byron, Shelley, and Keats.* London: Leonard Smithers, 1898, pp. 98-121.

In a conversation with Graham in 1879, Joseph Severn says that he had hoped for more from Keats than five perfect odes. He also claims to have been the one who pointed out to Keats the vase that was the inspiration for "Urn."

1880

Owen, Frances Mary. *John Keats: A Study*. London: C. Kegan Paul, 1880.

Has a biographical flavor. Also links the odes with Keats's other poetry and with one another to a small extent.

1881

Lanier, Sidney. *The English Novel and Essays on Literature*. Ed. Clarence Gohdes and Kemp Malone. 1883; rpt. Baltimore: Johns Hopkins Press, 1945.

An 1881 lecture. Praises "Melancholy" effusively as the height of lyric poetry. Based on the end of "Urn," argues that Keats was a moral poet rather than an art-for-art's sake one. Also, finds an intensity of despair over stasis in "Urn" based on the modern valuation of growth, increase, and movement.

Swinburne, Algernon Charles. *The Swinburne Letters*. Ed. Cecil Y. Lang. New Haven: Yale University Press, 1959-1962.

Swinburne quotes snatches of "Nightingale" in a letter to William Bell Scott, March 1, 1881.

1882

Caine, T. Hall. "That Keats Was Maturing." *Tinsley's Magazine*, 31 (August 1882): 197-200.

Quotes from "Urn" to show Keats's preoccupation with sensation and from "Nightingale" to indicate that he was, however, capable of looking on life's harsher side.

Cotterill, H. B. *An Introduction to the Study of Poetry*. London: Kegan Paul, Trench, 1882.

Uses lines 65-70 of "Nightingale" to demonstrate that Keats's poetry was too dreamy and unrealistic, though acknowledging its pathos and sublimity.

Oliphant, Margaret. "John Keats." In *The Literary History of England in the End of the Eighteenth and Beginning of the Nineteenth Centuries*. London: Macmillan, 1882. Vol. III, pp. 133-155.

The chapter on Keats consists of a mainly biographical

essay. It has high praise for the charm of "Nightingale," "Urn," and "Autumn."

Shairp, John Campbell. *Aspects of Poetry*. Boston: Houghton Mifflin, 1882.

Commends the sonorous harmonies of the odes in general, notices the Greek-ness of "Nightingale" and "Urn," and extols the sensuous delight in nature of "Autumn."

Swinburne, Algernon Charles. "John Keats." In *Encyclopaedia Britannica*. 9th ed. 1882; rpt. New York: Encyclopaedia Britannica Co., 1911. Vol. XV, pp. 708-710.

Cites the odes as the basis for Keats's deserved fame and calls them the loveliest possible lyrical poetry. Names "Autumn" and "Urn" the most perfect of the odes, "Nightingale" the most musical, radiant, and fervent, "Psyche" the most tender-fanciful, and "Melancholy" the subtlest in thought and feeling.

Wilde, Oscar. "The English Renaissance of Art." In *Essays and Lectures*. 1908; rpt. London: Methuen, 1909, pp. 111-155.

An 1882 lecture. Uses "Urn" as an example of the poetic virtue of including nothing harsh, painful, or debatable in a poem. Contrasts Keats with Byron and Wordsworth on this point.

1883

Milner, George. "On Some Marginalia Made By Dante G. Rossetti in a Copy of Keats' Poems." *Manchester Quarterly*, 2 (1883): 1-10. Rpt. *Englische Studien*, 61 (1927): 211-219.

Based on a study of D. G. Rossetti's marginalia in his Moxon edition of Keats (1868). Argues that Rossetti ranked "Urn" and "Nightingale" highest among Keats's works. "Psyche," "Autumn," and "Melancholy" are rated below "On First Looking Into Chapman's Homer," "The Eve of St. Mark," and "La Belle Dame Sans Merci."

Mortimer, John. "Did Keats Really Care for Music?" *Manchester Quarterly*, 2 (1883): 11-17.

Considers Rossetti's question written in the margin of his

copy of Keats beside "To Charles Cowden Clarke," lines 109-114: "Did he *really* care for music?" Discusses "Nightingale" and "Urn" briefly for their implications on the subject and stresses the music of Keats's poetry.

1884

"The American Edition of Keats." Rev. of *The Poems of John Keats, with the Annotation of Lord Houghton and a Memoir by Jno. Gilmer Speed. Atlantic Monthly*, 53 (March 1884): 422-429.

Based on the ending of "Urn," this argues that Keats felt the beauty of the earth to be a medium for divine revelation.

Arnold, William T., Introd. *The Poetical Works of John Keats*. London: Kegan Paul, Trench, 1884.

Names the odes and the best of the sonnets as Keats's best work. Treatment of the odes relies on source study.

Athenaeum, February 23, 1884, pp. 245-247.

Praises Keats as a conscious artist, noticing especially his metrics. Stanza seven of "Nightingale" is cited as having the virtue of the accents' falling on the quantitative syllables.

Robertson, John Mackinnon. "The Art of Keats." In *New Essays Towards a Critical Method*. New York: Bodley Head, 1897.

This 1884 essay ranks "Nightingale" as Keats's best ode because of its melody and word choice. The next best is "Melancholy," and then, decidedly below these two, come "Autumn" and "Urn," inferior because of their more prosaic qualities.

Stedman, Edmund C. "Keats." *Century Magazine*, NS 5 (February 1884): 599-602.

Celebrates enthusiastically the flawless language, melody, and tone of "Nightingale," along with the Greek perfection of "Urn."

1885

Courthope, William John. "Poetry, Music, and Painting: Coleridge and

Keats." In *The Liberal Movement in English Literature*. London: John Murray, 1885, pp. 159-194.

    Emphasizes the picturesque and sculpturesque qualities of "Nightingale" and "Urn."

"The Life and Works of John Keats." *Edinburgh Review*, 162 (July 1885): 1-36.

    This general essay on Keats's life and works mentions three of the odes: "Urn," "Nightingale," and "Psyche." Praises their lyrical qualities briefly and quotes from them.

1887

Colvin, Sir Sidney. *Keats*. In *English Men of Letters Series*. Ed. John Morley. 1887; rpt. New York: Harper, 1901.

    Discusses the themes of the odes, their metrical structure, and some of their sources. Finds "Urn" and "Psyche" to be inspired by the Greek world of imagination and art, "Melancholy" and "Nightingale" by moods of the poet's own mind, and "Indolence" by a weak combination of both.

"Fine Passages in Verse and Prose; Selected by Living Men of Letters." *Fortnightly Review*, NS 42 (September 1887): 430-454.

    Presents contemporary opinions as to the best verse in English literature. Quotes Edward Dowden's nomination of "Melancholy" and Augustine Birrell's choice of "Nightingale."

Hopkins, Gerard Manley. *Further Letters of Gerard Manley Hopkins.* Ed. Claude Colleer Abbott. 1956; rpt. London: Oxford University Press, 1970.

    In a letter to Coventry Patmore of October 20, 1887, Hopkins says that Keats found his right way in the odes.

Rossetti, William Michael. *Life of John Keats*. London: Walter Scott, 1887.

    Arranges the odes symphonically: 1) "Urn"; 2) "Psyche"; 3) "Autumn"; 4) "Melancholy"; and, 5) "Nightingale." Finds in them the common theme of "extreme susceptibility to delight, close-linked with afterthought." Views the ending of "Urn" as the key to Keats's thought, argues "Nightingale" to be the most perfect of the odes, and notes the imagery, diction, and music in "Melancholy."

1888

Arnold, Matthew. "John Keats." In *Essays in Criticism: Second Series.* 1888; rpt. London: Macmillan, 1905. Vol. II, pp. 100-121.

Blasts Keats for his displays of pure sensuousness, but finds, in the spiritual passion for beauty expressed in the last lines of "Urn" and elsewhere, signs of high character which did not have time to develop fully.

Courthope, William John. "Keats' Place in English Poetry." Rev. of *Keats,* by Sir Sidney Colvin. *National Review,* 10 (1888): 11-24.

Argues that Keats's poetry shows a morbidity of fancy which Keats acquired as a result of his physical ailments. Also discusses Keats's artistic workmanship, showing his metrical effects to be an attempt to reproduce in verse the form of sculpture and color of painting.

Rev. of *Keats,* by Sidney Colvin, and *Life of John Keats,* by William Michael Rossetti. *Quarterly Review,* 166 (April 1888): 308-388.

Praises the odes for their condensed pictorial expression, their Spenserian epithets, their instinct for color, form, and melody, and their classicism.

Tyrer, C. C. "The Sensuousness of Keats." *Manchester Literary Club Papers,* 14 (1888): 217-246.

This essay on the sensuous qualities of Keats's poetry praises the odes as Keats's greatest achievements and "Melancholy" as the greatest of the odes. Argues that the odes are sensuous, but never sensual. Keats used the sensuous in the odes, not for its own sake, but to help demonstrate a higher moral lesson. Thus, his was a sensuous ideality, unlike Shelley's pure idealism.

1890

Bouchier, Jonathan. "Keats." *Notes and Queries,* 7th Ser., 10 (July 5, 1890): 11.

An answer to Catti's query about the meaning of lines 5-7 of "Nightingale" *(Notes and Queries,* May 10, 1890). Suggests that the poet's heart aches, not because he is envious of the bird, but because he has an excess of happiness in the bird's happiness, which consists of singing in the manner described in the rest of the stanza.

Catti. "Keats." *Notes and Queries,* 7th Ser., 9 (May 10, 1890): 370.

A query as to the meaning of lines 5-7 of "Nightingale."

C.C.B. "Keats." *Notes and Queries,* 7th Ser., 10 (July 5, 1890): 11.

An answer to Catti's query about the meaning of lines 5-7 of "Nightingale" *(Notes and Queries,* May 10, 1890). Replies that the meaning is plain within the lines themselves, but goes on to quote from Keats's letters and from "Melancholy" other instances of Keats's empathic bent.

Woodberry, George Edward. "On the Promise of Keats." In *Studies in Letters and Life.* Boston: Houghton, Mifflin, 1890, pp. 47-65.

Quotes the last lines of "Urn" as an expression of Keats's creed.

1892

Groff, Alice. "Ideals of Beauty in Keats and Browning." *Poet Lore,* 5 (May 1893): 247-253.

Read before the Browning Society of the New Century Club on November 10, 1892. Treats Keats as a literal art-for-art's sake poet and interprets "Urn," ll. 49-50, in this way.

Mabie, Hamilton Wright. "John Keats: Poet and Man." In *Essays In Literary Interpretation.* 1892; rpt. New York: Dodd, Mead, 1897, pp. 138-174.

Interprets the ending of "Urn" according to the notion that God is an artist more obviously than he is a moralist. Beauty is not the ornament of righteousness but the soul of it.

Stedman, Edmund Clarence. *The Nature and Elements of Poetry.* Boston: Houghton, Mifflin, 1892.

Feels that the last two lines of "Urn" mar an "otherwise perfect poem" because of their didacticism.

1893

Lampman, Archibald. "The Character and Poetry of Keats." (1893). Ed.
E. K. Brown. *University of Toronto Quarterly,* 15 (July 1946): 356-372.

> This article comprises more than half of Lampman's essay
> on Keats written in 1893 and edited with a prefatory note by E.
> K. Brown in 1946. It takes "Urn," ll. 49-50, to be Keats's creed,
> interpreting "Beauty" as part of the Platonic Beauty-Truth-
> Goodness trichotomy. The approach is biographical, and a
> Platonic ideology governs the treatment of the odes.

1894

F.G.K. "The New Keats Ms." *Athenaeum,* December 29, 1894, pp. 894-
896.

> Describes the British Museum Egerton Manuscript #2780,
> which is a small volume of manuscript poems, some of them
> holographs, including "Nightingale," "Urn," "Melancholy,"
> and "Autumn." It was acquired by the British Museum from
> Prof. Jenks of Australia. Collates the texts of the poems with
> Forman's 1883 edition and prints the variants.

Gosse, Edmund. "Keats in 1894." In *Critical Kit-Kats.* 1896; rpt. New York:
Dodd, Mead, 1897, pp. 19-29.

> An address delivered at Hampstead on the occasion of the
> unveiling of the American Monument, July 16, 1894. Reads
> the ending of "Urn" as the conception of lofty beauty as the
> only consolation in a "jarring and bewildered world."

Howitt, William. "John Keats." In *Homes and Haunts of British Poets.* London:
George Routledge, 1894, pp. 292-300.

> Essay on Keats and his grave-site. Praises "Nightingale" for
> its poetic qualities and quotes stanzas two and three to illus-
> trate Keats's life-weariness.

[Stoddard, Richard Henry]. "After Many Days: A Study of Keats—II."
Scribner's Monthly, 15 (1894): 402-417.

> Tentatively orders the composition of the odes as follows:
> 1) "Nightingale"; 2) "Melancholy"; 3) "Urn"; and, 4) "Autumn."
> Takes the last lines of "Urn" as Keats's creed but gives highest

praise to "Nightingale" as "the translation of the untranslatable."

1895

Bridges, Robert Seymour. "The Odes." In *John Keats: A Critical Essay.* London: Lawrence and Bullen, 1895, pp. 54-61.

Analyzes the odes with a special interest as a poet in the way the elements of them affect the reader. Ranks "Autumn" highest based on its perfection, the only flaw being an awkwardness in line 24. Still, more enthusiastic about the splendour, intensity, and richness of "Nightingale." Criticizes the artificiality of its last stanza, though, and finds fault with the phrase "plaintive anthem" as well as with the rhyming of "elf" with "self." However, the last six lines gain highest praise. Finds weakness in "Melancholy"'s inconsistent conception of melancholy, and claims that in "Psyche" the imagery outstrips the idea, though that flaw turns out to be the source of the poem's main strength. Sees the theme of "Urn" as expressed in the first stanza to be the supremacy of ideal art over nature, but contends that the amplification of this theme is unprogressive, monotonous, and scattered. However, the poem is somewhat redeemed by the very fine closing lines.

Burne-Jones, Georgiana. *The Memorials of Edward Burne-Jones.* 1904; rpt. New York: Macmillan, 1906. Vol. II, p. 264.

Burne-Jones said in 1895 that ll. 69-70 of "Nightingale" were the crowning example of the kind of poetry he liked best: short pieces which made him tingle every time he read them.

Carrington, Thomas C. "John Keats, Poet." *Mid-Continent,* 6 (June 1895): 174-178.

Finds the strength of "Urn," "Psyche," and "Nightingale" to be their adoption of subjects familiar to the ordinary reader and their simplicity in style and treatment. Uses the end of "Urn" as evidence of Keats's lack of moral concern.

E.J.H. "Stray Thoughts About Keats." *The Critic,* 27 (October 26, 1895): 259-260.

Essay on the centenary of Keats's birth. Uses "Urn" to demonstrate that Keats tried to escape the sterner realities of life, yet finds in "Nightingale" evidence that had he lived he would have been humanized by sorrow.

Hallard, James Henry. "The Poetry of Keats." In *Gallica and Other Essays.* London: Longman, Green, 1895, pp. 119-127.

> Believes Keats the equal of Tennyson in the artistic use of words, and uses "Nightingale" as proof. Finds an intense feeling for nature in that poem as well.

Ingleby, Holcombe. "Keats's 'Ode to a Nightingale.'" *Notes and Queries,* 8th Ser., 8 (November 30, 1895): 429.

> Praises "Nightingale" but points out two flaws: asks for an interpretation of ll. 5-7 and suggests that "thine happiness" should be "thy happiness."

Schuyler, Montgomery. "The Centenary of Keats." *Forum,* 20 (November 1895): 356-363.

> Argues that Keats's real excellence was not in narrative or song, but in the more artificial forms of the sonnet and the ode.

Van Dyke, Henry. "The Influence of Keats." *Century Magazine,* NS 28 (October 1895): 910-914.

> Says that "Nightingale," "Autumn," and "Urn" show that Keats was essentially a juvenile poet, reflecting, as they do, the "Melancholy springtime of the heart." His strength, as in "Urn," is his ability to blend together many details into a central vision.

1896

Bouchier, Jonathan. "Keats's 'Ode to a Nightingale.'" *Notes and Queries,* 8th Ser., 9 (January 4, 1896): 18.

> A reply to Holcombe Ingleby's objection to Keats's use of "thine happiness" in "Nightingale." Points out that in the 1867 edition of Keats's poems, as well as in three others, the phrase is printed "thy happiness."

Hearn, Lafcadio. *Interpretations of Literature.* Ed. John Erskine. 1915; rpt. New York: Dodd, Mead, 1924, pp. 171-200.

Two chapters on Keats are in this collection of lectures delivered without notes at the University of Tokyo from 1896 to 1902 and reconstructed from the notes of students. Praises the odes over the longer poems and gives interpretations of "Nightingale," "Urn," and "Autumn," reconstructing for his Japanese audience the emotion and sentiment in them, occasionally translating Western experience into Eastern terms.

Higginson, Thomas Wentworth. "A Keats Manuscript." *Forum*, 21 (June 1896): 420-424.

Reproduces a photograph of the manuscript of the first two stanzas of "Melancholy" given to John Howard Payne by George Keats and subsequently owned by R. S. Chilton. Discusses textual variations between the manuscript and the poem's published form. This manuscript is now in the Robert H. Taylor Collection of the Princeton University library.

Mount, C. B. "Keats's 'Ode to a Nightingale.'" *Notes and Queries*, 8th Ser., 9 (January 4, 1896): 18.

Reply to Ingleby's questioning of the meaning of lines 5-7 of "Nightingale" (*Notes and Queries*, November 30, 1895). Asserts that it is the poet who disclaims envy in those lines. To Ingleby's second point—that "thine happiness" should be "thy happiness"—offers a counter-argument based on changing ideas of euphony, noting, however, that his Rossetti edition reads "thy happiness."

R. R. "Keats's 'Ode to a Nightingale.'" *Notes and Queries*, 8th Ser., 9 (January 4, 1896): 18.

Reply to Ingleby's request for an interpretation of lines 5-7 of "Nightingale." Suggests that the speaker's heart aches, not through envy of the bird's lot, but from an excess of sympathetic happiness. Also points out that his 1862 Milnes edition reads "thy happiness," not "thine happiness."

Saintsbury, George. *A History of Nineteenth Century Literature*. London: Macmillan, 1896.

This history of nineteenth-century poetry names Keats as the father of all that followed: "He begat Tennyson, and Tennyson begat all the rest." Claims "Urn" and "La Belle Dame

Sans Merci" to be Keats's best poems and sufficient to establish
him as a leader in English poetry.

West, Kenyon. "A Study of Keats." *Chautauquan*, 22 (March 1896): 691-
696.

>Emphasizes the universality of the odes. Even "Nightin-
gale," the most personal of the odes, reflects "haunting Melancholy characteristic of the great throbbing heart of the world."

1897

Downer, Arthur C. *The Odes of Keats, With Notes and Analyses and a Memoir.*
1897; rpt. Folcroft, Penn.: Folcroft Press, 1969.

>Gives a biographical sketch of Keats and a general study of
his poetry as introductory material to this book on the odes.
Provides background information on each ode concerning its
composition and the situation out of which Keats wrote it.
Then prints a text of the ode, followed by a metrical analysis.
Next comes a stanza by stanza explication. Treats "Nightingale," "Urn," "Psyche," "Autumn," "Melancholy," "Maia," and
"Indolence" in this manner. Concludes with an essay on the
history of the pre-Keatsian ode.

Fruit, John P. "Keats's 'Ode to a Nightingale.'" *Modern Language Notes*, 12
(November 1897): 193-196.

>Traces the development of the feeling that lies within each
stage of "Nightingale," showing how each feeling leads to the
next.

Herford, C. H. "John Keats." In *The Age of Wordsworth.* 1897; rpt. London:
George Bell, 1905, pp. 254-266.

>Argues that in "Urn" the poet takes refuge from his de-
spondent contemplation of life in the ideal eternity of art and
in "Nightingale" in the magic of romance. In "Melancholy" the
mood is one of joy in the richness of life mixed with a sense of
its fugitiveness. "Psyche" is a return to the pagan freedom of
"Endymion." And "Autumn" resolves the tension through a
mellow acceptance.

Meynell, Alice. "The Five Odes of Keats." *Pall Mall Gazette*, September 29,

1897. Seen in *The Wares of Autolycus: Selected Literary Essays of Alice Meynell.* Ed. P. M. Fraser. London: Oxford University Press, 1965, pp. 70-73.

Ranks the odes by excellence: "Nightingale," "Urn," "Autumn," "Melancholy," and "Psyche." Praises "Nightingale" highly for its display of intellectual imagination, claims "Urn" to be a beautiful work of the fancy, marred by its last two lines, ranks "Autumn" next because of its perfection but no higher because of its lack of depth, labels "Melancholy" a poem of rhetorical beauty, and slights "Psyche" for its weak sentimentality.

Pickard, C. E. "Keats Improved." *Critic,* NS 27 (June 5, 1897): 388.

A reply to Wilkinson's article on "Urn" in *Bookman,* May 1897. Compares the excellence of Keats's "Urn" to that of Gray's "Elegy" and to the "Twenty-third Psalm."

Wilkinson, William C. "Two Odes of Keats's—I. 'On a Grecian Urn.'" *Bookman* (America), 5 (May 1897): 217-219.

Sets out to prove that "Urn" is not only not a good poem, but in fact unworthy of its theme. Attacks the ode for violating in several places the cheerfully Greek tone established in the two opening stanzas. For several lines which Wilkinson finds thus inharmonious, he offers verses to replace them.

----------. "Two Odes of Keats's—II. 'Ode to a Nightingale.'" *Bookman* (America), 5 (July 1897): 377-380.

Maintains that "Nightingale" is flawed by illogic. It is a series of "incoherent musings" irreconcilable to any sentiments which the nightingale can properly inspire.

1898

Graham, William. "Keats and Severn." In *Last Links with Byron, Shelley, and Keats.* London: Leonard Smithers, 1898, pp. 98-121.

See 1879.

Rev. of *The Odes of Keats,* by A. C. Downer. *Athenaeum,* January 15, 1898, p. 85.

Points out the limits to the familiar conception of Keats as

Greek. His attitude toward women was un-Greek, as were the adornments of fancy found in "Urn."

Pratt, Alice Edwards. *The Use of Color in the Verse of the English Romantic Poets.* Chicago: University of Chicago Press, 1898, pp. 78-88.

The Keats chapter argues that Keats's color was true, not to nature, but to his imagination and that he intended to use milder, more soothing and steady colors as his poetry developed. In this context, it brings up "Urn," "Nightingale," and "Autumn" briefly.

1899

Harrison, Frederic. "Lamb and Keats." *Contemporary Review,* 76 (July 1899): 62-69.

An address given at the unveiling of the portraits of Lamb and Keats at the Passmore Edwards Free Library at Edmonton. Praises the odes for their passion, charm, color, and melody. "Urn" is said to be "truly Greek in imagination."

1900

Hunt, T. W. "The Poetry of John Keats." *Methodist Review,* 82 (May 1900): 432-445.

Cites "Autumn" and "Nightingale" as examples of Keats's love of nature, quotes from "Urn," ll. 11-12, to show that it is brief passages which form the foundation of Keats's reputation, and interprets the last lines of "Urn" as Keats's creed.

Mackenzie, David J. "John Keats." In *Byways Among Books.* Wick: W. Rae, 1900, pp. 65-95.

The Keats chapter devotes one paragraph to the odes, praising them and mentioning their importance to the English ode tradition.

Omond, T. S. *The Romantic Triumph.* 1900; rpt. New York: Charles Scribner's Sons, 1909.

The chapter covering the English Romantic Movement in literature quotes from "Nightingale" to illustrate romantic longing and praises the "statuesque dignity" of "Urn." In keeping with the purpose of this book, which is to discuss the movement, not individual works, no real criticism of the odes is offered.

1901

Symons, Arthur. "John Keats." *Monthly Review*, 5 (October 1901): 139-158. Seen in *The Romantic Movement in English Poetry*. New York: E. P. Dutton, 1909, pp. 298-314.

Surveys Keats's poetry and tries to capture the psychological attitude which lies behind it; in his words: "The poet in his poetry." Views Keats as a passionate lover of beauty who is sometimes metrically slipshod.

1903

C.C.B. "Keats's 'Ode to a Nightingale': The Original MS." *Notes and Queries*, 9th Ser., 11 (May 9, 1903): 372.

Reply to the editor's note to John Grigor's note (*Notes and Queries*, April 18, 1903). Argues briefly that Keats's usual spelling of fairy was "faery."

Colvin, Sir Sidney. "A Morning's Work in a Hampstead Garden." *Monthly Review*, 10 (March 1903): 130-141. Seen in *The John Keats Memorial Volume*. Issued by the Keats House Committee, Hampstead. New York: John Lane, 1921.

Reproduces a facsimile of the Houghton-Crewe Manuscript of "Nightingale" and argues against the validity of Charles Brown's account of the poem's composition. Gives a reading of the ode, especially emphasizing analysis of textual variants and treating it as the expression of a mood highly characteristic of Keats.

Grigor, John. "Keats's 'Ode to a Nightingale': The Original MS." *Notes and Queries*, 9th Ser., 11 (April 18, 1903): 305.

Reports Colvin's discovery of the Houghton-Crewe manuscript of "Nightingale," publicized previously in his *Monthly Review* article. Discusses briefly three of Keats's revisions newly brought to light by that manuscript.

1904

Bradley, A. C. "John Keats." In *Chamber's Cyclopedia of English Literature.* Philadelphia: J. B. Lippincott, 1904. Vol. III, pp. 99-107.

Distinguishes the odes for their expressiveness of feeling and discusses briefly the theme of the transitoriness of life versus the eternity of beauty in them.

Burne-Jones, Georgiana. *The Memorials of Edward Burne-Jones.* 1904; rpt. New York: Macmillan, 1906. Vol. II, p. 264.

See 1895.

Gwynn, Stephen. "Keats." In *The Masters of English Literature.* New York: Macmillan, 1904, pp. 369-379.

A brief, general treatment of Keats. Praises "Autumn," "Urn," and "Nightingale" highly. Values them for their boldness of language and for their sense of magic and mystery.

"To Autumn." *Century Magazine,* 47 (November 1904): 83-89.

A text of "Autumn" and a reproduction of the holograph, accompanied by illustrations by Maxfield Parrish.

1905

Bailey, John. "Keats." *Times Literary Supplement,* April 14, 1905, pp. 117-118.

Review of De Selincourt's edition, Drury's edition, and Sampson's edition. Mentions that "Autumn" shows Keats had an inclination to represent nature, unlike Shelley, in the "Ode to the West Wind," who interpreted it.

Bayne, Thomas. "Keats's 'Grecian Urn.'" *Notes and Queries,* 10th Ser., 3 (June 17, 1905): 464.

Notes that Keats's heifer "lowing at the skies" may be, unlike the "silken flanks," out of keeping with the facts of nature, but that it has a literary precedent in Ovid's *Metamorphoses,* III. i.20.

1906

Compton-Rickett, Arthur. "Keats and Rossetti." In *Personal Forces in Modern Literature.* New York: E. P. Dutton, 1906, pp. 112-139.

A book demonstrating various personality types among men of letters as reflected in their work. Includes the "Keats and Rossetti" section in a chapter on "The Poet." Extols the odes, "Nightingale" and "Urn" especially, for their qualities of symmetry, color (bringing details to life), and perspective (mixing the sensuous with the super-sensuous). Rossetti is shown to have these same virtues.

Dawson, W. J. "John Keats." In *The Makers of English Poetry*. 1906; rpt. Port Washington, New York: Kennikat Press, 1968, pp. 57-69.

Considers the odes briefly in the chapter on Keats. Praises them for their intensity of imagination, sense of enchantment, and youthful passion.

More, Paul Elmer. "John Keats." In *Shelburne Essays*. Fourth Series. 1906; rpt. Boston: Houghton Mifflin, 1922, pp. 99-128.

General treatment of Keats's works. Quotes from "Nightingale," "Melancholy," and "Urn" to show briefly that they have a common theme of sadness at the passing of beauty.

1907

Brooke, Stopford A. "Keats." In *Studies in Poetry*. 1907; rpt. Port Washington, New York: Kennikat Press, 1967, pp. 202-253.

The chapter on Keats in this collection of essays interprets the odes as well as the rest of Keats's major poetry under the thesis that Keats characteristically sought beauty and the beauty of nature because the impulse of the French Revolution was dead to him.

Goodall, G. R. "The Genius of Keats." *Manchester Literary Club Papers*, 33 (1907): 247-263.

Stresses Keats's use of nature in the odes and their musical quality. Also, points out the pictorial representation of the season in "Autumn."

Payne, William Morton. "John Keats." In *The Greater English Poets of the Nineteenth Century*. 1907; rpt. New York: H. Holt, 1909, pp. 1-32.

Views the odes as Keats's best poetry. Though various critics have found faults in them, the reason they will not bear strict logical analysis is that they are poems of the heart rather than of the intellect.

1908

Hancock, Albert Elmer. *John Keats: A Literary Biography*. Boston: Houghton Mifflin, 1908.

Says that the odes are less popular than the narrative works but that they appeal more strongly to those with cultured tastes. "Psyche" tempers passion into tenderness, "Autumn" paints nature objectively, "Melancholy" renders the profundity of emotion intellectual, and "Urn" expresses Keats's philosophy of idealism.

Hooker, Brian. "The Understanding of John Keats." *Forum* (New York), 40 (December 1908): 584-590.

Review of Hancock's biography of Keats. Uses the ending of "Urn" to demonstrate Keats's unwitting Christianity. Keats worshipped beauty, truth, and right, all of which are one and personified in God. Keats naturally worshipped God in man's truth and loveliness and in the earth's beauty.

1909

Gide, André. *Strait Is the Gate*. Trans. Dorothy Bussy. 1924; rpt. New York: Alfred A. Knopf, 1949.

The character Alissa Bucolin says in this 1909 novel that she would give up nearly all Byron and Shelley for Keats's four odes, and all of Hugo for a few of Baudelaire's sonnets.

Mabie, Hamilton Wright. "'Ode on a Grecian Urn' by John Keats, the Third of a Series of Great Poems with Introductions." *Outlook*, 91 (February 27, 1909): 473-477.

General biographical introduction to "Urn." Views the poem as a contrast to the other odes. Where they are effusive and texturally variegated, it is restrained and chiselled.

Magnus, Laurie. *English Literature in the Nineteenth Century: An Essay in Criticism*, New York: G. P. Putnam's Sons, 1909.

Cites the odes as exceptions to the adolescent quality that generally runs through Keats's poetry.

"The Posthumous Growth of Keats's Fame." *Current Literature*, 46 (January 1909): 59-60.

Review of Hancock's biography of Keats. Argues, on the basis of "Urn"'s ending, that Keats feeds man's need for beauty, a need which ultimately outlives social systems and politics.

Yeats, William Butler. *Memoirs: Autobiography—First Draft; Journal.* Ed. Denis Donoghue. London: Macmillan, 1972.

Yeats says in his journal on March 9, 1909, that great art is always a statement of traditional truths. The "revolt of individualism" came, he says, because tradition had become degraded. He uses "Nightingale" as an example of "a great work of art" which is rooted in the past.

1910

Courthope, William John. "Romanticism in English Poetry: Keats." In *A History of English Poetry*. 1910; rpt. New York: Russell and Russell, 1962. Vol. VI, pp. 320-356.

Devotes a chapter to Keats. The thesis of this chapter, which colors its interpretation of the odes, is that Keats had, on the one hand, a conviction of an unseen spirit existing in nature and, on the other, a painter's bent toward the pictorial and representative. These two forces combine in the odes to produce an expression of Abstract Beauty.

Saintsbury, George. *History of English Prosody*. London: Macmillan, 1910. Vol. III, pp. 116-132.

Treats the odes briefly as demonstrations of Keats's mastery of stanzaic poetry. Ranks "Nightingale," "Urn," and "Autumn" highly, but faults "Psyche" for its loose stanza arrangement.

1911

Hudson, William Henry. *Keats and His Poetry*. London: George G. Harrap, 1911.

A selection of Keats's poems joined together by biographical criticism. "Nightingale," "Urn," and "Melancholy" are treated as expressing sadness at mutability, and "Autumn" is viewed as a simple nature poem.

Mackail, J. W. "Keats." In *Lectures on Poetry*. New York: Longmans, Green, 1911.

    Considers the odes briefly as he illustrates what he takes to be Keats's most prominent poetic characteristic: continual growth and development.

Owen, Wilfred. *Wilfred Owen: Collected Letters*. Ed. Harold and John Bell. London: Oxford University Press, 1967.

    Wilfred Owen recommends "Nightingale" to his mother in a letter, April 2, 1911.

Trin. Coll. Camb. "Keats's 'Ode to a Nightingale.'" *Notes and Queries*, 11th Ser., 4 (December 23, 1911): 507.

    A query asking the relevance of ll. 68-70 from "Nightingale." The author wonders whether they might be an allusion.

1912

Bayley, A. R. "Keats's 'Ode to a Nightingale.'" *Notes and Queries*, 11th Ser., 5 (January 6, 1912): 11.

    Responds to the query in *Notes and Queries*, December 23, 1911, asking the relevance or reference of faery lands in "Nightingale" by quoting H. B. Forman's 1889 statement on the lines.

Bayne, Thomas. "Keats's 'Ode to a Nightingale.'" *Notes and Queries*, 11th Ser., 5 (January 6, 1912): 11.

    Reply to a query in *Notes and Queries*, December 23, 1911. Notes that the faery land of "Nightingale" comes from *Oedipus Colonus*.

C.C.B. "Keats's 'Ode to a Nightingale.'" *Notes and Queries*, 11th Ser., 5 (January 6, 1912): 11.

    Reply to a query appearing in *Notes and Queries*, December 23, 1911, asking the relevance and reference of ll. 68-70 of

"Nightingale." Objects that the question is literalistic and insignificant.

Cook, Albert S. "Keats and Cartwright." *Nation*, 95 (July 11, 1912): 34.

Admitting the lack of positive evidence, this letter to the editor builds a case that "Urn" was influenced by the poetry of William Cartwright in Humphrey Moseley's 1651 edition.

F. H. "Keats's 'Ode to a Nightingale.'" *Notes and Queries*, 11 Ser., 5 (January 6, 1912): 11.

Suggests that "forlorn" in line seventy of "Nightingale" refers to the tradition that faeries, though longer-lived than humans and more powerful, were outside the scheme of redemption and lacking immortal souls.

Pennialinus. "Keats's 'Ode to a Nightingale.'" *Notes and Queries*, 11th Ser., 5 (January 6, 1912): 11.

Response to the query in *Notes and Queries*, December 23, 1911. Suggests that the faery lands in "Nightingale" come from Keats's imagination rather than his reading.

Pinchbeck, W. H. "Keats's 'Ode to a Nightingale.'" *Notes and Queries*, 11th Ser., 5 (January 20, 1912): 58-59.

Suggests that lines 68-70 of "Nightingale" have their source in the *Arabian Nights*.

----------. Keats's 'Ode to a Nightingale.'" *Notes and Queries*, 11th Ser., 5 (March 2, 1912): 175.

Reply to Trin. Coll. Camb.'s query as to the exact tale of the *Arabian Nights* which influenced lines 68-70 of "Nightingale." Responds that, though it may have been the "Third Calendar," Keats probably responded generally to his reading of the tales as a whole.

Rannie, David Watson. "Keats's Epithets." *Essays and Studies by Members of the English Association*, 3 (1912): 92-113.

Discusses Keats's use of epithets, which he divides into three categories: 1) -ed; 2) -y; and, 3) compound. Argues that Keats's epithets are pictorial and not static. They are constructed for sense, not for sound, and they are not highly

imaginative. Examples from the odes, among other poems, are
used throughout.

Reed, Edward Bliss. *English Lyrical Poetry.* 1912; rpt. New York: Haskell
House, 1967.

Describes the odes enthusiastically, briefly, and generally,
and ranks "Autumn" and "Nightingale" highest.

Suddard, S. J. Mary. *Keats, Shelley, and Shakespeare: Studies.* Cambridge:
Cambridge University Press, 1912.

Argues that Keats was content with presenting separate
effects of light, sound, color, touch, and smell until he composed "Nightingale," when he came to learn the interdepen-
dence of the senses.

"Table Talk." *The Bookman Keats-Shelley Memorial Souvenir,* June 20, 1912,
pp. 3-8.

Announces the up-coming Keats-Shelley Memorial Matinee
on July 25 and 28, 1912, in which Mr. E. S. Willard was to recite
"Urn" dressed in ancient Greek costume before scenery arranged by Sir Lawrence Alma-Tadema and painted by Mr.
Joseph Harker.

Trin. Coll. Camb. "Keats's 'Ode to a Nightingale.'" *Notes and Queries,* 11th
Ser., 5 (February 10, 1912): 116.

Asks W. H. Pinchbeck which of the tales of the *Arabian Nights*
he had in mind when he suggested them as a source for lines
68-70 of "Nightingale" in *Notes and Queries,* January 20, 1912.

1913

Ascher, Isadore G., and Mary DeReyes. "John Keats." *The Poetry Review,* 3
(1913): 72-82.

Two short, general essays on Keats's poetry under a single
title, one by Ascher and one by DeReyes. Ascher mentions
"Nightingale" as the best lyric in English poetry up to its time.
DeReyes calls the odes Keats's best poetry, mentioning "Autumn," "Nightingale," and "Urn" briefly and praising Keats for
his ability to translate emotions into the terms of ordinary life.

Rhys, Ernest. *Lyric Poetry.* New York: E. P. Dutton, 1913.

   Briefly states the opinion that Keats took an over-artificial ode form and infused it with an impulsive melodiousness.

Spurgeon, Caroline F. E. *Mysticism in English Literature.* 1913; rpt. Cambridge: Cambridge University Press, 1922.

   Argues, based on "Endymion" (I, 744 ff.), that Keats was essentially a mystic. Quotes the last two lines of "Urn" as the essence of Keats's philosophy.

1914

Barbe, Waitman. *Great Poems Interpreted.* New York: Hinds, Noble, and Eldredge, 1914.

   Includes "Nightingale" and "Urn" among the thirty-one poems treated here. Gives an explication of each poem and a paraphrase in outline form.

Chubb, Edwin Watts. "Keats." In *Masters of English Literature.* 1914; rpt. Freeport, New York: Books for Libraries Press, 1967, pp. 230-247.

   Quotes and paraphrases the praises of various critics for "Nightingale" and "Urn."

1915

Hearn, Lafcadio. *Interpretations of Literature.* Ed. John Erskine. 1915; rpt. New York: Dodd, Mead, 1924, pp. 171-200.

   See 1896.

Powys, John Cooper. "Keats." In *Visions and Revisions: A Book of Literary Devotions.* New York: G. Arnold Shaw, 1915, pp. 183-196.

   Interprets the odes as filled with pain because of Keats's driving passion for physical sensation and the imminent fact that the physical must eventually be abandoned. Powys's feelings on this subject are expressed fervently.

1916

Herford, C. H. "Keats." In *The Cambridge History of English Literature.* Ed. A.

W. Ward and A. R. Waller. New York: G. P. Putnam's Sons, 1916. Vol. XII, pp. 87-103.

Devotes a little over two pages to the odes. Sees them as spontaneous in their composition and expressive of Keats's abiding love of beauty.

Hills, M. Robertson, Introd. *John Keats: Odes, Lyrics, and Sonnets.* Oxford: Clarendon Press, 1916.

Feels that "Nightingale," "Urn," and "Melancholy" present a contrast between life as it is and the eternal principle of beauty. "Autumn" reconciles these two forces and leaves us content.

1917

Burke, Robert E. "Keats and Giorgione—A Parallel." *Art and Archaeology,* 5 (March 1917): 133-135.

Claims an affinity between Giorgione and Keats which argues almost convincingly for the transmigration of souls. Likens "Melancholy" to "The Concert" and "Urn" to "The Venetian Pastoral."

Colvin, Sidney. *John Keats: His Life and Poetry, His Friends, and After-Fame.* 1917; rpt. New York: Octagon Books, 1970.

Devotes seven pages to the odes. Gives brief traditional explications of "Urn" and "Nightingale," describes "Psyche" and "Melancholy," and reprints "Autumn."

Leatham, James. *John Keats: The Poet of Beauty.* Cottingham: Cottingham Press, 1917.

Uses the odes as evidence that Keats was consciously trying to establish a theory of poetry based on beauty-worship.

Shanks, Edward. "Keats and His Critics." *New Statesman,* 10 (November 17, 1917): 157-158.

Review of Colvin's biography of Keats. Contends that, during the period in which Keats composed the odes, his powers were sensuous, not intellectual. "Urn" attempts the philosophical but fails to unite it successfully with the poetic.

1918

Cook, Edward [Tyas]. *Literary Recreations.* 1918; rpt. London: Macmillan, 1919, pp. 189-192 and 306-307.

Treats the odes twice. Gives a discussion of the pastime of ranking the odes in order of merit. And mentions the revision of "Nightingale" changing "the wide" to "magic" and "keelless" to "perilous" in lines 69-70.

1919

Babbitt, Irving. *Rousseau and Romanticism.* 1919; rpt. Cambridge: Houghton Mifflin, 1957.

Denies that beauty is truth. Invokes Helen of Troy as evidence, who was beautiful but neither good nor true.

Gilbert, Allan H. "The 'Furrow' in Keats's 'Ode to Autumn.'" *Journal of English and Germanic Philology,* 18 (October 1919): 587-592.

Charges Keats with verbal imprecision in the passage from the second stanza of "Autumn" which has the season sleeping in a furrow. Points out that by reaping time the furrows would have been destroyed by harrowing and that one sleeps in, not on, a furrow. Also points out possible literary sources for the general use of "furrow" to mean "grainfield."

1920

Clutton-Brock, Arthur. "The Promise of Keats." In *Essays on Books.* 1920; rpt. London: Methuen, 1921, pp. 115-128.

Points out how far Keats was from using natural speech in "Nightingale." In this view, Keats was a conscious craftsman.

Quiller-Couch, Arthur. *On the Art of Reading: Lectures Delivered in the University of Cambridge 1916-1918.* Cambridge: Cambridge University Press, 1920.

Uses "Urn" to demonstrate how one should teach a poem. Takes the point of the ode to be the eternal appeal of an arrested moment of innocent gaiety.

Squire, J[ohn] C[ollings]. "Keats's Fame." In *Life and Letters.* London: William Heinemann, [1920?], pp. 18-25.

This brief, personal evaluation of the odes is that they rank, along with "Hyperion," just below the greatest works of Shakespeare and Milton because they escape the over-luscious imagery of his earlier poetry and contain the strengths of character and intellect.

Williamson, Claude. "Concerning John Keats." In *Writers of Three Centuries, 1789-1914*. Philadelphia: George W. Jacobs, [1920], pp. 97-103.

Brief, general essay on Keats. Treats "Urn" and "Nightingale" as poems of the imagination as a means of perceiving the decay and unrest of life and the eternity of beauty.

1921

Bailey, John. "The Poet of Stillness." In *The John Keats Memorial Volume*. Issued by the Keats House Committee, Hampstead. New York: John Lane, 1921.

Approaches the odes as hymns to silence. "Nightingale," especially, concerns a passive, quiescent submission to outside influence, and it expresses a strong attraction for death-like states.

Bradley, A. C. "Keats and 'Philosophy.'" In *The John Keats Memorial Volume*. Issued by the Keats House Committee, Hampstead. New York: John Lane, 1921.

Defines Keats's use of the term "philosophy." Takes the ending of "Urn" as an expression of Keats's central article of faith.

De Selincourt, Ernest. "The Warton Lecture on Keats." In *The John Keats Memorial Volume*. Issued by the Keats House Committee, Hampstead. New York: John Lane, 1921.

Delivered before the British Academy on the centenary of Keats's death. Approaches the odes as intensely imaginative expressions of long-recognized thoughts and feelings. Explains "Autumn," "Nightingale," and "Urn" in terms of Keats's love of beauty and the function of art of preserving it.

Draper, William H. "John Keats." In *The John Keats Memorial Volume*. Issued by the Keats House Committee, Hampstead. New York: John Lane, 1921.

Says that the length of the odes is the source of their greatness: they are long enough to give full expression but not so long as to become diffuse.

Elliott, G. R. "The Real Tragedy of Keats (A Post-Centenary View)." *PMLA*, 36 (September 1921): 315-331.

Conceives that the real tragedy of Keats is that he was moving toward the writing of a more ethical kind of poetry which would have proven beyond his powers. Takes "Urn" as an example of his maturing poetry which attempted a deliberate interpretation of life.

Hamilton, Sir Ian. "John Keats." In *The John Keats Memorial Volume*. Issued by the Keats House Committee, Hampstead. New York: John Lane, 1921.

Hamilton was a British officer in World War I. He writes here in an elevated tone about the inspired motivation of his troops. Quoting ll. 49-50 of "Urn," he explains that his men saw beauty in the things they were fighting for and struggled in combat to insure them as reality.

"Keats." *Times Literary Supplement*, February 17, 1921, pp. 97-98.

This centenary essay discussing Keats's achievements, potentials, and place in literary history praises the odes as his best work. It offers them as the very definition of poetry itself.

Ker, William Paton. "Keats." In *Collected Essays of W. P. Ker*. Ed. Charles Whibley. London: Macmillan, 1925. Vol. I, pp. 224-241.

A lecture given on March 14, 1921. Argues that "Nightingale," "Urn," and "Autumn" are descendants of the pastoralism of the "Hymn to Pan" ("Endymion," I, 232-306) rather than the more intellectual "Psyche" or "Melancholy."

Lucas, E. V. "A Bird Sanctuary." In *The John Keats Memorial Volume*. Issued by the Keats House Committee, Hampstead. New York: John Lane, 1921.

This chatty, brief article reminisces about the author's delight in visiting Wentworth Place, now called Lawn Bank, and finding the garden in which Keats reportedly composed "Nightingale" to be a bird sanctuary. It urges the Keats Memorial Trustees to preserve it so, when they take control of the property.

Moult, Thomas. "John Keats and the Poetry of Our Time." *Fortnightly Review,* NS 109 (February 1921): 309-320.

Repeats Severn's account of the composition of "Nightingale" and praises the ode for its fusion of loveliness and thought. Feels that Keats, like many other poets, was at war with his own soul.

Newman, Sir George. *John Keats: Apothecary and Poet.* Sheffield: T. Booth, 1921.

Interprets the ending of "Urn" to mean that beauty is a stepping of the imagination towards or into the truth. This was the core of Keats's thinking.

Samuel, Herbert. "The Life and Poetry of John Keats." *Contemporary Review,* 119 (April 1921): 494-501.

General essay on the centenary of Keats's death. Briefly praises "Nightingale" as Keats's greatest ode, attacks ll. 49-50 of "Urn" as relatively meaningless, and points out a biographical background to "Melancholy."

1922

Crawford, Alexander Wellington. "Keats's 'Ode to the Nightingale.'" *Modern Language Notes,* 37 (December 1922): 476-481.

Notices that there are only two distinct images in "Nightingale": 1) the actual conditions of the morning when Keats composed the poem; and, 2) the darkness or "night."

Fausset, Hugh I'Anson. *Keats: A Study In Development.* 1922; rpt. London: Secker and Warburg, 1966.

Traces Keats's development as a poet. Discusses the odes as a transition stage between Keats's sensuousness and idealism. Keats had been a purely sensuous poet up until "Nightingale" and "Urn," when he linked sensuous beauty with truth and transcended the physical. "Melancholy" and "Psyche" represent temporary regressions, and "Autumn" is the purest expression of Keats's triumph over sensuousness.

Gide, André. *The Journals of André Gide.* Trans. Justin O'Brien. Vol. 2. New York: Alfred A. Knopf, 1948.

Gide records in his journal for November 12, 1922, that he learned by heart "Nightingale," "Psyche," and "Autumn."

Lynd, Robert. "Keats." In *Books and Authors.* London: Richard Cobden-Sanderson, 1922, pp. 45-62.

Treats the odes as a high achievement in the kind of poetry he argues that Keats wrote. The odes, and all of Keats's truly great poetry, arose from his love for Fanny Brawne. As a poet, Keats was more concerned with creating a beautiful picture of life than with expressing its reality.

Lyster, T. W. "Repetition in Keats." *Times Literary Supplement,* April 6, 1922, p. 228.

Points out in a letter that Keats made frequent use of repetition in his poetry, especially in the 1820 volume. Cites instances from "Urn," "Psyche," and "Melancholy."

1923

Greenwood, Sir Granville George. *Lee, Shakespeare, and a Tertium Quid.* London: Cecil Palmer, 1923.

Defends his assertion in *The Shakespeare Problem Restated* that William Shakespeare was not the author of *Hamlet, Othello,* et al., against Sir Sidney Lee's attack in *A Life of Shakespeare.* Argues that Keats was more likely to have been able to write "Nightingale" than Shakespeare was *Hamlet,* since Keats was not from so low a family as had been imagined, was possessed of genuine genius, and was backed by a solid education.

Massey, Bernard Wilfrid Arbuthnot. *The Compound Epithets of Shelley and Keats Considered from the Structural, the Historical, and the Literary Standpoints, With Some Comparisons, from the Greek, the Old English and the German.* Poznan: Poznanskie Towarzystwo Przyjaciol Nauk, 1923.

Lists the compound epithets of Keats according to various categories both of Greek grammar and of English, dividing the

English into epithets introduced by Old English, Middle English, sixteenth-, seventeenth-, and eighteenth-century English, and those introduced by Keats himself. Includes in the lists epithets from the odes.

1924

Shackford, Martha Hale. "Keats and Adversity." *Sewanee Review*, 32 (1924): 474-487.

Discusses "Nightingale" as expressing a personal sense of melancholy brought on by Keats's circumstances.

1925

Aiken, Conrad. "John Keats." *Dial*, 75 (June 1925): 475-490.

Review of Amy Lowell's biography of Keats. Points out that the odes, excepting "Autumn," share the common theme of the antinomy of beauty and death. "Melancholy" states the theme plainly. In "Nightingale," the poet seeks escape from the thought by considering the immortality of natural beauty. In "Urn" escape is found in the idea that art immortalizes beauty. And in "Psyche" the immortality for beauty is found in the consciousness of the observer. Overall, views the odes to contain more of pessimism than of idealism.

Faulkner, William. "Verse Old and Nascent: A Pilgrimage." *Double Dealer*, 7 (April 1925): 129-131. Seen in *William Faulkner: Early Prose and Poetry*. Ed. Carvel Collins. Boston: Little, Brown, 1962.

Finds a power and strength in the opening lines of "Urn." In "Nightingale," too, sees a masculine handling of spiritual beauty.

Ker, William Paton. "Keats." In *Collected Essays of W. P. Ker*. Ed. Charles Whibley. London: Macmillan, 1925. Vol. I, pp. 224-241.

See 1921.

Lowell, Amy. *John Keats*. Boston: Houghton Mifflin, 1925.

In a comprehensive approach to the odes, views "Psyche" as a half-successful experiment which paved the way for Keats's greater odes. "Urn" is a remarkable harmonization of his varying senses, thoughts, and beliefs. "Melancholy" presents the idea that grief is always present in beauty to the sensitive observer. "Nightingale" is a product of the free play of the imagination. And "Autumn" is an impersonal, pictorial poem lacking the undercurrent of meaning and emotion found in the other odes.

Murry, John Middleton. *Keats and Shakespeare: A Study of Keats' Poetic Life from 1816 to 1820.* London: Humphrey Milford, 1925.

Discusses Keats's poems as reflective of "the poet's soul which underlies them." Traces a growth in Keats's poetry, culminating in the odes, which almost reaches the kind of pure poetry Shakespeare wrote.

V. R. "Keats's Use of Capitals." *Notes and Queries,* OS 149 (July 4, 1925): 15.

A reply to J.W.N.'s query (*Notes and Queries,* June 6, 1925) concerning the capitalization of "Primrose" in "Ode to Maia." Argues that Keats capitalized "Beauty" in "Nightingale" to indicate personification.

1926

Evans, B. Ifor. "Keats and the Golden Ass." *Nineteenth Century,* 100 (August 1926): 263-271.

Traces the development of the Cupid and Psyche story of Apuleius through Mrs. Tighe and to Keats.

Garrod, H. W. *Keats.* 1926; rpt. Oxford: Clarendon Press, 1967.

Argues that Keats's odes were a development, not from the eighteenth century ode or hymn, but from the sonnet. Bases this conclusion in part on an analysis of the meter of the odes. Also demonstrates the odes to form a sequence in mood.

Havens, Raymond D. "Concerning the 'Ode on a Grecian Urn.'" *Modern Philology,* 24 (November 1926): 209-214.

Links "Melancholy" and "Urn" thematically. They both deal with sorrow arising from a consciousness of the transitoriness of much human joy. The understanding of the ending of "Urn" derives from the awareness of the importance of beauty

Havens derived from viewing the Roman aqueduct at Tarragona.

Thorpe, Clarence De Witt. *The Mind of John Keats.* 1926; rpt. New York: Russell and Russell, 1964.

Argues that in "Urn" Keats describes, not the scenes on the urn themselves, but the scenes upon which the creator of the urn modeled those on the urn. The scenes on the urn are important for Keats because he can see beyond them into the potter's imagination and beyond that into the universal aspects of the scenes.

1927

Auslander, Joseph and Frank Ernest Hill. "'Beauty is Truth, Truth Beauty.'" In *The Winged Horse: The Story of the Poets and Their Poetry.* Garden City: Doubleday, Doran, 1927, pp. 283-302.

A general and basic account of Keats's life and works. Treats the odes briefly as characterized by quietness, sadness, and sentimentality.

Cox, Morgan B. "More on False Shift." *Saturday Review,* 4 (October 8, 1927): 180.

Demonstrates the harmony of lines 68-70 of "Nightingale" with the rest of the poem, defending them against the charge of supernaturalism and maintaining that they allude to the exotic romanticism of medieval tales of chivalry.

Haight, Elizabeth Hazelton. *Apuleius and His Influence.* New York: Longmans, Green, 1927.

Traces the Psyche myth from Apuleius through William Adlington, Edmund Spenser, Thomas Heywood, Shakerley Marmion, Dr. Joseph Beaumont, Thomas Shadwell, Thomas Duffet, Gloucester Ridley, Mrs. Tighe, Hudson Gurney, John Keats, Elizabeth Barrett Browning, William Morris, Sir Lewis Morris, Robert Bridges, and Walter Pater.

Lawrence, D. H. "The Nightingale." *Forum,* 78 (September 1927): 382-387.

Contrasts the song of the actual nightingale with Keats's

depiction of it in his ode. There is nothing dreamy or forlorn about the real bird's song. It is Keats, not the bird, who longs for selflessness.

Lowden, Samuel Marion. "Ode on Melancholy." In *Understanding Great Poems*. Harrisburg, Penn.: Handy Book Corporation, 1927, pp. 121-128.

This is a guide to teaching "Melancholy." It includes some notes to the poem, a brief background to it, a paraphrase in outline form, an interpretation, and suggestions for classroom approaches. Lowden considers "Melancholy" to be untypical of Keats because it "faces the facts of life" instead of seeking escape in beauty.

Patterson, Margaret. "False Shift." *Saturday Review*, 3 (July 23, 1927): 1000.

This letter attacks lines 68-70 of "Nightingale" as a "false shift" from the more human elements earlier in the stanza. It calls the phrase "magic casements" "...a bit of elegant stuffing."

Weller, Earle Vonard. "Keats and Mary Tighe." *PMLA*, 42 (December 1927): 963-985.

Argues that Keats's influence by Mrs. Tighe was more extensive than has been previously supposed. Discusses "Nightingale"'s debt to Mrs. Tighe's "Psyche," and mentions parallels in "Urn" and "Psyche."

1928

Blunden, Edmund. *Leigh Hunt's* Examiner *Examined*. London: Cobden-Sanderson, 1928.

Suggests that Robert Hunt's Review in the *Examiner* in February 1820 of Mr. Moses' engravings of vases may have influenced "Urn."

Grierson, H. J. C. *Lyrical Poetry from Blake to Hardy*. 1928; rpt. London: Hogarth Press, 1950.

Adds Keats's five major odes to Spenser's "Epithalamion" and Milton's "Lycidas" as the only odes up to that time satisfying in imagination, evolution, and music. Ranks "Nightingale," "Autumn," and "Urn" over "Melancholy" and "Psyche" because of their greater subtlety and more elaborate evolution of thought.

Ker, W. P. *Form and Style in Poetry.* 1928; rpt. London: Macmillan, 1929.

Feels that both "Nightingale" and "Urn" are a "raid into the eternal world," the one into the world of the bird and the other into the world of the urn. Both poems interpret "that life of Beauty which is common to all the arts—the life of Mnemosyne or Memory."

Lamborn, E. A. Greening. *Poetic Values: A Guide to the Appreciation of the Golden Treasury.* 1928; rpt. Oxford: Clarendon Press, 1929.

Contains commentaries for each of the poems in Palgrave's *Golden Treasury.* Cites Wordsworth's "To the Cuckoo" as the inspiration for "Nightingale" and gives a brief discussion and notes. Traces "Autumn" back to Shakespeare's "Sonnet 97" and discusses the rhythm and rhyme of the ode.

Snow, Royall. "Heresy Concerning Keats." *PMLA,* 43 (1928): 1142-1149.

Argues that the subject of "Urn" is not abstract and permanent beauty but the more imminent beauty of the senses represented by the figures on the urn.

Spurgeon, Caroline F. E. *Keats's Shakespeare: A Descriptive Study.* 1928; rpt. Oxford: Clarendon Press, 1968.

Describes and reprints some of Keats's underlinings and annotations in his copy of Shakespeare. Links the murmuring pines of "Psyche" to *The Merchant of Venice,* IV, i, 80-82. And argues that "Autumn" exhibits a return to Keats's natural, Shakespearean self after a period of rejecting all that he loved best.

1929

Blunden, Edmund. "Keats and His Predecessors: A Note on the 'Ode to a Nightingale.'" *London Mercury,* 20 (1929): 289-292.

Finds sources for "Nightingale" in Horace, Milton, William Browne, and Shakespeare.

Bushnell, Nelson Sherwin. "Notes on 'Prof. Garrod's Keats.'" *Modern*

Language Notes, 44 (May 1929): 287-296.

Argues that the odes are not a development of the sonnet form. For one thing, they are just as elegaic as the Shakespearean sonnet whose elegaic quality Keats was supposedly trying to avoid. For another, the subject matter of the odes differs from the kind of topics he chose to write sonnets about.

Eliot, T. S. "Dante (1929)." In *Selected Essays*. 1932: rpt. New York: Harcourt, Brace, and World, 1964, pp. 199-237.

In his note to Section II of his essay on Dante, Eliot disagrees with Richards' view of "Urn," ll. 49-50, as a "pseudo-statement." Eliot finds the statement a blemish because it is meaningless.

Richards, Ivor Armstrong. *Practical Criticism: A Study of Literary Judgment*. 1929; rpt. London: Kegan Paul, Trench, Trubner, 1946.

Richards interprets "Urn," ll. 49-50, as what he calls elsewhere a "pseudo-statement," a statement made in poetry for the purpose of manipulating and expressing feelings, not as a declaration of doctrine.

Saito, Takeshi. *Keats's View of Poetry*. London: Cobden-Sanderson, 1929.

On the development of Keats's thought in his poetry. Briefly treats the odes as expressions of sorrow and sympathy for the miseries of the world.

Shipman, Mary Evelyn. "Orthodoxy Concerning Keats." *PMLA*, 44 (1929): 929-934.

Reply to Royall Snow's "Heresy Concerning Keats." Argues that Keats in "Urn" was thinking of abstract, not sensuous beauty.

1930

Bernbaum, Ernest. *Guide Through the Romantic Movement*. 1930; rpt. New York: Ronald Press, 1940.

Believes the ode to be the form best suited to express Keats's fondness for imagery, his seriousness, and his meditativeness.

Empson, William. *Seven Types of Ambiguity.* 1930; rpt. Norfolk, Connecticut: New Directions, 1953.

Discusses "Melancholy" in exemplification of the seventh type of ambiguity, in which two meanings of a word differ to the point of contradiction, indicating a division in the writer's mind. Keats is indicating that the desire for joy can only be fulfilled through the experience of melancholy.

[Kunitz, Stanley Jasspon]. "Dilly Tante Observes." *Wilson Bulletin for Librarians,* 4 (June 1930): 503-505.

Feels that "Melancholy" is decidedly inferior to Keats's best pieces. Lists twelve poems of the last fifteen years that are at least as good, including "The Waste Land," "Peter Quince At the Clavier," and "To Earthward."

Mallam, Phosphor. *An Approach to Poetry.* New York: Crowell, 1930.

The "Beauty" chapter devotes two or three pages to a consideration of the fourth stanza of "Urn." Argues that it achieves an effect of beauty through a harmony of the interrelationships of its parts surpassing the beauty of the sum of the parts alone.

Murra, Wilbur F. "The Prize Winning Letter." *Wilson Bulletin for Librarians,* 5 (September 1930): 64 and 96.

Interprets "Melancholy" as expressing a threefold, complex emotion consisting of melancholy, joy, and beauty. The theme of the poem is that we should transmute melancholy into joy by dressing it in the clothes of beauty.

Murry, J. Middleton. "Beauty Is Truth." *Symposium,* 1 (1930): 466-501.

In Murry's opinion, "Urn" is the development of a state of perception in which the perceiver is totally unaware of self and totally aware of the object of his percption. It is a state of raised consciousness that brings peace to the perceiver, though it cannot be maintained indefinitely.

Roberts, John Hawley. "Poetry of Sensation or of Thought?" *PMLA,* 45 (1930): 1129-1139.

Roberts' thesis is that much of Keats's poetry can be seen as an attempt to resolve the dilemma expressed in "Sleep and

Poetry" of which kind of poetry to write: poetry of sensations of poetry of thought. Poetry of sensation was more naturally appealing to Keats, but he felt he ought to write poetry of thought. Roberts argues that "Psyche" succeeds in combining sense and thought and that the other odes are purely poems of sense.

1931

[Kunitz, Stanley Jasspon]. "Dilly Tante Observes." *Wilson Bulletin for Librarians,* 5 (January 1931): 326-329.

Mentions that lines 49-50 of "Urn" do not merit the great attention Murry paid to them in *Studies in Keats.* They are not mystical, he says, only passionate.

1932

Crawford, Alexander Wellington. *The Genius of Keats: An Interpretation.* 1932; rpt. New York: Russell and Russell, 1967.

Finds a thematic conjunction in "Indolence," "Urn," "Melancholy," and "Nightingale." In "Urn," Keats raised the perception of beauty to the principle of beauty, an intellectual and universal concept. The odes concern the relationship between the beauty of art and life.

Gingerich, Solomon F. "The Conception of Beauty in the Works of Shelley, Keats, and Poe." *Essays and Studies in English and Comparative Literature, By Members of the English Department of the University of Michigan,* 8 (1932): 169-194.

Contrasts Keats's use of the word *beauty,* whose essence was taken from natural surroundings, with Shelley's, whose was more abstract. Keats discovered a lasting quality in beauty and realized that it had been as essential at the time of creation as reality, since beauty derives from harmony, and without harmony the universe would be thrown back into chaos.

Monroe, Harriet. "Keats." In *Poets and Their Art.* 1932; rpt. Freeport, New York: Books for Libraries Press, 1967, pp. 179-182.

Laments Keats's early death and assesses the grounds for his rank among the greatest poets, which are ascribed to "Urn,"

"Nightingale," "Melancholy," "Autumn," and a few other lyrics.

Richards, Ivor Armstrong. *Mencius On the Mind: Experiments In Multiple Definition.* New York: Harcourt, Brace, 1932.

Treats ll. 49-50 of "Urn" to Richards' system of Multiple Definitions, which he devised to solve the problems of trying to interpret a work conceived in a differing ideology from the reader's. Lists all the definitions of "beauty" and all of "truth," along with all the combinations in which those meanings might be used together.

Sickels, Eleanor M. *The Gloomy Egoist: Moods and Themes of Melancholy From Gray to Keats.* New York: Columbia University Press, 1932.

Discusses Keats's treatment of melancholy in "Nightingale" and "Melancholy" and compares it with traditional handlings of that theme.

1933

Catel, Jean. *John Keats et les Odes.* Marseille: Cahiers du Sud, 1933.

Feels that Keats intended "Psyche" to be empty of intellectual content. Translating "Tender is the night" as "Amoureux est le soir," Catel interprets "Nightingale" as the contemplation of a symbol of love. "Urn" develops both a melody which the spirit needs to explain and an image whose beauty is its own explanation. "Melancholy" concerns the sadness resulting from the brevity of earthly phenomena. And "Autumn," though charming on the surface, is essentially banal.

Eliot, T. A. "Shelley and Keats." In *The Use of Poetry and the Use of Criticism.* London: Faber and Faber, 1933, pp. 87-102.

Mentions that Keats's poetic greatness rests in the odes, especially "Psyche."

Praz, Mario. *The Romantic Agony.* Trans. Angus Davidson. 1933; rpt. London: Oxford University Press, 1970.

Sees in the seventh stanza of "Nightingale" the ecstasy of the exoticist who, alienated from himself and endowed with a discerning intuition, can perceive a unique essence behind the outward appearances of things.

Ridley, M. R. *Keats' Craftsmanship: A Study in Poetic Development.* Oxford: Clarendon Press, 1933.

Points out that Keats's ode stanza is comprised of a Shakespearean quatrain followed by a Petrarchan sestet. Also claims the Houghton-Crewe manuscript of "Nightingale" to be a fair copy rather than a first draft. Ridley's main interest in the odes, though, is in demonstrating Keats's composition process of "distillation," wherein lines and images are formed by compacting, intensifying, and combining parts of his other poetry.

Williams, Charles. "The Evasion of Identity: (ii) the 'Nightingale' and the 'Grecian Urn.'" In *Reason and Beauty in the Poetic Mind.* Oxford: Clarendon Press, 1933, pp. 63-81.

Traces the antipodes of the intellect and the imagination through Milton, Wordsworth, Marlowe, Shakespeare, and Keats. Argues that in "Nightingale" and "Urn" Keats abandoned the intellect for the imagination of beauty.

1934

Evans, Sir Benjamin Ifor. *Keats.* 1934; rpt. St. Clair Shores, Michigan: Scholarly Press, 1971.

Feels that all the odes rework the same material from different approaches: the importance of beauty emphasized in "Endymion."

Kirtlan, E. J. B. "The Relative Position of Keats, Shelley, and Byron, As Poets." *London Quarterly and Holborn Review,* 159 (April 1934): 233-237.

Assessing Keats as art-for-art's sake, Kirtlan believes that "Urn" is a journey of the imagination, triggered by looking at a Grecian urn, back to the ancient Hellenistic festivals depicted there.

Sherwood, Margaret. "Keats' Imaginative Approach to Myth." In *Undercurrents of Influence in English Romantic Poetry.* 1934; rpt. Freeport, New York: Books for Libraries Press, 1968, pp. 203-264.

Traces the development of Keats's use of myth. Seeks to discover how far he interpreted myth and how far he made it a form of self-revelation. Feels that, of the odes, it is only "Autumn" which shows any real growth in the use of myth. Examines "Autumn" briefly to show that it reflects the almost thoughtless, primitive feelings about earthly processes which form the essence of Greek myths.

1935

Bush, Douglas. "Notes on Keats's Reading." *PMLA*, 50 (1935): 785-806.

List of influences on Keats's poems. Mentions "Nightingale"'s debt to Dante's *Purgatory*, "Melancholy"'s to Gresset's "La Chartreuse" and "Autumn"'s to Thomson's "Castle of Indolence."

1936

Brooks, Cleanth, John Thibaut Purser, and Robert Penn Warren. *An Approach to Literature*. 3rd ed. 1936; rpt. New York: Appleton-Century-Crofts, 1952.

"Melancholy" is used as an example to teach poets' use of imagery. The theme of the ode is that sorrow is not found where one is usually taught to expect it, but in areas of greatest beauty, since beauty is always doomed to pall. The poem is built upon the image of tasting and the image of the temple rites.

Finney, Claude Lee. *The Evolution of Keats's Poetry*. Cambridge: Harvard University Press, 1936.

Reads "Urn," "Nightingale," "Melancholy," "Psyche," "Indolence," and "Autumn" in terms of what he calls Keats's "empirical humanism." This term refers to Keats's solution to the problem of the existence of evil in the world. Evil is a necessary expression of the ego which, although it causes pain, can also be a source of beauty, and which can serve to strengthen the soul as well. Tries to establish the ideology behind the odes based on Keats's life and his letters. Also discusses literary influences, traces the possession of manuscripts, and analyzes some textual variations.

Leavis, F. R. "Keats." *Scrutiny*, 4 (March 1936): 376-400. Seen in *Revalua-*

tion: Tradition and Development in English Poetry. 1936; rpt. New York: W. W. Norton, 1963, pp. 241-273.

The analysis of Keats's odes emphasizes his "exquisitely sure touch" as the quality which redeems their aestheticism. His vitality performs the same function.

1937

Bush, Douglas. "Keats." In *Mythology and the Romantic Tradition in English Poetry.* 1937; rpt. New York: W. W. Norton, 1969, pp. 81-128.

Traces the use of myth by poets from the early romantics to the present day. Sees Keats as essentially a torn poet, and analyzes the odes as expressing that quality (with the exception of "Autumn" which he feels is less troubled thematically). Keats was torn between the sensuous myth-handling of Shakespeare and Marlowe and the allegorical uses given it by Milton and Spenser. Thus, "Psyche" embodies a sensuous allegory, and "Nightingale" and "Urn," while espousing on the surface a yearning for the ideal, have almost equally strong currents of insistence upon the here and now. Bush's consideration of Keats comes in the context of his book's presentation of the romantic struggle, given the ugly results of the French and industrial revolutions, between escaping into the idealism of myth and embracing the role of instructor of social and moral values.

Haber, Tom Burns. "The Unifying Influence of Love in Keats's Poetry." *Philological Quarterly,* 16 (April 1937): 192-209.

Discusses "Melancholy," "Nightingale," and "Urn" briefly in the context of the topic of his essay: love in Keats's poetry.

James, David Gwilym. "Adam's Dream." In *Scepticism and Poetry: An Essay on the Poetic Imagination.* London: George Allen and Unwin, 1937, pp. 170-204.

The Keats chapter discusses lines 49-50 of "Urn" as referring to an act of the imagination, basing the argument on Keats's statement about Adam's dream.

Krutch, Joseph Wood. "What Porridge Had John Keats?" *Nation,* 144 (January 2, 1937): 25-26.

A review of A. C. Flexner's play "Aged Twenty-six," which was then appearing at the Lyceum. Mentions scenes in the play involving the composition of "Urn" and "Autumn."

Spender, Stephen. "Keats and Shelley." In *From Anne to Victoria: Essays By Various Hands*. Ed. Bonamy Dobree. 1937; rpt. Freeport, New York: Books for Libraries Press, 1967, pp. 574-587.

Criticizes Keats's poetry for being too divorced from the experience of real life, too dependent upon other poetry for its attitudes as well as its forms. The odes are an exception to this.

Wagenblass, John Henry. "Keats and Lucretius." *Modern Language Review*, 32 (October 1937): 537-552.

Uses lines from "Nightingale" and "Urn" as examples in his argument that Keats was influenced by Lucretius.

Winters, Yvor. *In Defense of Reason*. 1937; Denver: University of Denver Press, 1947.

Agrees with Eliot that the last lines of "Urn" are a blemish on the poem. The terms beauty and truth are too abstract to equate without explanation. The result is incomprehensible.

1938

Brooks, Cleanth, and Robert Penn Warren. *Understanding Poetry*. 1938; rpt. New York: Holt, Rinehart, and Winston, 1960.

This poetry text prints "Autumn," "Psyche," and "Urn," followed by study questions appropriate to each. It also prints "Nightingale" and discusses its use of imagery and its themes of death, alienation, and the ideal/actual.

Hewlett, Dorothy. *Adonais: A Life of John Keats*. New York: Bobbs-Merrill, 1938.

Treatment of the odes is largely biographical. Notes the influence of Haydon on "Urn," for example, and connects some descriptive lines in "Psyche" to Keats's journey to Keswick.

H. W. F. "Keats and Horace." *Notes and Queries*, OS 174 (June 18, 1938): 441.

The opening of "Nightingale" reminds the author of

Horace's "Epode Fourteen," though the resemblance is un-convincing of influence.

MacGillivray, J. R. "'Ode on a Grecian Urn.'" *Times Literary Supplement,* July 9, 1938, pp. 465-466.

Argues that "Urn" was influenced by Haydon's essays on Raphael's "The Sacrifice at Lystra" appearing in *The Examiner,* May 2 and 9, 1819.

Roberts, W. "'Ode on a Grecian Urn.'" *Times Literary Supplement,* August 20, 1938, p. 544.

Points out that Haydon's essay on Raphael appeared not only in *The Examiner* of May 2 and 9, 1819, as MacGillivray reported, but also in the *Annals of the Fine Arts* of that year, vol. 4, no. 13, pp. 226-247.

Rutland, William R. *Thomas Hardy: A Study of His Writings and Their Background.* 1938; rpt. New York: Russell and Russell, 1962.

Reports that Thomas Hardy owned a Moxon edition of Keats's poems and that "Nightingale" is quoted in *Desperate Remedies, Far From the Madding Crowd,* and *A Pair of Blue Eyes.*

St. Quintin, G. "The Grecian Urn." *Times Literary Supplement,* February 5, 1938, p. 92.

Argues that "ye" in line 50 of "Urn" refers to the figures on the urn because their only experience is with the beautiful world of the vase. Also, the urn is a "friend to man" because it is his means of escape into the realm of the imagination.

Tillyard, E. M. W. "Milton and Keats." In *The Miltonic Setting: Past and Present.* 1938; rpt. New York: Barnes and Noble, 1966, pp. 29-42.

Argues for Milton a prominent place in the development of Keats's poetry right up to the end of his life. Specifically, demonstrates both structural and thematic affinities between "Nightingale" and "Lycidas" as poems of tempting escape but eventual renewal.

1939

Fitzgerald, F. Scott. *The Letters of F. Scott Fitzgerald.* Ed. Andrew Turnbull. New York: Charles Scribner's Sons, 1963.

In a letter to Morton Kroll, August 9, 1939, Fitzgerald ranks "Urn" as a great English classic, along with *A Farewell To Arms, Dubliners, Huckleberry Finn,* and *Daisy Miller.*

"Ignoto." "Keats and Grammar," *Notes and Queries,* 174 (February 4, 1939): 81.

Reply to T. R. Glover's assertion in the presidential address to the Classical Association, 1938, that Keats had no hold on grammar. Insists on the grammatical correctness of the odes and suggests that perhaps Glover was referring to Keats's letters.

1940

Caldwell, James Ralston. "Beauty Is Truth...." In *Five Studies in Literature: University of California Publications in English.* Vol. 8. Berkeley, California: University of California Press, 1940, pp. 131-153.

Traces the beauty/truth equation to various writings of Hazlitt, including "On Gainsborough's Pictures," "On Imitation," "On the Elgin Marbles," "Conversations As Good As Real," "Picture Galleries in England," et al. Also connects Hazlitt's ideas on the nature of contrast in "On Poetry in General" to the ending of "Urn."

Du Bos, Charles. *What Is Literature?* New York: Sheed and Ward, 1940.

Interprets parts of "Nightingale" and "Urn" according to his definition of literature: "Literature is thought acceding to beauty in light." Views light according to Longinus' dictum that beautiful words are the light of the mind. Du Bos's approach is religious, since he feels that all light comes from above.

Fitzgerald, F. Scott. *The Letters of F. Scott Fitzgerald.* Ed. Andrew Turnbull. New York: Charles Scribner's Sons, 1963.

In a letter to Scottie, August 3, 1940, Fitzgerald asserts that every syllable of "Urn" is as inevitable as every note of Beethoven's Ninth Symphony. He claims to have read it about a hundred times and to have begun to understand it after the tenth. He also says that he can never read "Nightingale" without tears in his eyes.

Shuster, George Nauman. *The English Ode from Milton to Keats.* New York: Columbia University Press, 1940.

Says that in his odes Keats was not concerned with expressing an emotion but with creating a structure of images to suggest a mood or thought. Keats contributed beauty and richness of diction to the ode form.

Wood, William R. "An Interpretation of Keats's 'Ode on a Grecian Urn.'" *English Journal,* 29 (December 1940): 837-839.

Argues that "Ye" in the last line of "Urn" has "Cold Pastoral" as its antecedent. Thus, the last line and a half are spoken by the poet to indicate the inadequacy of the urn's aesthetic.

1941

Knight, G. Wilson. "The Priest-Like Task: An Essay on Keats." In *The Starlit Dome: Studies in the Poetry of Vision.* 1941; rpt. London: Methuen, 1959, pp. 258-307.

Emphasizes the recurring images in Keats's poetry and gives them a thematic significance. "Urn" studies the relationship between time and art. "Melancholy" celebrates the acceptance of sorrow. "Nightingale" is a release for Keats's identification of joy with pain, darkness with beauty, and nature with spiritual experience. "Autumn" is suggestive of deep contemplation. And "Psyche" concerns the separation of deep, instinctive desire from rationality.

1942

P. F. "The Education of Keats and Shelley: A Note with Some Queries." *Notes and Queries,* OS 183 (July 18, 1942): 45.

A reply to Raymond Mortimer's claim in *New Statesman,* June 20, 1942, that it would be useful, in comparing "Nightingale" with Shelley's "Skylark," to contrast Keats's education with Shelley's. Denies that any useful deduction about the poems can be made from studying the poets' educational backgrounds.

1943

Burke, Kenneth. "Symbolic Action in a Poem by Keats." *Accent*, 4 (autumn 1943): 30-42.

Considers "Urn" as an act performed by Keats which the reader is able to re-enact. Equates beauty with art and truth with science; then further associates art with act (in the sense of a thing performed) and science with scene (in the sense of a conception of what is). Thus, the final interpretation of the poem is, "Act is scene; scene, act." In the course of the poem, mental action transcends physical passivity.

Gide, André. *The Journals of André Gide.* Trans. Justin O'Brien. Vol. 4. New York: Alfred A. Knopf, 1951.

Gide records in his journal for February 17, 1943, that it took him a half-hour to commit "Nightingale" and "Autumn" to memory once more.

Larrabee, Stephen A. "Keats." In *English Bards and Grecian Marbles: The Relationship Between Sculpture and Poetry, Especially in the Romantic Period.* New York: Columbia University Press, 1943, pp. 204-232.

Adds to the list of suggestions for possible sources for the scenes on the urn some lines from Leigh Hunt's "The Story of Rimini" depicting a sacrifice from Poussin's "Polyphemus."

McLuhan, Herbert Marshall. "Aesthetic Pattern in Keats's Odes." *University of Toronto Quarterly*, 12 (January 1943): 167-179.

Argues that the odes are not self-expression but consciously crafted works of art. "Urn" has three themes which are given alternate stress, ending in an outright rejection of all forms of escape. In "Nightingale" there are two negative, or down, movements and two positive, or up. They are resolved by a "'rational' wakefulness" in the last stanza. "Autumn," however, is structured unremittingly according to a pattern of natural growth, ending like the others in an assertion of consciousness.

Pettit, Henry. "Scientific Correlatives of Keats's 'Ode to Psyche.'" *Studies in Philology*, 40 (1943): 560-567.

Traces the association of the soul with the brain in "Psyche" to the phrenological studies of Franz Joseph Gall and the

physiological studies of Sir Charles Bell. Gall related the soul
to the brain and Bell conceived of the brain as many-branched.

Williams, Blanche Colton. *Forever Young: A Life of John Keats*. New York: G.
P. Putnam's Sons, 1943.

> A narrative biography of Keats. Claims Keats's sadness at
> not being able to marry Fanny as the stimulus for writing
> "Melancholy." Similarly, he wrote "Urn" to ease the burden of
> sadness by triumphing in the identity of beauty and truth in
> both life and art.

1944

Brooks, Cleanth. "History Without Footnotes: An Account of Keats'
Urn." *Sewanee Review*,52 (1944): 89-101. This is reprinted in *The Well-
Wrought Urn* under the title of "Keats's Sylvan Historian: History With-
out Footnotes."

> Looks to the context of the entire poem to clear up am-
> biguities in particular passages of "Urn." Gives special em-
> phasis to paradox throughout the poem, especially to the fact
> that the urn, usually a silent figure, speaks at the end of the ode
> which has stressed silence all along. Views the final lines as
> supported by the dramatic context of the situation in the poem.

Ford, George Harry. *Keats and the Victorians: A Study of His Influence and Rise to
Fame, 1821-1895.* 1944; rpt. Hamden, Connecticut: Archon Books,
1962.

> Discusses the influence of "Urn," "Nightingale," and "Au-
> tumn" on Matthew Arnold and that of "Urn" and "Nightin-
> gale" on Tennyson.

Guérard, Albert Joseph. "Prometheus and the Aeolean Lyre." *Yale Review*,
33 (1944): 482-497.

> Points out the paradox in romanticism between the Pro-
> methean ideal of the exercise of the will and the prominent
> nineteenth-century metaphor for poetic creation, the Aeolean
> harp, which implies self-submersion. Discusses "Nightingale"
> in a page and a half to exemplify the Aeolean harp quality of
> romanticism.

Trevelyan, Raleigh. *The Fortress: A Diary of Anzio and After.* 1956; rpt. London: Leo Cooper, 1972.

> Diary of a British infantryman at Anzio beach. The April 24, 1944, entry records the author's meditations on "Nightingale" when reminded of the poem by the song of Italian nightingales.

1945

Basler, Roy P. "Keats' 'Ode on a Grecian Urn.'" *Explicator,* 4 (October 1945): #6.

> Contradicts Victor Hamm's assertion (*Explicator,* May 1945) that "Ye" in line 50 of "Urn" refers to the reader. Believes it refers to the urn.

Bate, Walter Jackson. *The Stylistic Development of Keats.* 1945; rpt. New York: The Humanities Press, 1958, pp. 125-141 and 182-188.

> Contains chapters on the May odes and on "Autumn." Regards the odes as the height of Keats's stylistic development. Treats the ode form as an outgrowth of the sonnet form, and provides statistical data to support his analysis of such stylistic elements as the use of bilabials, stress inversions, caesurae, run-on lines, word origins, and spondees.

Caldwell, James Ralston. *John Keats' Fancy: The Effect on Keats of the Psychology of His Day.* 1945; rpt. New York: Octagon Books, 1972.

> Views "Melancholy" as a poem about beauty in general which expresses the sadness inevitably concomitant with joy, beauty, and ecstasy. "Nightingale" and "Urn" are specific illustrations of the general principles outlined in "Melancholy."

Hamm, Victor M. "Keats' 'Ode on a Grecian Urn,' Lines 49-50." *Explicator,* 3 (May 1945): #56.

> Finds three voices in the poem: 1) the speaker commenting on the urn; 2) the urn speaking to eternity; and; 3) the poet commenting to the speaker.

Hampson, Norman. "Keats and Ourselves." *Times Literary Supplement,* December 22, 1945, p. 607.

> Answer to the *TLS* article of November 10, 1945. Replies

that "Autumn," not "Urn," represents Keats's final view of life. In "Urn" Keats rejects escape into art, but in "Autumn" he embraces the real world.

The editor responds in a brief note that "Autumn" is a descriptive, not a substantive poem, and reasserts his belief that "Urn" is the best statement of Keats's philosophy.

Huxley, Aldous. *The Perennial Philosophy.* New York: Harper and Brothers, 1945.

Associates Keats's meaning for "truth" in "Urn" with the usual definition of "fact," but also, secondarily, with the Johannine phrase "to worship God in truth."

"Keats and Ourselves." *Times Literary Supplement,* November 10, 1945, p. 535.

Points out the appropriateness of the 150th anniversary of Keats's birth to the re-opening of the Keats House in Hampstead after war damage repairs have been made. Cites lines 49-50 of "Urn" as the heart of Keats's view of life and points out the applicability of the ode as a friend to the man of 1945 who has been through woe.

Pitcher, S. M. "Keats's 'Ode to a Nightingale.'" *Explicator,* 3 (March 1945): #39.

Traces the moods in "Nightingale" from happiness at the bird's song, through heightened ecstasy, to the soberness of a requiem. It is the tragic vein of poetry which purges the speaker as the bird's song alone could not, yet still he is left with a feeling of uneasiness.

Russell, Bertrand. *A History of Western Philosophy, And Its Connection with Political and Social Circumstances from the Earliest Times to the Present Day.* New York: Simon and Schuster, 1945.

Uses "Urn" briefly to exemplify the inaccurate view that Greek religion and ritual were cheerful.

Stoll, Elmer Edgar. "The Validity of the Poetic Vision: Keats and Spenser." *Modern Language Review,* 40 (1945): 1-7.

Argues that in "Urn," Spenser's "Bower of Bliss" episode, and especially "Nightingale," we find poetry functioning not as a reflection of the real world but as an expression of a feeling or set of feelings. With poetry of this sort, we mistake the intention by demanding accuracy to perceptible phenomena; all we should look for is a consistency within the vision or feeling.

1946

Kenyon, Katherine M. R. "Keats and Ourselves." *Times Literary Supplement,* January 26, 1946, p. 43.

A letter to the editor. Discusses the things that were a source of pain for Keats as he was writing the odes: Haydon's callousness, Bailey's behavior, Tom's death, his own illness, poverty, and the belief that George had cheated him.

Pettigrew, Richard C. "Keats's 'Ode on a Grecian Urn.'" *Explicator,* 5 (November 1946): #13.

Attacks the explications of lines 49-50 of "Urn" given by Hamm and Basler and gives a demonstration of their invalidity, but poses no specific interpretation for these lines. As a whole, feels that Keats did not find escape undesirable in either "Nightingale" or "Urn," but that he found it impossible to maintain.

Stauffer, Donald A. *The Nature of Poetry.* New York: W. W. Norton, 1946.

Gives a brief explanation of the structure of "Nightingale," which is common in Keats's poetry: it begins and ends with a concrete statement. The concrete is worked up to a higher and higher level of abstract significance in the poem until it falls back into the concrete again. Argues that "Autumn" and "Melancholy" are organized in a number of harmonious images around a unifying theme.

Tate, Allen. "A Reading of Keats (II)." *The American Scholar,* 15 (spring 1946): 189-197. This is a continuation of "A Reading of Keats (I)." *The American Scholar,* 15 (winter 1945): 55-63.

Puts "Nightingale" and "Urn" as well as most of Keats's poetry into the *ut pictura poesis* tradition and examines "Nightingale" and "Urn" with regard to the limits of that tradition, i.e., the inability to express movement, action, or development effectively.

Thompson, L. C. "Shelley and Keats." *Times Literary Supplement*, June 29, 1946, p. 307.

> In this letter Thompson suggests that lines 58, 76, 448, 450, 452, 453, 534, 535, 536, 557, 580, 586, 675, and 686 of "Alastor" influenced "Nightingale."

1947

Beyer, Werner William. *Keats and the Daemon King*. New York: Oxford University Press, 1947.

> Traces the influences of C. M. Wieland's *Oberon* on "Psyche," "Nightingale," and "Urn." Interprets beauty at the end of "Urn" to mean spiritual beauty, which is united with truth in the person of God.

Denwood, Marley. "Markham and Marlowe." *Times Literary Supplement*, February 8, 1947, p. 79.

> Letter to the editor. Claims a parallel between Keats's second line of "Nightingale" and line 13 of Marlowe's translation of Ovid's *Amores*, iii, 6.

Empson, William. "Thy Darling in an Urn." *Sewanee Review*, 55 (1947): 691-697.

> Reviews Brooks's *The Well-Wrought Urn*, emphasizing the essay on "Urn." Offers an interpretation of the ode based more on feeling than Brooks's was.

Fogle, Richard H. "A Note on Keats's 'Ode to a Nightingale.'" *Modern Language Quarterly*, 8 (1947): 81-84.

> This article, which is worked in its entirety into the text of *The Imagery of Keats and Shelley*, approaches the odes as expressions of acceptance of the "inseparability of the elements of human experience." "Nightingale" is the record of the poet's state of intense, but fleeting, aesthetic and imaginative poignancy.

Ford, Newell F. "Some Keats Echoes and Borrowings." *Modern Language Quarterly*, 8 (1947): 455-458.

> Among a miscellaneous collection of echoes and borrowings

in Keats, Ford says that lines 69-70 of "Nightingale" may reflect Coleridge's "Fears in Solitude," line 87.

Gordon, R. K. "Keats and Milton." *Modern Language Review*, 42 (1947): 434-446.

Argues for Milton's influence on much of Keats's poetry. Suggests that "Nightingale," "Psyche," and "Autumn" were influenced by *Paradise Lost*.

Kilby, Clyde S. "Keats' 'Ode to a Nightingale,' line 35." *Explicator*, 5 (February 1947): #27.

Argues for removing the exclamation point in line 35 of "Nightingale" to indicate that the speaker's wish to fly to the nightingale has not been fulfilled at that point.

Muir, Kenneth. "Shakespeare and Keats." *Times Literary Supplement*, July 5, 1947, p. 337.

In this letter, Muir finds an echo for the ending of "Nightingale" in Shakespeare's *Merry Wives*, III, v.

Powell, E. D. B. "Marlowe and Keats." *Times Literary Supplement*, April 5, 1947, p. 157.

Replies to Marley Denwood's letter to *TLS* of February 8, 1947. Argues that line 2 of "Nightingale" was influenced by Ovid's *Amores*, iii, 7, and not by Marlowe's translation of it.

Rashbrook, R. F. "Keats's 'Beauty Is Truth, Truth Beauty.'" *Notes and Queries*, OS 192 (November 1, 1947): 472-474.

Finds influences on the closing of "Urn" in Hazlitt's essay "On the Elgin Marbles," Raphael's admonition to Adam in *Paradise Lost*, and Beaumont and Fletcher's *The Maid's Tragedy*, V. iv.

----------. "Keats's 'Ode to Psyche.'" *Notes and Queries*, OS 192 (September 6, 1947): 385-388.

Lists some influences on "Psyche": "Lycidas," the *Faery Queene*, Peele's "David and Bethsabe," Spenser's "An Hymne of Love," Burton's *Anatomy of Melancholy*, and Beaumont and Fletcher's *The Maid's Tragedy*.

Ryle, G. "Keats' 'Beauty Is Truth.'" *Notes and Queries,* OS 192 (November 15, 1947): 503.

Notes that the equation of beauty and truth can be found in Shaftesbury's "An Essay of Wit and Humour" in *Characteristics* (1711), vol. 1, p. 142.

Scudder, Harold H. "Keats's 'Beauty Is Truth.'" *Notes and Queries,* OS 192 (May 31, 1947): 236-237.

Argues that the source for line 49 of "Urn" is Boileau, *Epitre IX, Au Marquis de Seignelay* (1675), line 43.

Stallman, Robert Wooster. "Keats the Apollonian: The Time-and-Space Logic of His Poems as Paintings." *University of Toronto Quarterly,* 16 (1947): 143-156.

Basing his approach in the terms and concepts of Spengler's *Decline of the West,* Stallman argues that in his major poems Keats has an Apollonian sense of time which renders it in terms of the "point-present now." He demonstrates briefly that "Autumn," "Melancholy," "Psyche," and "Nightingale" embody a sense of time which depicts pictorially an extra-temporal suspension of past and future in one co-existent moment, and he gives a brief reading of "Urn" as Keats's best expression of this concept.

Starnes, D. T. "Spenser—and Keats's 'Ode to Psyche.'" *Notes and Queries,* OS 192 (August 1947): 341-342.

Argues that "Psyche" was influenced by Spenser's "Epithalamion" and "Amoretti."

Stubbs, Peter. "Keats's 'Beauty Is Truth.'" *Notes and Queries,* OS 192 (September 20, 1947): 417.

Presents J. R. Caldwell's argument that lines 49-50 of "Urn" were influenced by the end of Hazlitt's essay "On the Elgin Marbles." Makes no attempt to add to or qualify Caldwell's argument.

Wilcox, Stewart C. "Keats' 'Ode on a Grecian Urn.'" *Explicator,* 6 (October 1947): # 2.

Answers Brooks's reading of the line from "Urn," ". . . and not a soul to tell/Why thou art desolate can e'er return." Brooks felt that it means no stranger to the town will ever discover it and ask why it is empty. Wilcox argues that it means no one from the town can re-enter the living realm to explain the town's emptiness.

1948

Beatty, Frederika. "Theocritus in Hampstead." *Classical Journal,* 43 (March 1948): 327-332.

Argues that "Urn" and "Autumn" were influenced by Francis Fawkes's translation of Theocritus' *Idyls.*

Chew, Samuel C., and Richard D. Altick. "John Keats." In "The Nineteenth Century and After (1789-1939)." In *A Literary History of England.* Ed. Albert C. Baugh. 1948; rpt. New York: Appleton, Century, Crofts, 1968, pp. 1241-1251.

Short survey of Keats's life and work. Gives brief attention to the odes and omits comment on "Melancholy" altogether. Offers concise thematic descriptions of the odes and recommends the study of their background, development, influences, and inter-relationships.

Eberly, Ralph D. "Keats' 'Ode on Melancholy.'" *Explicator,* 6 (April 1948): #38.

Exposes the contrapuntal construction of "Melancholy"'s two themes. The surface theme urges one to turn to beauty to discover true melancholy. The other finds delight in even the saddest experiences.

Ford, Newell F. "Keats, Empathy, and 'The Poetical Character.'" *Studies in Philology,* 45 (1948): 477-490.

Explains the lapses of logic in Keats's treatment of the deserted town in "Urn" and the bird's immortality in "Nightingale." In Keats's aesthetic experience, the empathic fusion of subject and object was so strong that he lost contact with his normal self and his surroundings. In such a state, temporary lapses of logic are easily understandable.

Gay, R. M. "Keats's 'Ode on a Grecian Urn.'" *Explicator,* 6 (April 1948): #43.

Suggests that the change in "Urn" from "thou" to "ye" in the last stanza was due to a desire for euphony.

Gide, André. *The Journals of André Gide*. Trans. Justin O'Brien. Vol. 2. New York: Alfred A. Knopf, 1948.

See 1922.

Gorell, Ronald Gorell Barnes. *John Keats: The Principle of Beauty*. London: Sylvan Press, 1948.

Treats the odes as expressions of Keats's concern for beauty.

Hill, Dorothy Kent. "What Are 'Greek Vases'?" *Classical Journal*, 43 (1948): 223-224.

Postulates that the real vase Keats was describing in "Urn" was a marble urn of the late Greek or, more likely, the early Roman period.

Keister, Don A. "Keats's 'Ode to a Nightingale.'" *Explicator*, 6 (March 1948): #31.

Argues against Kilby's claim (*Explicator*, February 1947) that the exclamation point in line 35 of "Nightingale" should be replaced by a comma.

McDermott, William C. "Keats and Sosibios." *Classical Journal*, 44 (October 1948): 33-34.

Assigns possible sources for the various details on the urn in Keats's ode. Attributes influence to the Townley vase, the Borghese vase, the Sosibios vase, the Holland House vase, and the Panathenaic procession in the frieze of the Parthenon.

McPeek, James A. S. "Keats and the Palice of Honour." *Philological Quarterly*, 27 (1948): 273-276.

Argues that "Urn" was influenced by Gavin Douglas' *Palice of Honour*, based on a similarity of thought and rhetoric.

1949

Bellinger, Rossiter R. "The First Publication of 'Ode on a Grecian Urn.'" *Notes and Queries*, 194 (October 29, 1949): 478-479.

Points out an advertisement in *The Morning Chronicle* for Wednesday, January 19, 1820, which includes a notice for the *Annals of the Fine Arts,* No. 15, in its column of "Books Published This Day." On the basis of this, concludes that "Urn" was first published on Wednesday, January 19, 1820.

Bowra, Cecil Maurice. *The Romantic Imagination.* 1949; rpt. New York: Oxford University Press, 1961, pp. 126-148.

Bowra's study of "Urn" is predicated on his thesis that for Keats truth was reached not through reasoning but through the imagination. He presents a source study of the original vases which may have influenced Keats. He outlines a tripartite structure for the poem of introduction, body, and conclusion. And he views the ode as an attempt to express the timeless rapture of the creative act.

Connolly, Thomas E. "Sandals More Interwoven and Complete: A Re-Examination of the Keatsean Odes." *English Literary History,* 16 (1949): 299-307.

Studies the metrics of the odes, combining the results of Garrod and Ridley, and pointing out that Keats altered the sonnet form in the odes to produce a more intra-organized structure.

Fairchild, Hoxie Neale. "Keats." In *Religious Trends in English Poetry.* 1949; rpt. New York: Columbia University Press, 1961. Vol. 3, pp. 452-501.

Considers Keats to be a poet of pure sensuous delight, devoid of philosophical or religious substance. Interprets the odes as arising from the surge of emotions Keats felt at his failure to resolve life's problems. The theme common to all the odes is that ". . . art is better than life and death is better than art."

Fogle, Richard Harter. *The Imagery of Keats and Shelley.* 1949; rpt. Hamden, Connecticut: Archon Books, 1962.

Gives a statistical survey of the kinds of imagery in the odes and their frequency of appearance. Overall, judges Keats's imagery to be empathic; Keats projected himself into his object of contemplation with his feelings as well as with his thoughts.

Highet, Gilbert. *The Classical Tradition: Greek and Roman Influences on Western Literature.* New York: Oxford University Press, 1949.

Places Keats's odes in a direct line of descent from Horace. However, Keats removed the public element. His odes are intended for no hearers.

Murry, John Middleton. "The 'Ode to a Nightingale.'" In *Katherine Mansfield and Other Literary Portraits.* London: Peter Nevill, 1949, pp. 45-50.

Argues that "Nightingale" is a poem of victory, not despair. It suspends in time a moment of beauty and affirms the potential of the imagination to render any human experience beautiful.

Rashbrook, R. F. "Keats's 'Ode to a Nightingale.'" *Notes and Queries,* 194 (January 8, 1949): 14-16.

Points out over a dozen influences on "Nightingale" without evaluation, including *Hamlet,* Beaumont and Fletcher's *A Wife for a Month,* and Tourneur's *The Revenger's Tragedy.*

Sypher, Wylie. "Portrait of the Artist as John Keats." *Virginia Quarterly Review,* 25 (summer 1949): 420-428.

Views Keats as the originator of what Joyce was later to call the epiphany, the static perception of an object which leads to a sense of higher truth through a transvaluation. Feels "Urn" to represent a successful epiphany, and "Nightingale," "Melancholy," and "Psyche" unsuccessful ones.

Wilcox, Stewart C. "Keats' 'Ode on a Grecian Urn.'" *Explicator,* 7 (April 1949): #47.

Argues that both last two lines of "Urn" were spoken by the vase to mankind.

1950

Bateson, F. W. *English Poetry: A Critical Introduction.* 1950; rpt. London: Longmans, Green, 1966.

Views "Urn" as an expression of the split between the extreme competitiveness of the nineteenth-century middle class on the rise (truth) and the desire to escape from the pressure of an uneasy conscience (beauty).

Belshaw, Harry. "Keats on the Mount of Transfiguration." *London Quarterly and Holborn Review,* 175 (1950): 320-324.

Interprets "Nightingale" as an analog to the tale of Jesus on the Mount of Transfiguration, using Keats's influence on Dean Stanley's hymn on that subject as a link between the two.

Blunden, Edmund Charles. *John Keats.* 1950; rpt. New York: Longmans, Green, 1969.

Reports that the excellence of the odes was overlooked in their early years because of the popularity of the long poem at that time. The odes excel in their dreaminess, but they do return to the actual.

Ford, Newell F. "Empson's and Ransom's Mutilation of Texts." *Philological Quarterly,* 29 (1950): 81-84.

Contends that Empson's version of "Melancholy" in *Seven Types of Ambiguity* contains twenty-two textual errors. John Crowe Ransom adopts these errors unthinkingly in *The New Criticism.*

Green, David B. "Keats, Swift, and Pliny the Elder." *Notes and Queries,* OS 195 (November 11, 1950): 499-501.

Suggests that Pliny the Elder may possibly be the source for Keats's references to bees and to poisonous honey in "Melancholy."

Murry, J. Middleton. "Keats and Coleridge: A Note." *Keats-Shelley Memorial Bulletin,* 3 (1950): 5-7.

Argues briefly that "Nightingale" was influenced by Coleridge's poem "The Nightingale." Discusses other Coleridge influences on Keats as well.

Rashbrook, R. F. "Keats and *Hamlet.*" *Notes and Queries,* OS 195 (June 10, 1950): 253-254.

Notes here several parallels between "Nightingale" and *Hamlet,* pointing out pertinent biographical associations as well.

----------. "Keats's Ode 'To Autumn.'" *Notes and Queries,* OS 195 (February 18, 1950): 78-79.

Argues that "Autumn" was influenced by Webster's "The Duchess of Malfi," Shakespeare's "Much Ado About Nothing," "The Merchant of Venice," and "Cymbeline," Milton's "Comus" and "First Psalm," and Spenser's "Faerie Queene."

Vivante, Leone. "Keats." In *English Poetry and Its Contribution to the Knowledge of a Creative Principle.* 1950; rpt. Carbondale, Illinois: Southern Illinois University Press, 1963, pp. 182-204.

Considers "Urn," "Nightingale," and "Psyche" as exemplary of the thesis of this book: that there is a frequent theme in literature of a creative principle, a spontaneous energy, a spirit of essence.

Wilcox, Stewart C. "The Unity of 'Ode on a Grecian Urn.'" *Personalist,* 31 (1950): 149-156.

Argues that "Urn" is a unified poem which justifies the much-disputed last two lines. Sees the work as a series of contrasts which are emotionally apprehended and then intellectually resolved.

Wood, Frank. "Rilke's 'Keats-Bild.'" *Germanic Review,* 25 (October 1950): 210-223.

Compares Keats's poetry to Rilke's. Relates the theme of "Urn" to that of "Auf eine Lampe" and contrasts "Urn"'s structure with Rilke's "Sonnet to Orpheus."

1951

Borges, Jorge Luis. "The Nightingale of Keats." In *Other Inquisitions, 1937-1952.* Trans. Ruth L. C. Simms. Austin: University of Texas Press, 1964, pp. 112-124.

First published around 1951. Addresses the critical problem of the bird's immortality in "Nightingale." Argues that Keats's concept was Platonic—that the individual bird in the poem represented the type of the species (Borges differs slightly here from Amy Lowell who felt that Keats was referring directly to the species in the poem). Offers as an explanation for the frequent misreading of these lines the assertion that the English mind is Aristotelian by nature, not Platonic.

Brower, Reuben Arthur. *The Fields of Light: An Experiment in Critical Reading.* 1951; rpt. London: Oxford University Press, 1968.

Demonstrates methods of analytical reading which reveal the "imaginative organization" of literary works. Gives a reading of "Autumn" which shows how the images in the poem come to have a metaphorical significance.

Empson, William. *The Structure of Complex Words.* New York: New Directions, 1951.

Gives a reading of "Urn" which interprets it as a strong expression of Keats's feeling. This is in response to Brooks, whose antipathy for biographical criticism makes his treatment of the ode impatient of Keats's expressions of personal feeling.

Ford, Newell F. *The Prefigurative Imagination of John Keats: A Study of the Beauty-Truth Identification and Its Implications.* 1951; rpt. Hamden, Connecticut: Archon Books, 1966.

Argues that Keats exercised, during moments of rapture, a prefigurative notion of truth based on his letter to Bailey, November 22, 1817, which led him to identify the imaginative perception of beauty with truth. Traces this concept through "Nightingale" and "Urn."

Gérard, Albert. "Coleridge, Keats, and the Modern Mind." *Essays in Criticism,* 1 (1951): 249-261.

Asserts Keats's modernity over Coleridge. Gives a brief discussion of "Nightingale." The poem exemplifies for Gérard the affective quality of Keats's idealism which makes it appeal to modern man. The questions at the end reflect our contemporary dilemma: how can you believe in a value system which is affective and personal in origin? If you doubt yourself, you doubt the system.

Gide, André. *The Journals of André Gide.* Trans. Justin O'Brien. Vol. 4. New York: Alfred A. Knopf, 1951.

See 1943.

Hartung, George W. "A Note on Keats's 'To Autumn.'" *Notes and Queries,* OS 196 (March 31, 1951): 143.

Says "Autumn," ll. 3-6, is paralleled by Spenser's "Colin Clouts Come Home Again," ll. 600-603.

Jump, J. D. "Thomas Philpott and John Dryden. And John Keats!" *Notes and Queries*, OS 196 (December 8, 1951): 535-536.

Jump is concerned primarily with suggesting Philpott as a source for some lines in Dryden. However, he hesitates to claim influence outright because of two lines of Philpott which cannot have influenced Keats's phrase "drowsy numbness," but which seem to have.

Pratt, Willis W. "A Note on Keats and Camoens." *Notes and Queries*, OS 196 (June 9, 1951): 253-254.

In discussing the influence of Mickle's translation of Camoens' *Lusiad* on Keats, Pratt mentions that it serves as the source for the opening stanza of "Nightingale."

Raymond, William O. "'The Mind's Internal Heaven' in Poetry." *University of Toronto Quarterly*, 20 (April 1951): 215-232.

Studies the way various poets handled the senses in their work. Includes brief discussions of "Nightingale" and "Urn." Treats Keats as deeply concerned with the senses, yet transcendent of them.

Rivers, Charles L. "Influence of Wordsworth's 'Lines Composed a Few Miles Above Tintern Abbey' Upon Keats' 'Ode to a Nightingale.'" *Notes and Queries*, OS 196 (March 31, 1951): 142-143.

Adds strength to Finney's claim that line 23 of "Nightingale" may have been influenced by "Tintern Abbey." Specifically cites lines 27 and 35-41 of Wordsworth's poem, in addition to the lines 52-53 that Finney mentions.

Robson, W. W. "Professor Trilling and the 'New Critics.'" *Dublin Review*, 255 (1951): 54-62.

Main purpose is to indicate the shortcomings of New Criticism. In the process, points out that if the first part of the beauty/truth equation is stressed, the lines are viewed as pure aestheticism, but if the second part is emphasized they become a statement of socialist realism. Historical criticism avoids these confusions.

Wormhoudt, Arthur. "Cold Pastoral." *American Imago*, 8 (September 1951): 275-285.

Analyzes the beauty/truth identification from the point of view of Freudian psychoanalysis. Defines Keats's truth as an unconscious, instinctive truth and beauty as the result of sublimated sexual desire.

1952

Auden, W. H., and Norman Holmes Pearson, Introd. *Poets of the English Language*. Ed. W. H. Auden and Norman Holmes Pearson. London: Eyre and Spottiswoode, 1952.

Explains the romantic rejection of the metaphysical poets along with Dryden and Pope by asserting that the real novelty of romantic poetry was structure, not diction. Illustrates the associative structure of "Nightingale" as an example of the romantic antipathy to syllogistic structure.

Ford, Newell F. "Keats's Romantic Seas: 'Ruthless' or 'Keelless'?" *Keats-Shelley Journal*, 1 (1952): 11-22.

Argues that Keats's first draft of line 70 of "Nightingale" read "keelless" rather than "ruthless," based on an examination of Keats's customary uses of these words.

Gwynn, Frederick L. "Keats, Autumn, and Ruth." *Notes and Queries*, OS 197 (October 25, 1952): 471-472.

Asserts that the personification of autumn in Keats's ode is female and that she is based on Ruth the Moabitess.

Haddakin, Lilian. "Keats's 'Ode on a Grecian Urn' and Hazlitt's Lecture 'On Poetry in General.'" *Notes and Queries*, OS 197 (March 29, 1952): 145-146.

Haddakin's thesis is that "Urn" represents an answer to, not an outgrowth of Hazlitt's lecture "On Poetry in General," published in the spring of 1818. Hazlitt contends that painting is less stimulating to the imagination than poetry and that Greek statues likewise are incapable of moving the imagination. Keats's ode contradicts this view of its very conception.

Holloway, John. "The Odes of Keats." *Cambridge Journal*, 5 (April 1952): 416-425.

Argues that the odes are a "unified sequence" and says that
the best way to understand them is to "make them interpret
each other." To this end, proposes to look at the odes to discover "the Odes as poems" and "Keats the writer." Interprets
the odes as variations on the mood expressed in "Indolence."

Pearson, Norman Holmes. "Lena Grove." *Shenandoah,* 3 (spring 1952): 3-7.

Discusses Faulkner's use of "Urn" in *Light in August,* which it
treats as a mystery novel.

Spens, Janet. "A Study of Keats's 'Ode to a Nightingale.'" *Review of English
Studies,* NS 3 (1952): 234-243.

Defends the immortality of the bird and the change of its
song from happy to sad by tracing the emotional development
of the speaker through the poem.

1953

Adams, Robert M. *"Trompe-l'Oeil* in Shakespeare and Keats." *Sewanee
Review,* 61 (1953): 238-255.

Traces the development of the use of *trompe-l'oeil* from
Shakespeare to Keats. Shows "Psyche," "Nightingale," and
"Urn" to be structured by the *trompe-l'oeil,* a device more often
used in the plastic arts, wherein one frame of reality is over-
lapped by another, such as occurs in a painting when a real
pencil might be glued to the canvas among other painted objects. In literature, *trompe-l'oeil* most often takes the form of
shifting levels of perception. For example, Adams points out
Keats's use of this device at the end of "Urn" when the poem
turns to comment upon itself.

Daniel, Robert. "Odes to Dejection." *Kenyon Review,* 15 (1953): 129-140.

Defines an ode to dejection as a romantic reverie taking
place in a vividly realized setting, usually out of doors. Compares the structure of "Nightingale" to that of Coleridge's
"Dejection: An Ode," which influenced it.

Datta, A. "Keats's Ode Sequence: A Study of Miltonic Design." *Saugar
University Journal,* 1 (1953-54): 53-61.

Views the odes as a strongly unified sequence. They record

the poet's attempt at faith in the power of love, nature, and art to overcome life's ills. The climax is "Nightingale," the height of Keats's approach to optimism; then he sinks toward despair, with a final, but abortive attempt at recovery in "Urn."

Davie, Donald. "'Essential Gaudiness': The Poems of Wallace Stevens." *Twentieth Century*, 153 (June 1953): 455-462.

Compares the structure of Stevens' "Le Monocle de Mon Oncle" with that of a Keats ode. It is discursive, advancing from point to point.

Fogle, Richard Harter. "Keats's 'Ode to a Nightingale.'" *PMLA*, 68 (1953): 211-222.

Considers the romantic qualities of "Nightingale." It describes a choice and rare experience in which the speaker feels the stress between the ideal and the actual in terms of pleasure and pain, imagination and reason, plenitude and privation, permanence and change, natural and human, art and life, freedom and bondage, waking and dream.

Hough, Graham. "Keats." In *The Romantic Poets*. 1953; rpt. London: Hutchinson University Library, 1963, pp. 156-194.

Discusses the odes in the section on negative capability. Treats them as expressions of Keats's concern for the passing of beauty. They are the summit of Keats's poetry.

Lowry, Malcolm. "Strange Comfort Afforded by the Profession." In *New World Writing: Third Mentor Selection*. New York: New American Library, 1953, pp. 331-344.

In this short story, the main character, Sigbjorn Wilderness, visits the Keats-Shelley House in Rome, is much concerned with Keats and his death throughout, and mentions "Nightingale" and parodies "Melancholy" briefly.

Masson, David I. "Vowel and Consonant Patterns in Poetry." *Journal of Aesthetics and Art Criticism*, 12 (December 1953): 213-227.

Uses parts of "Nightingale" as examples in the argument that certain patterns of vowels and consonants occur in passages of lyrical feeling or sensuous description.

Perkins, David. "Keats's Odes and Letters: Recurrent Diction and Imagery."*Keats-Shelley Journal,* 2 (1953): 51-60.

> Points out numerous examples of phrasing in the odes which had been preceded by similar words in the letters.

Read, Herbert. "The True Voice of John Keats." *Hudson Review,* 6 (1953): 90-105.

> Argues that the study of Keats shows a continual growth toward the poetic voice of a pure English and that he finally reached that voice in "The Fall of Hyperion." Accordingly, views the odes as a regression to a less mature style.

Swaminathan, S. R. "Three Odes of Keats." *Saugar University Journal,* 1 (1953-54): 1-35.

> Discusses the thought and imagery of "Psyche," "Nightingale," and "Urn." Treats them as essentially mystical poems in which Keats yearns for a state of eternal stasis. Approaches "Psyche" and "Nightingale" as studies in the immortality of the soul. "Urn" concerns the possibility of a unification of beauty and truth in eternity, not in the temporal world.

Veerappaji, M. S. "A Comparison Between Wordsworth's 'To the Cuckoo' and Keats's 'Ode to a Nightingale.'" *Literary Criterion* (Mysore), summer 1953, pp. 22-25.

> Argues in this comparison that the two poems are representative of their authors. Keats's is marked by depth of feeling and sensuousness of detail, Wordsworth's by simplicity and delight in nature.

Wasserman, Earl Reeves. *The Finer Tone: Keats's Major Poems.* Baltimore: Johns Hopkins Press, 1953.

> Asserts a reading of "Urn" and "Nightingale" based on the concepts of the "Pleasure Thermometer" ("Endymion," I, 777 ff.) and the "bourne of heaven" ("Endymion," I, 293-302). "Urn" leads us to the "bourne of heaven," the boundary between the sensory and the spiritual where what is beautiful to the senses passes over into what is true to the spirit. When the essence of the sensory object is reached (the point of transition being, in Burke's words, a "mystic oxymoron"), the contemplation of art can take us to the bourne. In "Nightingale," we see

the poet fall from an awareness of the "bourne of heaven" and attempt to regain it, while the bird, in contrast, seems from the poet's point of view to rise higher into it.

Whitley, Alvin. "The Message of the Grecian Urn." *Keats-Shelley Memorial Bulletin*, 5 (1953): 1-3.

Prints the various transcript readings of lines 49-50 of "Urn" in his discussion of who says what to whom at the end of the ode. Sees three possible interpretations: 1) both lines are spoken by the urn to the reader; 2) the first five words by the urn and the rest by the poet to the reader; and, 3) the first five words by the urn and the rest by the poet to the urn. Argues for interpretation #1 based on the tripartite division of the lines found in all transcripts.

Woodruff, Bertram L. "Keats's Wailful Choir of Small Gnats." *Modern Language Notes*, 68 (April 1953): 217-220.

Postulates as a source for Keats's wailful choir of mourning gnats an 1817 book by two English naturalists: *An Introduction to Entomology* by William Kirby and William Spence.

1954

Bland, D. S."'Logical Structure' in the 'Ode to Autumn.'" *Philological Quarterly*, 33 (1954): 219-222.

Applies the methods of analyzing composition in a painting to analyzing "To Autumn," looking for principles of movement which lead us through the poem. Finds the sense of taste predominant in stanza I, sight in II, and hearing in III. Also, stanza I suggests morning, II afternoon, and III evening.

Blunden, Edmund. "Keats's Odes: Further Notes." *Keats-Shelley Journal*, 3 (1954): 39-46.

Blunden's consideration of Keats's education leads him to conclude that Keats's odes are Horatian, except for "Psyche," which he finds Pindaric.

Gittings, Robert. *John Keats: The Living Year, 21 September 1818 to 21 September 1819*. 1954; rpt. New York: Barnes and Noble, 1968.

Gives a biographical treatment of the odes with heavy reliance on source study. "Psyche" was written in the optimism of spring and in the hope of romance, "Nightingale" and "Urn" were written under the shadow of recent tragic personal events, "Melancholy" was composed in an exhaustion, and "Autumn" reflects the serenity of his retreat to Winchester.

Gombrich, E. H. "Visual Metaphors of Value in Art." In *Symbols and Values: An Initial Study: Thirteenth Symposium of the Conference on Science, Philosophy, and Religion.* Ed. Lyman Bryson, Louis Finkelstein, R. M. MacIver, and Richard McKeon. New York: Harper and Brothers, 1954, pp. 255-281.

Uses the beauty/truth identification to reflect the nineteenth-century esthetic values of sincerity and honesty, the prescription that called on the artist to express truthfully his personality or mood.

Hamilton, K. M. "Time and the Grecian Urn." *Dalhousie Review,* 34 (autumn 1954): 246-254.

Argues that an underlying theme of "Urn" is the possibility of a victory over time in eternity. Man's only glimpse of this higher truth comes through his contemplation of ideal beauty.

Patterson, Charles Ivey. "Passion and Permanence in Keats's 'Ode on a Grecian Urn.'" *English Literary History,* 21 (1954): 208-220.

Argues that "Urn" favors the vitality of a sadly transient life over the possibility of an always-beautiful but sterile permanence.

Roth, Robert N. "The Houghton-Crewe Draft of Keats's 'Ode to a Nightingale.'" *Papers of the Bibliographical Society of America,* 48 (1954): 91-95.

Gives a brief history of the question of whether the Houghton-Crewe manuscript is the first draft of "Nightingale"; then asserts that it is not. Argues that Keats wrote the first draft on four or five scraps, as Brown reported, and then came inside and made a copy on the letter-size paper of the manuscript.

Schrero, Elliot M. "Keats' 'Ode on a Grecian Urn.'" *Chicago Review,* 8 (1954): 77-86.

Treats "Urn" as the representation of the speaker's reverie or contemplation of the urn and traces the various stages of feelings and changes of attitudes through the poem. According to this view, the last lines present, not a statement of dogma, but a reflection of the speaker's final set of mystical feelings and attitudes about the urn.

Van Ghent, Dorothy. "Keats's Myth of the Hero." *Keats-Shelley Journal*, 3 (1954): 7-25.

Argues that Keats's body of poetry attains a dramatic unity through using the theme of the mythical hero who undergoes a consistently structured adventure involving an affliction with a "strife of opposites," a descent underground (or ascent to a pinnacle), a curing of the state, and an attaining of identity. Discusses each of the odes, along with Keats's other major works, with respect to this pattern and the Greek myths that underlie it.

Wolfson, Lester Marvin. "A Rereading of Keats's Odes: the Intrinsic Approach in Literary Criticism." Diss. University of Michigan 1954.

Written under Clarence Thorpe. Presents New Critical readings of Keats's major odes plus "Indolence." Gives explications for each ode and analyzes it for its ideas, metaphors, and metrics. Final chapter discusses the common features of the odes as a group.

1955

Bass, Robert D. "Keats's Debt to Mrs. Robinson." *Times Literary Supplement*, August 26, 1955, p. 500.

Argues that Keats's "Nightingale" ode was influenced by the poetry of Mrs. Mary Robinson, especially her "Ode to the Nightingale."

Daniel, Robert, and Monroe C. Beardsley. "Reading Takes a Whole Man." *College English*, 17 (October 1955): 28-32.

Refutes Frank Towne's contention (*College English*, November 1953) that feelings are the main value of poetry. Gives a brief discussion of Keats's use of time and personification in "Autumn," showing the poem to be structurally and intellectually complex.

Foa, Giovanna. *John Keats in 1819: "Ode on a Grecian Urn"; "La Belle Dame Sans Merci"; "The Eve of St. Agnes."* Milano: La Goliardica, 1955.

Argues that the theme of "Urn" is that man, through art, may reach the "bourne of heaven," where the earthly and the ethereal meet.

Grundy, Joan. "Keats and William Browne." *Review of English Studies*, NS 6 (January 1955): 44-52.

Discusses the influence of *Britannia's Pastorals* (I.iii.163-166) on "Nightingale."

Jeffrey, Lloyd N. "Two Notes on Keats's 'Endymion.'" *Notes and Queries*, 200 (October 1955): 446-447.

One of two points in this note is that the first four lines of stanza eight of "Nightingale" have their source in "Endymion," (II, 275-280).

Ker, William Paton. "John Keats." In *On Modern Literature: Lectures and Addresses*. Ed. Terrence Spencer and James Sutherland. Oxford: Clarendon Press, 1955, pp. 121-135.

Approaches the odes as unpersonal, philosophical poetry. "Nightingale" and "Urn" present a glimpse into the eternity of art in which a representation of the past has life outside of time for the perceiver.

Murchie, Guy. *The Spirit of Place in Keats*. London: Newman Neame, 1955.

Reconstructs Keats's life within the frame of the various places he lived. Gives a brief discussion of "Psyche," "Nightingale," and "Urn," asserting that their excellence derives from a greater control Keats developed through his philosophy of soul-making. Ranks "Urn" highest based on the ennobling truth of the last two lines.

Shackford, Martha Hale. "The 'Ode on a Grecian Urn.'" *Keats-Shelley Journal*, 4 (1955): 7-13.

Interprets "Urn" as a triumphant assertion of faith in man's ability to achieve a perfection in art which will continue to inspire and comfort men.

Spens, Janet. Rev. of *The Finer Tone*, by Earl Wasserman. *Review of English Studies*, 6 (1955): 96-98.

Approves Wasserman's reading of "Urn" but attacks his

essay on "Nightingale." Feels that the poet's sympathy is not separated from the bird until late in the poem.

Spitzer, Leo. "The 'Ode on a Grecian Urn,' or Content vs. Metagrammar." *Comparative Literature*, 7 (1955): 203-225.

Answer to Wasserman's reading of "Urn." Argues that *explication de texte*, not metagrammar, is the key to understanding "Urn." Sees the urn as a newly discovered object; the conflict in the poem stems from the speaker's urge to make a historical or archaeological reaction to the urn and the urn's insistence that the only adequate response is personal and aesthetic.

Stevenson, Ada L. "Keats's Debt to Mrs. Robinson." *Times Literary Supplement*, September 16, 1955, p. 541.

Suggests, in contradiction to Robert Bass's *TLS* article of August 26, 1955, that what seem to be influences by Mary Robinson on Keats are actually influences by Milton which were felt by both Mary Robinson and Keats.

Williams, Porter. "Keats's Well-Examined Urn." *Modern Language Notes*, 70 (May 1955): 342-345.

Argues that the last line and a half of "Urn" is addressed to the urn.

1956

Adams, M. Ray. "Keats' 'Ode on Melancholy,' 25-28." *Explicator*, 14 (May 1956): #49.

Argues that the "strenuous tongue" in "Melancholy" implies the tasting of not only the sweetness of joy but also the bitterness of experience.

Allott, Kenneth. "Keats's 'Ode to Psyche.'" *Essays in Criticism*, 6 (July 1956): 278-301.

In the midst of analysis of sources of "Psyche," Allott asserts that the ode opens weakly but improves rapidly and that the happiness in the poem is defensive or defiant.

Cook, Reginald L. "Frost on Analytical Criticism." *College English*, 17 (May 1956): 434-438.

Reports the opinions about how poetry should be taught which Frost expressed at the Breadloaf Conference. Frost used "Autumn" to exemplify his teaching method, which stems from the belief that poetry has as its object entertaining the reader by making play with things the reader already knows. Thus, his treatment of "Autumn" focuses on an accurate perception of the senses.

----------. "Frost on Frost: The Making of Poems." *American Literature*, 28 (March 1956): 62-72.

Reports that Frost quoted lines 65-70 of "Nightingale" at the Breadloaf Conference to illustrate the way words work upon one another.

Crowder, Richard. "Anne Bradstreet and Keats." *Notes and Queries*, NS 3 (1956): 386-388.

Sees parallels between stanzas 26-29 of Anne Bradstreet's "Contemplations" and Keats's "Nightingale."

Faulkner, William. *Lion in the Garden: Interviews with William Faulkner, 1926-1962*. Ed. James B. Meriwether and Michael Millgate. New York: Random House, 1968.

In a 1956 interview with Jean Stein Vanden Heuvel, Faulkner commented by way of illustrating the necessity of an artist's dedication to his art:"If a writer has to rob his mother, he will not hesitate; the 'Ode on a Grecian Urn' is worth any number of old ladies."

Foa, Giovanna. *John Keats in 1819: "Lamia," "Ode to a Nightingale," "Ode to Autumn."* Milano: La Goliardica, 1956.

Interprets "Nightingale" as the representation of an attempt to pass over into the "bourne of heaven." However, man cannot maintain such a state as the bird can. "Autumn" records a greater acceptance of life's joys and sorrows and a consequent advancement toward the bourne.

Fox, Robert C. "Keats' 'Ode on a Grecian Urn,' I-IV." *Explicator*, 14 (June 1956): #58.

Finds in the two scenes on the urn a contrast between

secular and religious, natural and supernatural, and human and divine.

Hopkins, Gerard Manley. *Further Letters of Gerard Manley Hopkins.* Ed. Claude Colleer Abbott. 1956; rpt. London: Oxford University Press, 1970.

See 1887.

Nelson, Lowry. "The Rhetoric of Ineffability: Toward a Definition of Mystical Poetry." *Comparative Literature,* 8 (1956): 323-336.

Discusses "Nightingale" as a secularized mystical work similar to those of Dante and St. John of the Cross.

Pollard, Arthur. "Keats and Akenside: A Borrowing in the 'Ode to a Nightingale.'" *Modern Language Review,* 51 (1956): 75-77.

Argues that lines 40-46 of "Nightingale" were influenced by Akenside's "To the Evening Star."

Reeves, James. *The Critical Sense: Practical Criticism of Prose and Poetry.* London: Heinemann, 1956.

A text on the method of practical criticism. Gives a reading of "Autumn," treating it as achieving a balanced fusion of mind and senses.

Shen, Yao. "Accident or Universality." *Western Humanities Review,* 10 (1956): 77-79.

Notes the similarity between lines 11-12 of "Urn" and lines 35-37 of "Song of a Guitar" by Pai Chu Yi.

Trevelyan, Raleigh. *The Fortress: A Diary of Anzio and After.* 1956; rpt. London: Leo Cooper, 1972.

See 1944.

Unger, Leonard. "Keats adn the Music of Autumn." In *The Man in the Name: Essays on the Experience of Poetry.* Minneapolis: University of Minnesota Press, 1956, pp. 18-29.

Shows the interrelationship of "Autumn" with the other odes based on a common concern with the association of beauty and melancholy. Also discusses the imagery and the structure of the poem.

Watkins, Floyd C. "Thomas Wolfe's High Sinfulness of Poetry." *Modern Fiction Studies,* 2 (winter 1956-57): 197-206.

Points out that Wolfe used lines 11-12 of "Nightingale" at the end of the twenty-fourth chapter of *Look Homeward, Angel.*

Wilcox, Stewart C. "The Seasonal Motif in Keats's Ode 'To Autumn.'" *Philological Quarterly,* 35 (1956): 194-195.

Denies D. S. Bland's assertion that the structural movement of "Autumn" is diurnal. Instead, argues that the poem moves seasonally from fruitfulness through harvest to post-harvest migration.

1957

Abel, Darrel. "Frozen Movement in *Light in August.*" *Boston University Studies in English,* 3 (spring 1957): 32-44.

Mainly concerns Faulkner's treatment of time in *Light in August.* Gives consideration to the influence of "Urn" on the novel.

Bate, Walter Jackson. "Keats's Style: Evolution Toward Qualities of Permanent Value." In *The Major English Romantic Poets: A Symposium in Reappraisal.* Ed. Clarence D. Thorpe, Carlos Baker, and Bennet Weaver. Carbondale, Illinois: Southern Illinois University Press, 1957, pp. 217-230.

When he gets to the odes in his essay on the evolution of Keats's style, Bate balks in the face of voluminous previous scholarship and only mentions the successful use of the dramatic by "Nightingale" and "Urn."

Brooks, Cleanth. "The Artistry of Keats: A Modern Tribute." In *The Major English Romantic Poets: A Symposium in Reappraisal.* Ed. Clarence D. Thorpe, Carlos Baker, and Bennett Weaver. Carbondale, Illinois: Southern Illiniois University Press, 1957, pp. 246-251.

Argues that Keats's odes appeal to the modern taste in the same way that Donne's poetry does: they represent a fusion, or the approach to a fusion, of emotion or sense and intellect.

Burrow, John. "Keats and Edward Thomas." *Essays in Criticism,* 7 (October 1957): 404-415.

Most of this essay establishing the influence of Keats upon the poetry of Edward Thomas, poet and critic, is taken up with tracing the influence of Keats's odes, which Thomas considered Keats's greatest work.

Geppert, Eunice Clair. "A Handbook to Keats's Poetry." *DA,* 17 (1957) 2608 (Texas).

Names manuscripts, transcripts and their locations, gives dates of first publication, discusses texts, cites dates of composition, traces geneses of the poems and circumstances of composition, names sources for the poems, and presents criticism and after-history.

Hood, Thurman Los. "The 'Ode on a Grecian Urn': Its Basis in Books, Part I." *Trinity Review* (Trinity College, Hartford, Conn.), 11 (spring-summer 1957): 3-8.

Lists influences on "Urn," including Potter's *Antiquities of Greece,* Longus's *Daphnis and Chloe, The Faerie Queene,* Sandys' Ovid, Chaucer's "The Flower and the Leaf," Wieland's *Oberon,* and Shakespeare's "Sonnet 101."

Hunter, Edwin R. "A Note on Keats's Idea of Beauty." *Tennessee Studies in Literature,* 2 (1957): 81-85.

Alleges that truth in "Urn" was the truth of the ancient Greek sense of beauty which the poet discovered in the urn. Emphasizes time as the revealer of the beauty/truth identification in the sense that what has endured as truth has been perceived as beautiful by both ancients and moderns.

Jarrett, James L. *The Quest for Beauty.* Englewood Cliffs, New Jersey: Prentice-Hall, 1957.

Prentice-Hall Philosophy Series book on aesthetics. Dismisses lines 49-50 of "Urn" as too vague to deal with. Also, claims the reference to Ruth in lines 65-67 of "Nightingale" to be psychological rather than historical.

Langbaum, Robert. *The Poetry of Experience: The Dramatic Monologue in Modern Literary Tradition.* New York: Random House, 1957.

Views "Nightingale" as "the poetry of experience" growing out of the nineteenth century and largely influencing twentieth-century poetry, a kind of poetry in which an observer imaginatively penetrates an object to arrive at the meaning of that object.

Lennam, T.N.S.. "A Nightingale Amongst the China." *Dalhousie Review*, 36 (winter 1957): 402-405.

Traces the influence of "Nightingale" on Rupert Brooke's "The Great Lover."

Pearce, Donald. "Yeats and the Romantics." *Shenandoah*, 8 (spring 1957): 40-57.

Analyzes the contrapuntal nature of "Nightingale" and "Sailing to Byzantium."

Pettet, E. C. *On the Poetry of Keats.* 1957; rpt. Cambridge: Cambridge University Press, 1970.

Relying on Keats's earlier work, reads "Urn" as the expression of a simple, non-metaphysical vision of ideal bliss which can be approached, though not sustained, through art. The final lines are an affirmation of the value of that kind of vision. Includes an appendix refuting the views of Brooks, Murry, Bowra, and Wasserman. In the chapter on "Nightingale," relies heavily on "Endymion" and "On Fancy" to prove that the poem is mainly about death, not a mystical state of vision. Feels the climax of the poem to be at the end of the sixth stanza when the poet fully realizes the implications of death. Includes an appendix tracing the formation of many of "Nightingale"'s images through his earlier poetry. In the chapter on "Melancholy," contends that the poem is primarily an expression of a conventional romantic "pleasing woe" attitude, mixed with a lesser degree of Keats's genuine psychological insight.

Richards, Ivor Armstrong. "Beauty and Truth." In *Complementarities: Uncollected Essays.* Ed. John Paul Russo. Cambridge, Massachusetts: Harvard University Press, 1976, pp. 215-225.

Talk six of the "Sense of Poetry" series broadcast on WGBH-TV, Boston, in the winter of 1957-1958. While asserting that there is no single, correct interpretation of "Urn," suggests that the ending is a reflection of what has gone before, not an advancement of the thought. Puts the beauty-truth identification in the tradition established by Plato and carried on by Spenser and defines terms throughout the poem.

Walsh, William. "John Keats." In *From Blake to Byron.* Vol. V of *The Pelican Guide to English Literature,* ed. Boris Ford. 1957; rpt. Baltimore: Penguin, 1963, pp. 220-239.

> Only discusses one poem at any length: "Nightingale." Emphasizes the ambiguity of many of the words and phrases in the poem and stresses the importance of silence throughout the work.

Wigod, Jacob D. "Keats's Ideal in the 'Ode on a Grecian Urn.'" *PMLA,* 72 (March 1957): 113-121.

> Argues that Keats in "Urn" was affirming the imagination as capable of grasping the ideal which exists in the eternal and which is reflected by real beauties here on earth.

Yost, George. "An Identification in Keats's 'Ode to Psyche.'" *Philological Quarterly,* 36 (October 1957): 496-500.

> Argues against Garrod that "Love," in line 67 of "Psyche," refers not to Psyche but to Cupid, based largely on Mrs. Tighe's "Psyche."

1958

Abrams, M. H. "Belief and Disbelief." *University of Toronto Quarterly,* 27 (January 1958): 117-136.

> Argues that our appreciation of "Urn" is not independent of our belief in the dignity, seriousness, and importance of the last two lines.

Battenhouse, Henry M. "John Keats." In *English Romantic Writers.* Woodbury, New York: Barron's Educational Series, 1958, pp. 201-227.

> Short survey of the romantic writers in twenty-two sections. Devotes four pages to a general setting-forth of the odes.

Berkelman, Robert. "Keats and the Urn." *South Atlantic Quarterly,* 57 (1958): 354-358.

> Sees three possibilities for who says what to whom at the

end of "Urn": 1) the urn speaks to man; 2) the poet speaks to man; and, 3) the poet speaks to the urn and its figures. Argues for #3.

Berry, Francis. "Keats: The Subjunctive Realized, or a New Mood." In *Poets' Grammar: Person, Time and Mood in Poetry.* London: Routledge and Kegan Paul, 1958, pp. 130-142.

Uses "Nightingale" to exemplify the theory that Keats developed the concept of a third grammatical mood between indicative and subjunctive. If the indicative expresses the actual and the subjunctive the desired, Keats's new mood, what Berry calls the Intense Present, captures a state in which the actual becomes the desired without sacrificing the essence of either quality. The song of the nightingale is the distillation of this concept in the poem, spanning as it does the real and the ideal.

Bostetter, Edward E. "The Eagle and the Truth: Keats and the Problem of Belief." *Journal of Aesthetics and Art Criticism,* 16 (March 1958): 362-372.

Traces Keats's vacillating attraction between the metaphysical, ethical, and factual on the one hand and the beautiful, creative, and imaginative on the other. Treats the odes as variations on the theme of the meaning of the artistic experience. Concludes that Keats ultimately felt belief impossible under the unavoidable scrutiny of science and that he resolved the conflict by turning to what I. A. Richards has called "pseudo-statement."

Bradbrook, Frank W. "Marlowe and Keats." *Notes and Queries,* NS 5 (March 1958): 97-98.

Traces the influence of Marlowe's *Dr. Faustus* on "Melancholy."

Cauthen, I. B. "The Shield and the Urn." *Keats-Shelley Journal,* 7 (1958): 23-28.

Finds the source for the Grecian urn in Keats's ode in Book 18 of Chapman's Homer, which includes a description of the shield of Achilles.

Davenport, Arnold. "A Note on 'To Autumn.'" In *John Keats: A Reassess-*

ment. Ed. Kenneth Muir. 1958; rpt. Liverpool: Liverpool University Press, 1969, pp. 96-102.

Connects "Autumn" with Dante, Coleridge, the Bible, and Shakespeare. The theme of the ode is that something must be sacrificed in order that something else may be gained.

Graham, Sheilah, and Gerold Frank. *Beloved Infidel: The Education of a Woman.* New York: Henry Holt, 1958.

In her memoir, Sheilah Graham tells of F. Scott Fitzgerald's reciting portions of "Urn" to her.

Hood, Thurman Los. "Literary Materials of the 'Ode on a Grecian Urn.'" *Trinity College Library Gazette,* 2 (December 1958): 3-17.

A piecing-together of sections from "The 'Ode on a Grecian Urn': Its Basis in Books" by Hood published in two parts in the *Trinity Review* in 1957 and 1958.

----------. "The 'Ode on a Grecian Urn': Its Basis in Books, Part II." *Trinity Review* (Trinity College, Hartford, Conn.), 12 (May 1958): 9-16.

Lists influences on "Urn," including Theocritus' "Idyl I," Sidney's *Arcadia,* Shakespeare's sonnets, and Shaftesbury's *Characteristicks.*

Jaeger, Hans. "Heidegger and the Work of Art." *Journal of Aesthetics and Art Criticism,* 17 (1958): 58-71.

Interprets "Urn" in light of an essay by Heidegger on the origin of a work of art entitled "Der Ursprung des Kunstwerkes" and based on lectures given in 1935-36. Explains that truth in Keats's ode comes through the harmony, the balance, and the repose that we associate with beauty. In the poem, "eternity in art" is balanced against "transitoriness on earth" to create a beauty in which is found truth. This parallels Heidegger's balance of the terms "world" and "earth."

James, David Gwilym. *Three Odes of Keats: The W. D. Thomas Memorial Lecture, Delivered at the University College of Swansea on November 13, 1958.* Cardiff, Wales: University of Wales Press, 1959.

Argues that the controlling force over Keats's odes was his reading of *King Lear.* Shakespeare's tragedy fertilized Keats's growing tragic vision. "Nightingale" and "Urn" poignantly contrast the temporal with the eternal, and "Autumn" synthesizes them in the calm inseparability of birth and death. "Hyperion," also under the control of *Lear*, is a key to understanding the odes. It presents the end of the reign of Saturn over a world of primitive innocence and the ascension of Apollo over a world of wrongdoing and pain, the world we know.

Jones, Leonidas M. "The 'Ode to Psyche': An Allegorical Introduction to Keats's Great Odes." *Keats-Shelley Memorial Bulletin*, 9 (1958): 22-26.

Interprets "Psyche" as an introduction to "Melancholy," "Nightingale," and "Urn." "Psyche" was Keats's allegorical announcement of his intention to become a psychological poet, glorifying the imagination's power to enrich human experience. "Nightingale" then went on to use the imagination to give a new approach to death; "Melancholy" used it to show the painful side of beauty; and "Urn" used it to catch a glimpse of the infinite.

Kornbluth, Alice Fox. "Keats's 'Ode on a Grecian Urn,' 1-2." *Explicator*, 16 (June 1958): #56.

Explains the loquacity of the urn at the end of the ode by the fact that it had not yet been ravished by its husband, quietness.

Lyon, Harvey T., ed. *Keats' Well-Read Urn*. 1958; rpt. Folcroft, Pennsylvania: Folcroft Press, 1970.

Prints Keats's odes in the first chapter of his casebook on "Urn," along with textual variants taken from Garrod's 1939 edition. Next, prints selections from twenty-nine of Keats's letters which may add to an understanding of "Urn." Finally, offers selections from eighty-eight commentators on the ode.

Masson, David I. "The Keatsian Incantation: A Study of Phonetic Patterning." In *John Keats: A Reassessment*. Ed. Kenneth Muir. 1958; rpt., Liverpool: Liverpool University Press, 1969, pp. 159-180.

Outlines in some detail a linguistic method of analyzing sound patterns in poetry and establishes six elementary pattern types. Then examines in detail sound patterns in "The Eve of St. Agnes" and the late odes, concentrating especially on the penultimate stanza of "Nightingale." Argues that the effect of Keats's sound pattern was an incantatory spell.

Muir, Kenneth. "The Meaning of the Odes." In *John Keats: A Reassessment.* Ed. Kenneth Muir. 1958; rpt. Liverpool: Liverpool University Press, 1969, pp. 64-74.

> Connects the ideas in the odes with Keats's life, letters, and reading. "Psyche" records a search for a surrogate religion. "Nightingale" expresses the desire to escape from reality but the realization that no escape is possible. "Urn" contrasts the beauty, significance, and eternality of art with the transitoriness and meaninglessness of life. "Melancholy" announces that enjoyment is always accompanied by melancholy. And "Autumn" reflects the season without drawing any lesson.

Slote, Bernice. *Keats and the Dramatic Principle.* Lincoln: University of Nebraska Press, 1958.

> Views "Nightingale" and "Urn" as embodying dramatic conflicts of forces. "Urn"'s paradox is cold/warm, death/life. "Nightingale"'s is the wish to escape and the knowledge of its impossibility.

Stillinger, Jack. "Keats's Grecian Urn and the Evidence of Transcripts." *PMLA,* 73 (1958): 447-448.

> Arguing that Keats likely proofread "Urn" for the 1820 volume and denouncing the reliability of the transcript versions, Stillinger insists on adopting the 1820 volume text of "Urn."

1959

Blackstone, Bernard. *The Consecrated Urn: An Interpretation of Keats in Terms of Growth and Form.* New York: Longmans, Green, 1959.

> Considers the odes as a choral whole. "Indolence," the first movement, states the themes: love, ambition, art. These are developed in "Psyche," "Nightingale," and "Urn." "Melancholy" brings them together in the minor, and "Autumn" restates them in final chorus in the major.

Bonjour, Adrien. "Blushful Wine and Winking Bubbles—Or Keats's Nightingale Revisited." *English Studies,* 40 (1959): 300-303.

> Looks closely at lines 15-18 of "Nightingale" to conclude that the beaker is personified into the image of a blissful toper.

Overall, finds the duality of the lure of death and the longing
for immortality not resolved in the poem.

Hollander, John. "The Metrical Emblem." *Kenyon Review,* 21 (1959):
279-296.

This essay on the linguistic analysis of poetry refutes F. R.
Leavis's reading of lines 19-20 of "Autumn," preferring a
linguistic rather than a metaphorical approach to the effect
of the sound of the lines.

Hooker, Charlotte Wood Schrader. "Dream Vision in the Poetry of
Keats," *DA,* 20 (1960), 3728 (Tulane).

Completed in 1959. Discusses Keats's poetry in terms of his
belief that "What the imagination seizes as Beauty must be
truth." The imagination envisions beauty in "Psyche" and "Indolence." "Nightingale" describes joy in beauty and anguish at
its brevity. "Melancholy" declares the necessary connection
between beauty and sadness. And "Urn" and "Autumn" show
the comprehensive vision which results from accepting that
connection.

Hopkins, Gerard Manley. *The Journals and Papers of Gerard Manley Hopkins.*
Ed. Humphry House. London: Oxford University Press, 1959.

See 1864.

Jack, Ian. "'The Realm of Flora' in Keats and Poussin." *Times Literary Supplement,* April 10, 1959, p. 212.

Suggests that Keats took his conception of Flora in "Nightingale" from Poussin's painting "L'Empire de Flore."

James, David Gwilym. *Three Odes of Keats: The W. D. Thomas Memorial Lecture,
Delivered at the University College of Swansea on November 13, 1958.* Cardiff,
Wales: University of Wales Press, 1959.

See 1958.

Maxwell, Ian R. "Beauty Is Truth." *Journal of the Australasian Universities
Language and Literature Association,* 10 (May 1959): 100-109.

Interprets the last three lines of "Urn" as a contrast to the
Abbe d'Aubignac's *La Pratique du Theatre,* which insisted that in
painting the pleasing disposition of colors on the canvas must

operate within the bounds of verisimilar representation. For Keats, however, beauty created its own verisimilitude.

Perkins, David. "Hardy and the Poetry of Isolation." *English Literary History,* 26 (June 1959): 253-270.

Discusses isolation in Hardy's poetry. Compares briefly "Nightingale" and "The Darkling Thrush."

----------. *The Quest for Permanence: The Symbolism of Wordsworth, Shelley, and Keats.* 1959; rpt. Cambridge, Massachusetts: Harvard University Press, 1969.

Treats each of the odes in his consideration of Keats's use of symbolism. Argues that Keats was weighing in the odes the relative values of the concrete satisfactions of enacting process and the visionary comfort of retreating into permanence. Keats's method was to invent symbols for process or permanence and debate the acceptability of these symbols in his odes.

Rev. of *Three Odes of Keats,* by David Gwilym James. *Times Literary Supplement,* April 10, 1959, p. 215.

Suggests that "Nightingale," "Urn," and "Autumn" do not progress toward a final statement of peace and perfection. Instead, "Autumn" expresses a "declining urge that led Keats to give up "Hyperion," and to write no more major poems after this ode."

Ryals, Clyde de L. "The Nineteenth Century Cult of Inaction." *Tennessee Studies in Literature,* 4 (1959): 51-60.

Traces the artist's alienation from society back to the nineteenth-century over-emphasis on the imagination and, at the same time, on practical values. Discusses the odes briefly as an example of Keats's preoccupation with a dream world.

Swinburne, Algernon Charles. *The Swinburne Letters.* Ed. Cecil Y. Lang. New Haven: Yale University Press, 1959-1962.

See 1870 and 1881.

Thorpe, Clarence D. Rev. of *Keats' Well-Read Urn,* by Harvey T. Lyon. *Philological Quarterly,* 38 (April 1959): 154-155.

Pools the ideas presented in Lyon's book to arrive at this consensus of "Urn"'s qualities and ideas: "Heightened perception as a function of art"; "paradox and contrast in life and art"; "reconciliation of opposites in great works of art"; "the principle of renunciation and acceptance"; "the enduring qualities of art juxtaposed to the eternal qualities of human nature"; and "the supremacy of the imagination" in artistic creation.

1960

Aoyama, Fujio. "On Keats's Ode 'To Autumn.'" *Thought Currents in English Literature*, 33 (December 1960): 131-146.

Thinks "Autumn" is a representation of Keats's truth/beauty equation. Traces influences on the ode to Chatterton's *Aella*, Collins' "Ode to Evening," Thomson's "The Seasons," and Dante's *Inferno*.

Durant, Jack D. *Atlantic Monthly*, 206 (October 1960): 38.

Letter to the editor. Denies the validity of Gerald Johnson's reading of lines 49-50 of "Urn" (*Atlantic Monthly*, July 1960). Johnson had taken the last two lines as an aphorism, but Durant insists that they are not a philosophical statement. The "ye," he says, refers to the urn, not to mankind. Durant goes on to disagree with Johnson's view of the South.

Evert, Walter H., Jr. "The Apollonian World of John Keats: A Study of His Poetic Theory and Practice." *DA*, 21 (1961), 3457 (Princeton).

Completed in 1960. Treats "Nightingale" in terms of Keats's poetic theory.

Harrison, Thomas P. "Keats and a Nightingale." *English Studies*, 41 (1960): 353-359.

Suggests that "Nightingale" reflects the song of a real nightingale throughout the ode. The actual bird's song, like the poem, begins cheerfully but waxes melancholy.

Haydon, Benjamin Robert. *The Diary of Benjamin Robert Haydon*. Ed. Willard Bissell Pope. Cambridge: Harvard University Press, 1960. Vol. II, p. 318.

See 1821.

Highet, Gilbert. "Keats's Greek Ode: The Poet and the Urn." In *The Powers of Poetry*. New York: Oxford University Press, 1960.

An introduction to the reading of poetry. The chapter on Keats's "Urn" seeks primarily to explain Keats's inclusion of two such separate scenes on the urn by way of Nietzsche's theory of the Apollonian and the Dionysian in Greek art.

Johnson, Gerald W. "To Live and Die in Dixie." *Atlantic Monthly*, 206 (July 1960): 29-34.

Quotes lines 49-50 of "Urn" in arguing that the South has been living in a dream of its own beauty and ignoring the issue of civil rights. Contends that southerners have taken Keats's dictum completely to heart and have become complacent in the beauty of their section of the country.

Perluck, Herbert A. "'The Heart's Driving Complexity': An Unromantic Reading of Faulkner's 'The Bear.'" *Accent*, 20 (winter 1960): 23-46.

This treatment of Faulkner's use of "Urn" in "The Bear" asserts that Keats felt that reality and truth reside in dream.

Rosenheim, Edward W. *What Happens in Literature: A Student's Guide to Poetry, Drama, and Fiction*. Chicago: Chicago University Press, 1960.

A basic book about how to read literature. Uses "Autumn" to illustrate the elements of imagery and sound in poetry.

Schanzer, Ernest. "'Sailing to Byzantium,' Keats, and Anderson." *English Studies*, 41 (1960): 376-380.

Ascribes influence on "Sailing to Byzantium" and "The Tower" to "Nightingale," and asserts that the goddess unites permanence with youth, joy, and love in "Psyche."

Schulz, Max F. "Keats's Timeless Order of Things: A Modern Reading of 'Ode to Psyche.'" *Criticism*, 2 (winter 1960): 55-65.

Sees "Psyche" as an early expression of Keats's notion of the philosophical truth of beauty. The ode affirms faith in an immutable quality in beauty and love.

Southam, B. C. "The Ode 'To Autumn.'" *Keats-Shelley Journal*, 9 (1960): 91-98.

Gives an explication of "Autumn," interpreting its lines through the paradoxical idea that the passage of time which makes life possible also makes death inevitable.

1961

Bloom, Harold. *The Visionary Company: A Reading of English Poetry*. 1961; rpt. Ithaca, New York: Cornell University Press, 1971.

Feels that in "Psyche" outward forms of worship are rejected in favor of the inner worship of the imagination. Yet, the limits of the imagination are seen, too, and love is finally suggested as the proper medium for religious apprehension. In "Nightingale," there is an unresolved tension between creativity as a heightened state of awareness and creativity as a delusion. "Melancholy" presents the idea that the natural is beautiful only because it is ephemeral. However, Keats is not merely disillusioned by his realization that joy is linked to sorrow, insisting as he does on pursuing the beautiful intensely. Keats's values in "Urn" are firmly in the human and the natural, yet the urn has value for man because of its freedom from time, which constitutes its truth. "Autumn" resolves the conflicts of the other odes; it is an acceptance of process which precludes grief at termination.

Boulger, James D. "Keats' Symbolism." *English Literary History*, 28 (September 1961): 244-259.

Discusses Keats's use of symbolism in "Nightingale," "Lamia," "The Eve of St. Agnes," and "Urn." Shows a progression from the futility of the nature symbol in "Nightingale" to the success of the art symbol in "Urn" as a means of resolving the conflict between the permanence of beauty and the limitations of the individual.

Flood, Ethelbert. "Keats' Nightingale Ode." *Culture* (Quebec), 22 (December 1961): 392-402.

Responds to "Nightingale" as a description of the state of vital perception induced by poetry, in which all that burdens man's daily existence is quickened and clarified. Such moments of transcendence are, however, fleeting.

Heinen, Hubert. "Interwoven Time in Keats's Poetry." *Texas Studies in Literature and Language,* 3 (1961): 382-388.

Mentions that Keats is treating time as interwoven in lines 11-14 of "Nightingale." Instead of calling up images of the taste of similar wines, the wine here reminds the poet of its own past and brings it into the present.

Hollingsworth, Keith. "'Vathek' and the 'Ode to a Nightingale.'" *Times Literary Supplement,* October 27, 1961, p. 771.

Suggests that the fifth stanza of "Nightingale" was influenced by William Beckford's Arabian romance, *Vathek* (1786).

Hutton, Virgil. "Keats' 'Ode on a Grecian Urn.'" *Explicator,* 19 (March 1961): #40.

Takes the phrase "still unravished" in "Urn" to mean, "always untransported with emotion." Also, argues the maxim at the end of the ode to apply only to the urn.

MacLeish, Archibald. "The Arable World: Poems of Keats." In *Poetry and Experience.* Boston: Houghton-Mifflin, 1961, pp. 173-199.

Treats "Melancholy" as an assertion that the contradictions of human experience are one. "Nightingale" and "Urn," however, present discoveries of that oneness. The paradox in "Nightingale" is that in order to reach the nightingale we must leave our mortal world behind us. The paradox of "Urn" lies in the contradiction of eternity and the present.

Patterson, Charles Ivey. "The Keats-Hazlitt-Hunt Copy of *Palmerin of England* in Relation to Keats's Poetry." *Journal of English and Germanic Philology,* 60 (1961): 31-43.

Argues that Keats was influenced by the copy of *Palmerin of England* translated by Southey which Keats borrowed from Taylor and Hessey. The main interest in the article is in showing that two passages of *Palmerin* (III, pp. 283-299 and IV, pp. 177-201) establish a rejection of the superiority of art over nature as the theme of "Urn."

Peckham, Morse, and Seymour Chatman. *Word, Meaning, Poem.* New York: Thomas Y. Crowell, 1961, pp. 344-370.

"Nightingale" is included in this college level poetry text.

Chatman provides a lexical gloss and syntactical diagram of the poem, and Peckham offers an "Interpretational Hypothesis," or detailed reading. He conceives the dramatic situation of the ode to be that of a speaker whose unity of mind and body dissolves in a loss of self-identity because of the pain of his environment. The speaker attempts to project his identity into a nightingale's harmonious world, but in the end he is forced to realize the inadequacy of such escape as a final solution to his dilemma, and is left questioning the possible value of his experience.

Reid, B. L. "Keats and the Heart's Hornbook." *Massachusetts Review,* 2 (1961): 472-495.

Argues here that the odes express an essentially tragic view of life. Sees them as the last stage in Keats's poetic development of a tragic vision and uses the letter to George and Georgiana of April 1819 to show Keats's transition into this view of life.

Roth, Leon. "Religion and Literature." *Hibbert Journal,* 60 (October 1961): 24-34.

Uses lines 11-12 of "Urn" as an example of the common ground between religion and literature: they both imply a belief in a spiritual world according to which the material world should be interpreted.

Scarfe, Francis. "Keats's Use of the Negative." *Études Anglaises,* 14 (1961): 1-9.

Argues that the use of the negative is a characteristic of Keats's poetry. Uses "La Belle Dame Sans Merci" to establish this tendency and traces its development briefly through the odes up to its peak in "Urn" where it achieves an affirmation.

Sethuraman, V. S. "'Soul-Making' in 'To a Nightingale.'" *Indian Journal of English Studies,* 2 (1961): 121-124.

Sees "Nightingale" as an expression of Keats's theory of soul-making, as found in his letter to the George Keatses, April 21, 1819, in which the intelligence acquires an identity through experience.

Swaminathan, S. R. "The Odes of Keats." *Keats-Shelley Memorial Bulletin,*

12 (1961): 45-47.

Argues that "Nightingale," "Urn," and "Psyche" all have the immortality of the soul as their theme.

1962

Balslev, Thora. *Keats and Wordsworth: A Comparative Study.* Copenhagen: Norwegian Universities Press, 1962.

Argues the influence of "To the Cuckoo" on "Nightingale" and mentions that "Urn" derives in part from "Upon the Sight of a Beautiful Picture" and "The fairest, brightest hues of ether fade."

Bullough, Geoffrey. *Mirror of Minds: Changing Psychological Beliefs in English Poetry.* London: Athlone Press, 1962.

Concerns the development of psychological theory as it is reflected in poetry. Discusses "Nightingale" and "Urn" briefly as exemplifying the theory that the mind works through association.

Combellack, C. R. B. "Keats's Grecian Urn as Unravished Bride." *Keats-Shelley Journal,* 11 (1962): 14-15.

Asserts that Keats used the term "unravished" in "Urn" to refer to the vase's being unbroken. He used "bride" to counteract any possible associations with death which might have been associated with the urn, an object so frequently used in funerals.

Cornelius, D. K. "Keats' 'Ode on a Grecian Urn.'" *Explicator,* 20 (March 1962): #57.

Argues that the last line and a half of "Urn" represent the observer of the vase's realization of the limitations of aesthetic experience. The urn has failed to respond pertinently to any of his questions posed in stanzas one and four.

Empson, William. "Rhythm and Imagery in English Poetry." *British Journal of Aesthetics,* 2 (January 1962): 36-54.

Explains lines 19-20 of "Autumn" as a "muscular image" and the center of the ode.

Freeman, Arthur. "Keats's 'Ode on Melancholy,' 24." *Notes and Queries*, 207 (May 1962): 184.

Treats line 24 as an adaptation of the Elizabethan figure in which the spider sucks poison out of the same flower the bee sucks honey.

Gérard, Albert. "Romance and Reality: Continuity and Growth in Keats's View of Art." *Keats-Shelley Journal*, 11 (1962): 17-29.

Argues that "the main theme of 'Urn' is not the supremacy of art over life, but rather the function of art in life." Art acts as a way for man to perceive the presence of the ideal in the actual.

Hagelman, Charles W. "Keats's Medical Training and the Last Stanza of the 'Ode to Psyche.'" *Keats-Shelley Journal*, 11 (1962): 73-82.

Demonstrates Keats's reliance in "Psyche" upon the anatomical and physiological knowledge of Astley Cooper and Joseph Henry Green.

Hecht, Anthony. "Shades of Keats and Marvell." *Hudson Review*, 15 (1962): 50-71.

Compares "Nightingale" with Marvell's "The Garden" and concludes that Keats was indicating a separation of the rational intellect from the imagination. This exercise of the supra-rational imagination is what Keats meant by negative capability.

Kenyon, Katherine M. R. "When Did Keats and Fanny Brawne Become Engaged?" *Keats-Shelley Memorial Bulletin*, 13 (1962): 4-7.

Argues that Keats became engaged to Fanny Brawne on May 1, 1819, and that this emotional event is reflected in the hopefulness of "Psyche," written on April 30, and in the growing optimism of the subsequent "Nightingale" and "Urn."

MacLeish, Archibald, and Mark Van Doren. *The Dialogues of Archibald MacLeish and Mark Van Doren*. Ed. Warren V. Bush. New York: Dutton, 1964.

This conversation took place on June 18, 1962. MacLeish expresses his admiration for the passion for life which "Nightingale" conveys and which "Urn" requires of—and even brings about in—its perceptive reader.

Marilla, E. L. "Three Odes of Keats." In *Essays and Studies on English Language and Literature.* Ed. S. B. Liljegren. Copenhagen: Uppsala, 1962.

Traces a strain of Neoplatonism through "Melancholy," "Nightingale," and "Urn." These odes reflect the concept of man as a spark of the Divine Being, confined within a physical body and destined to long for release into that world which it has only an imperfect perception of.

Miller, Lois T. "A Single Gaggling Eye: An Analysis of Sidney Keyes' 'Greenwich Observatory.'" *English Journal,* 51 (January 1962): 62-63.

A portion of this brief article is taken up in a comparison of "Urn" and Sidney Keyes' "Greenwich Observatory."

Swanson, Roy Arthur. "Form and Content in Keats's 'Ode on a Grecian Urn.'" *College English,* 23 (1962): 302-305.

Argues that "Urn" is Classical in form (since it employs the symmetrical figures of chiasmus and anaphora and emphasizes the golden mean) and Romantic in content (since it invites the reader to complete the vision of the urn in his head). *In toto,* the poem acts as a reconciliation of the Classical and the Romantic.

1963

Bate, Walter Jackson. *John Keats.* 1963; rpt. New York: Oxford University Press, 1966.

Aware that no single interpretation of the odes satisfies anyone except its exponent, Bate conducts instead a detailed analysis of the odes. He discusses their meter and integrates them stylistically and thematically with Keats's other works. He also records the history of their composition, insofar as it is determinable, and cites influences on the odes. In general, he takes the theme of the odes, excepting "Psyche," to be the acceptance of or the escape from process.

Bostetter, Edward E. *The Romantic Ventriloquists: Wordsworth, Coleridge, Keats, Shelley, and Byron.* Seattle: University of Washington Press, 1963.

Concerns the romantic imagination. Discusses Keats's odes to support the thesis that Keats shifted ideological positions between "Hyperion" and "The Fall of Hyperion." Keats began believing in the truth of beauty and in the holiness of the heart's affections, but ended realizing that such a belief was no longer possible in the light of the scientific attitude. Some of the material in Bostetter's treatment of the odes here comes from his 1958 essay, "The Eagle and the Truth."

D'Avanzo, Mario Louis. "Recurrent Metaphors for Poetry in John Keats's Works." *DA,* 24 (1964), 3745 (Brown).

Completed in 1963. Offers a reading of "Psyche" based on the recurring figures and images of Keats's other work dealing with poetry, poetry-making, and poetic inspiration.

Fitzgerald, F. Scott. *The Letters of F. Scott Fitzgerald.* Ed. Andrew Turnbull. New York: Charles Scribner's Sons, 1963.

See 1939 and 1940.

Gross, George Clayburn. "Keats's 'Presider': The Influence of Shakespeare on Keats." *DA,* 24 (1963), 726 (Southern California).

The odes were influenced by Shakespeare in the areas of intensity, movement of imagery, use of allegory, and the relationship of beauty and truth. "Urn," especially, is the epitome of what Keats learned from Shakespeare.

Halpern, Martin. "Keats's Grecian Urn and the Singular 'Ye.'" *College English,* 24 (January 1963): 284-288.

Sees four possible interpretations of who says what to whom at the end of "Urn": 1) the poet addresses mankind; 2) the urn addresses mankind; 3) the poet addresses the figures on the urn; and 4) the poet addresses the urn itself. Argues for #4 based on evidence of the use of "ye" in the singular in Keats's time.

Jack, Ian. "Keats." In *English Literature: 1815-1832.* Oxford: Clarendon Press, 1963, pp. 105-129.

Stresses Keats's expression of concern for beauty in the odes and de-emphasizes their philosophical content. Discusses mainly their subject matter and their metrics.

Kudo, Naotaro. "What a Japanese Thinks of Keats and Shelley." *Keats-Shelley Memorial Bulletin,* 14 (1963): 8-16.

Says that the Japanese are attracted to "Autumn" for its

description of the English landscape seen so often on Japanese television. They appreciate "Nightingale" for the sensuousness of its color and "Urn" for its serenity.

Robinson, Dwight E. "Ode on a 'New Etrurian' Urn: A Reflection of Wedgwood Ware in the Poetic Imagery of John Keats." *Keats-Shelley Journal,* 12 (1963): 11-35.

Argues that Keats's model for the Grecian urn was one of the imitations of the Borghese vase done by Josiah Wedgwood which were very much in vogue among middle class Englishmen at the time Keats wrote his poem.

Rodway, Allan. "Keats." In *The Romantic Conflict.* London: Chatto and Windus, 1963, pp. 227-244.

Contends that Keats had a strong interest in social issues which caused him frustrations resulting in an interest in escapism. However, in the odes he is able to reconcile the real and the ideal and face actuality.

Skutches, Peter. "Keats' Grecian Urn and Myth." *Iowa English Yearbook,* 8 (fall 1963): 45-51.

Basing his interpretation on Keats's letter to George and Georgiana Keats of February 14-May 3, 1819, Skutches feels that in "Urn" the poet loses himself empathically within the frieze on the urn in an aesthetic-religious experience, but cannot maintain this state.

Spender, Stephen. *The Struggle of the Modern.* Berkeley: University of California Press, 1963.

Feels that the last two lines of "Urn" express Keats's identification of imagination with reality. The lines, to Spender, are abundantly clear.

Ward, Aileen. *John Keats: The Making of a Poet.* 1963; rpt. New York: Viking Press, 1967.

Asserts that Keats wrote the odes during a period of perfect balance when he was confident in his writing and his love and when he could rejoice in the beauty of spring. They share the theme of the attempt to arrest change through intense contemplation.

Whiting, George W. "Charlotte Smith, Keats, and the Nightingale." *Keats-Shelley Journal*, 12 (winter 1963): 4-8.

Argues that Keats is indebted to Charlotte Smith's sonnets "Farewell to the Nightingale," "Sonnet to the Nightingale on Her Departure," and "On the Departure of the Nightingale" for both the subject matter and the vocabulary of "Nightingale."

1964

Austen, Allen. "Keats's Grecian Urn and the Truth of Eternity." *College English*, 25 (March 1964): 434-436.

Citing Keats's letter to Bailey of November 22, 1817, as evidence, Austin argues that "Urn" "dramatizes the idea that imaginative perception reveals the truth of eternity."

Baker, J. "Poets of Their Time." *Times Literary Supplement*, September 10, 1964, p. 845.

Traces both the reference to Ruth in "Nightingale" and the personification of autumn in "Autumn" to the same passages in the Bible.

Beall, Chandler. "Eugenio Montale's 'Sarcofaghi.'" In *Linguistic and Literary Studies in Honor of Helmut A. Hatzfeld*. Ed. Alessandro S. Crisafulli. Washington, D.C.: Catholic University of America, 1964.

Argues that the "Sarcofaghi" section of Eugenio Montale's *Ossi di Seppia* (1925) was influenced heavily by "Urn."

Benjamin, Adrian. "'Ode to. a Nightingale.'" *Time Literary Supplement*, February 6, 1964, p. 112.

Reply to Marghanita Laski's letter to *TLS*, January 2, 1964. Asserts that the last line and a half of "Urn" are addressed to the urn.

Bevan, Jack. "'Ode to a Nightingale.'" *Times Literary Supplement*, February 13, 1964, p. 112.

Reply to Benjamin's letter to *TLS*, February 6, 1964. Denies that Keats expresses a need for a burning forehead or that the phrase "Cold pastoral" is used in a pejorative sense.

Burgess, C. F. "Keats' 'Ode on a Grecian Urn,' 2." *Explicator*, 23 (December 1964): #30.

Explains the sense of "foster-child" in line 2 of "Urn." The urn's natural parents were the mind and hands which created it. Its foster parent was the silence of the hiding place which preserved it over the centuries.

Carben, Edward. "John Keats: Pioneer of Modern Existentialist Thought." *Trace*, 55 (winter 1964): 322-330.

Connects the ideas in "Nightingale" and "Melancholy" with the existentialist thinking of Camus. In expressing the link between the opposites of beauty and mortality, joy and melancholy, and life and death, Keats recognized the absurd tension between subjective and objective nature.

Chayes, Irene H. "Rhetoric As Drama: An Approach to the Romantic Ode." *PMLA*, 79 (1964): 67-79.

Uses "Nightingale" to demonstrate how the romantic ode was a combination of the seventeenth century ode, with its emphasis on drama in the Aristotelian sense, and the eighteenth century ode, with its emphasis on the devices of language.

Clayton, Thomas. "'Ode to a Nightingale.'" *Times Literary Supplement*, April 16, 1964, p. 317.

Response to Stahl's letter to *TLS*, March 19, 1964. Argues that the first half of line 49 of "Urn" is spoken by the urn to the poet and that the next line and a half is spoken by the poet to the urn.

Felperin, Howard. "Keats and Shakespeare: Two New Sources." *English Language Notes*, 2 (December 1964): 105-109.

Claims that "Urn" was influenced by Shakespeare's "The Phoenix and the Turtle" and "Nightingale" was influenced by Richard Barnfield's "The Passionate Pilgrim" (mistakenly attributed to Shakespeare in Keats's Thomas Wilson 1806 reprint of John Benson's 1640 edition of Shakespeare's poems).

Gaull, Marilyn S. "Keats and Wordsworth: Their Historical and Literary Relationship." *DA*, 25 (1964), 2957 (Indiana).

Traces Keats's beauty-truth identification back to Words-worth's "Ode: Intimations of Immortality."

Grube, John. *"Tender Is the Night:* Keats and Scott Fitzgerald." *Dalhousie Review,* 44 (winter 1964-65): 433-441.

Demonstrates Fitzgerald's use of the moon as a symbol in *Tender Is the Night* and says that it derives from lines 36-37 of "Nightingale," which were elided from the epigraph to the novel.

Guy, E. F. "Keats's Use of 'Luxury': A Note on Meaning." *Keats-Shelley Journal,* 13 (1964): 87-95.

Defines Keats's use of "luxury" as a state of intense sensual-ity. Associates line 52 of "Nightingale" with Keats's letter to Fanny Brawne, July 25, 1819.

Heller, Erich. "The Theology of the Grecian Urn." *The Listener,* 72 (December 31, 1964): 1037-1039.

In his discussion of Hegel's distinction between Classical and Romantic, Heller repeatedly uses "Urn" as his example of the romantic view, which, aware of the gap between the spiritual and the real, yearns for a time when beauty was truth.

Hobsbaum, Philip. "The 'Philosophy' of the Grecian Urn: A Consensus of Readings." *Keats-Shelley Memorial Bulletin,* 15 (1964): 1-7.

Outlines three kinds of responses to lines 49-50 of "Urn": 1) the aesthete sees them as a statement about the nature of beauty; 2) the philosopher sees them as a statement about truth; and, 3) the aesthetic philosopher, finding value in the paradox of the poem, avoids the lines as much as possible. In Hobsbaum's view, any interpretation which serves the needs of the reader is valid.

James, G. Ingli. "'Ode to a Nightingale.'" *Times Literary Supplement,* February 20, 1964, p. 153.

Reply to Benjamin's letter to *TLS,* February 6, 1964. Agrees that the last two lines of "Urn" are addressed to the vase, but adds that "ye" is used to express an ironic respect for the urn.

Kroeber, Karl. *The Artifice of Reality: Poetic Style in Wordsworth, Foscolo, Keats, and Leopardi.* Madison: University of Wisconsin Press, 1964.

"Melancholy" is the only one of the odes which doesn't present a personal experience; instead, it outlines abstractly the psychological orientation of the other odes. "Psyche" shows the experience of the power of an obsolete religion through the imagination. "Nightingale" celebrates the process by which the human mind uses sensory experience to spring into a higher plane of perception; it ultimately must return to the natural, but the natural then takes on a new meaning. "Urn" expresses the imagination's ability to bring forth the inner vitality of the universe; love is the stimulus for the imagination in this action.

Laski, Marghanita. "'Ode to a Nightingale.'" *Times Literary Supplement,* January 2, 1964, p. 16.

Claims that "envy" in the first stanza of "Nightingale" has the meaning of "pride," "a sense of being enviable," and "self-gratification." Thus, the bird sings, not because it is aware of being enviable, but out of its own happiness.

MacLeish, Archibald, and Mark Van Doren. *The Dialogues of Archibald MacLeish and Mark Van Doren.* Ed. Warren V. Bush. New York: Dutton, 1964.

See 1962.

Rhydderch, William. *Times Literary Supplement,* March 5, 1964, p. 191.

This letter claims that both lines 49 and 50 of "Urn" are spoken by the vase to man.

Ruotolo, Lucio P. "Keats and Kierkegaard: The Tragedy of Two Worlds." *Renascence,* 16 (1964): 175-190.

Asserts that Keats and Kierkegaard held similar views regarding the necessity of achieving a self through refusal to give oneself over totally to either the real or the ideal. Interprets "Urn" as a statement of Christian existentialism, a dialectic between the real and the ideal with no synthesis and ending in an absurdist declaration.

Seright, Orin Dale. "Syntactic Structures in Keats' Poetry." *DA,* 26 (1965), 1033 (Indiana).

Completed in 1964. Argues that nouns used as noun modifiers drop to a low percentage in the odes while the percentage of compound modifiers reaches its highest point.

Southall, Raymond. "'Ode to a Nightingale.'" *Times Literary Supplement,* March 5, 1964, p. 199.

This letter argues that both "Nightingale" and "Urn" end with the poet's awareness of the limitations of their respective vehicles of imaginative transport, the bird and the urn.

Stahl, E. L. "Ode to a Nightingale.'" *Times Literary Supplement,* March 19, 1964, p. 238.

Agrees with William Rhydderch's March 5, 1964 view that the entire last two lines of "Urn" are spoken by the urn to man, but for a different reason. Claiming popularity for the discussion of the beauty/truth relationship in the nineteenth century, Stahl parallels Keats's view with Schiller's in "Die Kunstler" in which the idea is expressed that truth can only be apprehended sensuously by man, but that after death it can be perceived more directly. However, Stahl adds that there is no evidence that Keats knew Schiller's poem first hand.

Wagner, Robert D. "Keats: 'Ode to Psyche' and the Second 'Hyperion.'" *Keats-Shelley Journal,* 13 (1964): 29-41.

Treats "Psyche" as a step towards achieving the vision in the second "Hyperion" of the limits of the imagination. Because the poet builds Psyche's altar within the confines of his brain and because the narrator in "Hyperion" achieves a greater knowledge than that of the gods, reality triumphs over the powers of the imagination in them, putting Keats out of the main romantic tradition.

Wilson, Katharine M. *The Nightingale and the Hawk: A Psychological Study of Keats' Ode.* London: George Allen and Unwin, 1964.

Claims that "Nightingale" is the description of an experience of the Self according to the thought of Jung.

1965

Bellairs, John. "Variations on a Vase." *Southern Review* (Adelaide), 1 (1965): 58-68.

Attacks Brooks, Burke, and Wasserman for their interpretations of "Urn." Denies that "Urn"'s basic structure is dramatic and objects to these critics' habit of over-emphasizing certain words and phrases, as well as to their excessive paradox-consciousness. Bellairs' own thesis for the meaning of "Urn" is more literal: the beautiful permanence of art over the painful transience of human experience.

Bloom, Harold. "Keats and the Embarrassments of Poetic Tradition." In *From Sensibility to Romanticism: Essays Presented to Frederick A. Pottle.* Ed. Frederick W. Hilles and Harold Bloom. New York: Oxford University Press, 1965, pp. 513-526.

Considers "Psyche," "Nightingale," and "Autumn" with respect to the negative weight Keats felt from poetic tradition. "Psyche" represents a conscious departure from tradition; Keats chooses to be the priest of a goddess never worshipped before. "Nightingale" breaks from tradition by choosing the human, laden though it is with necessary death. And "Autumn" replaces the traditional poets' paradise with a cyclical vision which includes life, growth, and death.

Cutting, Vivien. *The Listener,* 73 (January 14, 1965): 61.

A letter to the editor. Criticizes Erich Heller's over-emphasis of lines 11-12 of "Urn" in his essay in *The Listener,* December 31, 1964.

Frechet, R. "Yeats's 'Sailing to Byzantium' and Keats's 'Ode to a Nightingale.'" In *W. B. Yeats, 1865-1965, Centenary Essays on the Art of W. B. Yeats.* Ed. D.E.S. Maxwell and S. B. Bushrui. Ibadan: Ibadan University Press, 1965, pp. 217-219.

Compares "Nightingale" with Yeats's "Sailing to Byzantium."

Gleckner, Robert F. "Keats's Odes: The Problems of the Limited Canon." *Studies in English Literature,* 5 (autumn 1965): 577-585.

Points out the problems in treating the odes as a unified group of poems. For one thing, the sequence of the odes is often determined according to the critic's thesis concerning the development of a theme within them; that sequence changes from critic to critic. Also, there is difficulty determining which of Keats's poems belong in a grouping of his odes.

Godfrey, D. R. "Keats and the Grecian Urn." *Hermathena,* 100 (summer 1965): 44-53.

Argues that lines 49-50 of "Urn" are spoken by the urn and that they are true for the art of ancient Greece but lacking as a guide to modern experience.

Hill, Archibald A. "Some Points in the Analysis of Keats's 'Ode on a Grecian Urn.'" In *Essays in Literary Analysis*. Austin: Dailey Diversified Services, 1965, pp. 95-105.

Discusses the implications of nineteenth-century British pronunciation on the rhyming in "Urn" and examines the first two and last two lines of the ode.

Kimura, Akiko. "A Study of John Keats: The Evolution of Keats's Idea of Beauty." *Essays and Studies in British and American Literature* (Tokyo), 13 (September 1965): 1-33.

Feels that Keats's sense of reality was so strong that it prevented him from abandoning himself wholly to the sensuous enjoyment of beauty and imagination, though he longed to do so. Kimura's readings of the odes are conventional.

Mackenzie, Manfred. "A Reply." *Southern Review* (Adelaide), 1 (1965): 70-73.

Defends Burke against Bellairs' attack in the same issue of *Southern Review*. Defines Burke's terms which Bellairs found incomprehensible and explains the basis of Burke's approach.

Magaw, Malcolm. "Yeats and Keats: The Poetics of Romanticism." *Bucknell Review*, 13 (December 1965): 87-96.

Compares Keats to Yeats as a romantic poet, concentrating on "Nightingale," "Urn," and "Sailing to Byzantium."

Moorman, Mary. *William Wordsworth: A Biography*. 1965; rpt. Oxford: Clarendon Press, 1966.

Says that a phrase from Wordsworth's "The Resting Place" was influenced by "Nightingale."

Quinn, Michael. "The Objectivity of Keats's Ode 'To Autumn.'" *Critical Survey*, 2 (winter 1965): 146-150.

Argues that "Autumn" is not an objective poem in the usual sense of the word. It is not a work which excludes a personal response to the season; rather, the construction of the poem is based on just such a response. The first stanza presents the filling of autumn to the point of overflow. The response to that over-fullness comes in stanza two in the form of the welcome relief of harvest. The response to that experience comes in stanza three, where we find the song of autumn in praise of the cleansing accomplished in stanza two. These responses are personal, not objective.

Teich, Nathaniel. "Criticism and Keats's 'Grecian Urn.'" *Philological Quarterly*, 44 (1965): 496-502.

Uses a textual analysis of the last two lines of "Urn" to organize this account of past critics' answers to "who says what to whom" at the end of the ode. Concludes that the reason for such diversity of opinion as is to be found is that Keats's lines were the expression of a yet-unformed mind. Lines 49-50 do not represent a satisfyingly whole viewpoint; thus, critics have completed that view according to their own wisdoms.

Waldron, Philip. "A Reply." *Southern Review* (Adelaide), 1 (1965): 68-70.

Defends Brooks and, to a lesser extent, Wasserman from John Bellairs' attack in the same issue of the *Southern Review*. The excessive paradox-hunting is an attempt by Brooks to illustrate one of the characteristics of poetry which has been overlooked. *The Well-Wrought Urn* is an admitted *tour de force*.

1966

Benton, Richard P. "Keats and Zen." *Philosophy East and West*, 16 (January-April 1966): 33-47.

Associates the loss of self-identity as a means to a higher discovery in "Nightingale" with the Zen concept of *satori*, the awakening of the Buddha nature.

Blackstone, Bernard. "The Mind of Keats in His Art." In *British Romantic Poets: Recent Revaluations.* Ed. Shiv K. Kumar. New York: New York University Press, 1966, pp. 257-275.

Conceives "Truth" in lines 49-50 of "Urn" to be constantly changing. Keats's dictum places truth in the natural, organic order of things, and that implies mutability.

Boggs, W. Arthur. "Permanence and Impermanence: Keatsian Mutability." *Trace,* 62 (fall-winter 1966): 358-369.

> Discusses Keats's seven greatest works ("The Eve of St. Agnes," "La Belle Dame Sans Merci," "Urn," "Melancholy," "Nightingale," "Lamia," and "Autumn") in light of the permanence/impermanence theme which runs through all of them.

Bush, Douglas. *John Keats: His Life and Writings.* 1966; rpt. New York: Collier Books, 1967.

> Compact, general book on Keats. Gives readings for the odes, discusses their diction, puts them in the context of literary tradition, relates them to other nineteenth-century literature, mentions their sources, evaluates them, establishes their themes, and relates them to Keats's other works as well as to each other.

Green, David B. "An Early Reprinting of Three Poems from Keats's 1820 Volume." *Papers of the Bibliographical Society of America,* 60 (1966): 363.

> Announces the discovery that "Urn" and "Psyche" were printed in the 1820 Rivington's *Annual Register.*

Halpern, Martin. "Keats and the 'Spirit That Laughest.'" *Keats-Shelley Journal,* 15 (1966): 69-86.

> Demonstrates Keats's integration of humor into his poetic vision. Discusses the thematic role of humor in "Melancholy," arguing that the comic exaggeration in the first and in the omitted stanzas of such a serious poem supports the joy-in-sorrow idea.

Hudnall, Clayton Edward. "Metaphorical Projection and the Picturesque in the Writings of John Keats." *DA,* 27A (1967), 3841 (Illinois).

> Completed in 1966. Uses Keats's important poems to argue that Keats's poetry moved from a picturesque concern with the outward and physical to a more mature inner vision.

Jacobs, Roderick A. "A Poem for the Junior High." *English Journal,* 55 (January 1966): 98-100.

> Compares "Nightingale" with W. W. Gibson's "The Ice-

Cart" for structure and theme, concluding that the latter is better suited to a junior high school curriculum.

Kauvar, Gerald Bluestone. "Figurative Relationships in the Poetry of Keats." *DA*, 27A (1967), 1787 (Duke).

Completed in 1966. Devotes a chapter to "Nightingale" and the thematic relationships among its figurative language and some of Keats's other poems.

Kohli, Devindra. "Inner Resonance: A Note on the Odes of John Keats." *Quest*, 48 (January-March 1966): 33-42.

Argues that Keats's odes embody deep moral insights. Finds in each of them a strong commitment to life as it is, even in the face of suffering and loss.

Laski, Marghanita. "The Language of the Nightingale Ode." *Essays and Studies*, 19 (1966): 60-73.

Traces the various kinds and stages of ecstasy found in "Nightingale" according to the analysis of ecstasy made in her book *Ecstasy: A Study of Some Secular and Religious Experiences* (Bloomington: Indiana University Press, 1961).

Lee, Brian. "The New Criticism and the Language of Poetry." In *Essays On Style and Language: Linguistic and Critical Approaches to Literary Style*. London: Routledge and Kegan Paul, 1966, pp. 29-52.

Devotes six pages to discussing the views of "Urn" of Wasserman, Spitzer, Burke, and others.

Madden, J. S. "Melancholy in Medicine and Literature: Some Historical Considerations." *British Journal of Medical Psychology*, 39 (June 1966): 125-130.

Traces historically two approaches to melancholy, an unfavorable view of it as an illness and a favorable one associating it with intelligence and artistic creativity. Argues "Melancholy" represents the unfavorable view.

Man, Paul de. "Introduction." In *John Keats: Selected Poetry*. Ed. Paul de Man. New York: New American Library, 1966, pp.ix-xxxvi.

Views the pattern of Keats's work as hopefully prospective in a progression of Ovidian metamorphosis involving a detach-

ment from both sympathetic love, which is painfully aware of
life's limitations, and poetic dream, which thrives on ideal potential. Treats odes in this context, finding a counterpart to
"Nightingale" and "Urn" in "What can I do to drive away."

Mayerson, Caroline W. "Keats's 'Ode to a Nightingale,' 31-33." *Explicator*,
25 (November 1966): #29.

Argues that lines 31-33 of "Nightingale" allude to Pegasus.

Notopoulos, James A. "'Truth-Beauty' in the 'Ode on a Grecian Urn' and
the Elgin Marbles." *Modern Language Review*, 61 (1966): 180-182.

Discusses the influence of the Elgin Marbles on "Urn."

Pearce, Donald. "Flames Begotten of Flame." *Sewanee Review*, 74 (July-
September 1966): 649-668.

Links "Nightingale" with Horace and Yeats. Denies that
such a phenomenon as "influence" exists, suggesting instead
that there was a "potential poem" which Keats drew on to compose his ode. In so doing, if he used some of Horace's words, it
was because they both were trying to give actuality to the
same, or part of the same, potential poem.

Polgar, Mirko. "Keats's Beauty-Truth Identification in the Light of
Philosophy." *Keats-Shelley Memorial Bulletin*, 17 (1966): 55-62.

Emphasizes Keats's insistence on the power of the imagination. It is in the exercise of the imagination, which is not deceit-
ful, that beauty becomes truth. Where Keats used imagination
to reach this conclusion, Aquinas used philosophical reason to
reach a similar one: the unity of beauty, truth, and goodness.

Pollin, Burton R. "Keats, Charlotte Smith, and the Nightingale." *Notes and
Queries*, 13 (May 1966): 180-181.

Argues that "Nightingale" was influenced by Charlotte
Smith's "On the Departure of the Nightingale."

Rhodes, Jack Lee. "A Study in the Vocabulary of English Romanticism:
'Joy' in the Poetry of Blake, Wordsworth, Coleridge, Shelley, and
Byron." *DA*, 27A (1967), 3434 (Texas).

Completed in 1966. Discusses the concept of joy in "Melancholy."

Smith, Barbara Herrnstein. "'Sorrow's Mysteries': Keats's 'Ode on Melancholy.'" *Studies in English Literature*, 6 (autumn 1966): 679-691.

Sees "Melancholy" as spoken by a person in Melancholy's power instructing someone else where the goddess' dwelling is and how to get there.

Visick, Mary. "'Tease us out of thought': Keats's 'Epistle to Reynolds' and the Odes." *Keats-Shelley Journal*, 15 (1966): 87-98.

Discusses the role of romance in "Nightingale" and "Urn" as established in Keats's verse "Epistle to Reynolds."

Warncke, Wayne. "Keats' 'Ode on a Grecian Urn.'" *Explicator*, 24 (January 1966): #40.

Emphasizes that the real value of "Urn" lies not in the beauty of the urn but in the function of the poem in relating that work of art to real life. In this view, Keats was presenting the act of experiencing a work of art, not by completely losing oneself in it, but by remaining conscious, in the face of the beauty of art, of human woe.

1967

Brooks, Cleanth. "The Language of Poetry: Some Problem Cases." *Archiv fur das Studium der neueren Sprachen und Literaturen*, 203 (April 1967): 401-414.

Examines Keats's repetition of the word "fade" in "Nightingale." Demonstrates its use as a structural device by analyzing its irony, which Brooks regards broadly as "something like qualification by context."

D'Avanzo, Mario L. *Keats's Metaphors for the Poetic Imagination*. Durham, North Carolina: Duke University Press, 1967.

Considers the odes in his study of Keats's imagery. The thesis is that Keats repeatedly used certain metaphors and images to represent and describe the process of poetic inspiration, such as the moon, sleep, dreams, the grot, the elf, wine, the bower, et al.

Dickstein, Morris. "The Divided Self: A Study of Keats' Poetic Development." *DA*, 28A (1968), 4168 (Yale).

Completed in 1967. Views the odes as built upon the dialectic of a divided consciousness rather than on visionary flight.

Jack, Ian. *Keats and the Mirror of Art*. 1967; rpt. Oxford: Clarendon Press, 1968, pp. 201-243.

Shows Keats's debt to painting for many of the excellences of his poetry. Contains chapters on "Psyche," "Urn," and "Autumn." Suggests relationships between "Psyche" and paintings by Raphael, Giulio Romano, Luca Giordano, Canova and others, and grounds the poem in its literary sources as well. Discusses the various vases, urns, and paintings of vases and urns which may have served as models for "Urn" and examines the way Keats may have transmuted their elements into poetry. And presents "Autumn," too, in terms of painting, emphasizing especially the works which may have suggested the images of autumn in the second stanza.

Krieger, Murray. *"Ekphrasis and the Still Movement of Poetry; or Laokoon Revisited."* In *The Poet as Critic*. Ed. Frederick P. W. McDowell. Evanston, Illinois: Northwestern University Press, 1967, pp. 3-26.

Discusses Keats's use in "Urn" of ekphrasis, the literary imitation of a piece of plastic art. The frozen world of plastic art is imposed upon the fluid world of literary relationships to still them.

Little, G. L. "Keats' 'Ode on Melancholy.'" *Explicator*, 25 (February 1967): #46.

Argues that "Melancholy" distinguishes between passively succumbing to melancholy and actively accepting it. A kind of permanence can be achieved over time and death by embracing melancholy in a creative way.

Mayhead, Robin. *John Keats*. Cambridge: Cambridge University Press, 1967.

Forty pages of the 126-page book are devoted to a reading of the odes. "Melancholy" demonstrates the possibility of conquering sadness by concentrating on something real outside the sufferer. "Nightingale" strives towards a faith that beauty does not always die. The vase in "Urn" is seen as a symbol of permanence with the power of diverting us temporarily from

life's sorrows. "Psyche" concerns the nature of poetic composition. And "Autumn" accepts impermanence by attaching
it to a larger, cyclical permanence.

Owen, Wilfred. *Wilfred Owen: Collected Letters.* Ed. Harold and John Bell.
London: Oxford University Press, 1967.

See 1911.

Purcell, H. D. "The Probable Origin of a Line in Keats's 'Ode to a Nightingale.'" *Notes and Queries,* OS 212 (January 1967): 24.

Says "Nightingale" was influenced by Act V of Thomas
Heywood's *A Challenge for Beauty.*

Rogers, Robert. "Keats's Strenuous Tongue: A Study of 'Ode on
Melancholy.'" *Literature and Psychology,* 17 (1967): 2-12.

This Freudian essay argues that the basis of the melancholy
in the ode is oral and sexual, stemming from the manic-depres-
sive state of mind Keats developed as a result of childhood
rejection by his mother.

----------. "Reply by Mr. Rogers." *Literature and Psychology,* 17 (1967): 41-43.

Replies to Ward's assertion in the same issue of this journal
that the real subject of "Melancholy" is metaphysical rather
than sexual by saying that he had claimed that view himself in
his essay and offered the sexual view, not as the only interpretation possible, but as a way to help complete our reading of
the poem.

Stevenson, John. "Arcadia Re-Settled: Pastoral Poetry and Romantic
Theory." *Studies in English Literature,* 7 (autumn 1967): 629-638.

This essay on the romantic versus the enlightenment view
of the pastoral uses the phrase "Cold pastoral" from "Urn" to
exemplify the romantic shift in attitude toward the pastoral
from artificial to integral.

Thompson, Phyllis Rose. "The 'Haiku Question' and the Reading of
Images." *English Journal,* 56 (April 1967): 547-551.

Encourages teachers to teach their students to respond to
poetry loaded with sensuous imagery by first introducing

them to the Haiku. Applies the technique of Haiku interpretation to "Autumn," concentrating on analysis of the images.

Ward, Aileen. "The Psychoanalytical Theory of Poetic Form: A Comment." *Literature and Psychology*, 17 (1967): 30-37.

> Replies to three psychoanalytic interpretations of literary works. One is Robert Rogers's "Keats's Strenuous Tongue," from the same volume of this journal. Condemns Rogers's method of interpreting "Melancholy," accusing him of taking words and phrases out of context, over-emphasizing the sexual aspects of the poem, and pushing the psychoanalytic approach farther than it can justifiably go.

Winters, Yvor. *Forms of Discovery: Critical and Historical Essays on the Forms of the Short Poem in English.* [Chicago]: Alan Swallow, 1967.

> Devotes two and a half pages to condemning the odes as adolescent.

1968

Adams, Richard P. *Faulkner: Myth and Motion.* Princeton: Princeton University Press, 1968.

> Argues that Faulkner was attracted to "Urn" because of its contrast between motion and arrest.

Ball, Patricia M. *The Central Self: A Study in Romantic and Victorian Imagination.* London: Athlone Press, 1968.

> The romantic poets each had two kinds of imaginative expression, what Keats called the "egotistical sublime" and the "chamelion." Like Langbaum, Ball feels that the romantic poets were trying to come to terms with their own personalities after the collapse of the eighteenth century rationalism. She approaches the odes as expressions of the "egotistical sublime."

Buchen, Irving H. "Keats's 'To Autumn': The Season of Optimum Form." *CEA Critic*, 31 (November 1968): 11.

> Points out the references to both spring and winter in the last stanza of "Autumn." Feels that Keats was using the season of autumn as a transition between spring and winter, lending

total affirmation to neither one. Autumn gives form to the life experience, and that is its value.

Faulkner, William. *Lion in the Garden: Interviews with William Faulkner, 1926-1962.* Ed. James B. Meriwether and Michael Millgate. New York: Random House, 1968.

See 1956.

Gittings, Robert. *John Keats.* Boston: Little, Brown, 1968.

Sets "Psyche" apart from the other odes both in quality and in form. Groups together "Urn," "Melancholy," "Nightingale," and "Indolence" as expressing from different points of view Keats's theory of soul-making. "Autumn" differs from the other odes in its calm; where the others strain with the philosophy they present, "Autumn" accepts it.

Haworth, Helen E. "Keats and the Metaphor of Vision." *Journal of English and Germanic Philology,* 67 (July 1968): 371-394.

Explores Keats's use of vision metaphor. Argues that Keats used expressions of experiencing a vision as equivalents for the action of the imagination. The vision of autumn personified is used as a clear example of this. Haworth extends this principle to apply to "Nightingale" and "Psyche" (as well as to other poems): they are not mystical in their subject matter. Rather, they concern the poet's individual imagination which is based in the concrete world he knows.

Hayter, Alethea. "Keats." In *Opium and the Romantic Imagination.* Berkeley: University of California Press, 1968, pp. 306-328.

Briefly treats the mood of "Nightingale" and "Melancholy" as stemming from an opium-induced indolence.

Hinkel, Howard Hollis. "The Two Worlds of John Keats: A Study of His Poetry as Attempts to Reconcile the Disparity Between Intuited and Observed Reality." *DA,* 29A (1969), 3098 (Tulane).

Completed in 1968. Sees the odes as a reassertion of Keats's early trust in the truth of the imagination which had faltered briefly after "Endymion."

Jeffrey, Lloyd N. "A Freudian Reading of Keats's 'Ode to Psyche.'" *Psychoanalytic Review,* 55 (summer 1968): 289-306.

Analyzes "Psyche" according to Freud's "The Theme of the
Three Caskets." Finds Freudian equivalents for death in the
ode in references to sleep, concealment, pallor, dumbness,
secrecy, mystery, and silence, and argues that love (Cupid) is
often unconsciously substituted for death (Psyche) as an act of
wish-fulfillment.

Johnson, Richard Edward. "Settings of Innocence and Experience in the
Poetry of Keats." *DA,* 30A (1969), 2487 (Tulane).

Completed in 1968. Claims that "Urn" and "Nightingale"
achieve a balance between the philosophical, skeptical mind
and the empathic, disinterested self.

Leoff, Eve. "A Study of John Keats's 'Isabella.'" *DA,* 29A (1968), 874
(Columbia).

Argues that "Psyche" marks the conscious change Keats
made from the influence of Boccaccio.

Lozano, Ann. "Phonemic Patterning in Keats's 'Ode on Melancholy.'"
Keats-Shelley Journal, 17 (1968):15-29.

Studies the phonemic patterning in "Melancholy" to draw
hypotheses about Keats's poetics.

Mathur, D. K. "The Meaning of 'Pure Poetry' in Keats and Baudelaire."
Quest (Bombay), 59 (autumn 1968): 52-59.

In discussing Keats and Baudelaire as writers of "pure
poetry," Mathur suggests a comparison of "Nightingale" with
"Le Voyage."

Matthey, F. "Interplay of Structure and Meaning in the 'Ode to a Nightingale.'" *English Studies,* 49 (1968): 303-317.

Applies Allott's tripartite, pyramidal structure of "Isabella,"
"The Eve of St. Agnes," and "Lamia" to "Nightingale." Stanzas
I-III show the poet falling into a swoon. In IV and V he awakens
into enchantment. And from VI through VII he returns to a
hostile world.

Sendry, Joseph, and Richard Giannone. *A Critical Study Guide to Keats: The
Odes.* Los Angeles, California: Littlefield, Adams, 1968.

Gives critical readings of the odes, discusses their form and meter, provides glosses for words and lines, and traces influences on the odes.

Smith, Barbara Herrnstein. *Poetic Closure: A Study of How Poems End.* Chicago: University of Chicago Press, 1968.

Briefly examines the structures of "Nightingale" and "Urn" with regard to their endings. "Nightingale" effects closure by shifting from present to past tense to announce that the experience is over. In "Urn," Keats overstated his case at the end in an attempt to reach a solid conclusion.

Solis, Gustavo Diaz. "Six Odes of Keats." In *Exploration in Criticism: Eleven Papers on English and American Literature.* [Caracas]: Universidad Central de Venezuela, [1968].

This lecture on Keats's odes is a continuation of a discussion of the nature of lyric poetry begun in an English literature course. Solis discusses the odes as lyric poetry, gives New Critical readings of them, and analyzes their structures.

Stillinger, Jack. "Introduction: Imagination and Reality in the Odes of Keats." In *Twentieth Century Interpretations of Keats's Odes: A Collection of Critical Essays.* Ed. Jack Stillinger. Englewood Cliffs, New Jersey: Prentice-Hall, 1968, pp. 1-16.

Sees the odes as variations on the basic pattern of a flight from reality into ideality and then a return to reality again with a changed perception of it. Treats "Psyche" tentatively as following this pattern of escape and return-with-a-difference. "Nightingale" and "Urn" fit better, while "Melancholy" and "Autumn" express the post-return point of view. Traces the development of the ideology which lies behind the odes and gives a brief historical account of Keats's reputation.

----------. "Appendix: Who Says What to Whom at the End of 'Ode on a Grecian Urn'?" In *Twentieth Century Interpretations of Keats's Odes: A Collection of Critical Essays.* Ed. Jack Stillinger. Englewood Cliffs, New Jersey: Prentice-Hall, 1968, pp. 113-114.

Gives most of the textual variations for lines 49-50 of "Urn" and arranges the interpretations of who is speaking to whom in them into four categories: 1) poet to reader; 2) poet to urn; 3) poet to figures on the urn; and 4) urn to reader.

Talbot, Norman. *The Major Poems of John Keats.* Sydney: Sydney University Press, 1968.

Gives readings of "Urn," "Nightingale," and "Autumn," sometimes allowing the value of more than one reading for a particular passage. Argues that in "Nightingale" the imaginative fancy is rejected because of its forlorn unhumanity. In "Urn," Keats captured the ecstasy of the moment between expectation and achievement; the last two lines are the urn's expression of the value of that moment. And in "Autumn," Keats created a tension by balancing the process of the season against the static poses of autumn.

1969

Anderson, James Blakely, Jr. "Ambiguity and Paradox in the Poetry of Keats." *DA,* 30A (1969), 2474 (Tulane).

Traces the semantic ambiguity in "Urn," the ambiguous state of "living death" in "Nightingale," the paradox of "pleasing sorrow" in "Melancholy," and the paradoxes of the real and the ideal, the concrete and the abstract, and the mortal and the immortal in "Nightingale" and "Urn."

Beer, Gillian. "Aesthetic Debate in Keats's Odes." *Modern Language Review,* 64 (October 1969): 742-748.

Conceives of the odes as derived from Keats's awareness that different art forms have not only different modes of expression but also different areas of expressiveness. "Psyche" explores the relationship between the poetic imagination and myth; "Nightingale" between poetry and music; and "Urn" between poetry and visual art.

Brown, Charles Armitage. "Life of John Keats." In *The Keats Circle.* Ed. Hyder Edward Rollins. Cambridge, Mass.: Harvard University Press, 1969. Vol. II, pp. 52-96.

See 1836.

Dickie, James. "The Grecian Urn: An Archaeological Approach." *Bulletin of the John Rylands Library,* 52 (autumn 1969): 96-114.

Approaches "Urn" as a study in the contrasts of the two scenes on the vase—the one Dionysian and the other Apol-

lonian. Traces the individual images in the scenes back to their
original sources on original vases and drawings.

Ferguson, Oliver W. "Warton and Keats: Two Views of Melancholy."
Keats-Shelley Journal, 18 (1969): 12-15.

Traces parallels between "Melancholy" and Thomas Warton's poem "The Pleasures of Melancholy."

Fusco, Robert J. "The Concrete Versus the Abstract in 'Ode on a Grecian
Urn.'" *Massachusetts Studies in English*, 2 (spring 1969): 22-28.

Argues that Keats began his career writing on the maternal
principle, which posits a one-to-one relationship between a
word and the thing it stands for. However, later Keats began
shifting to the paternal, in which a word signifies an essence
common to all members of the species to which it refers. The
result is that "Urn," among other works, displays a tension
between the abstract (paternal) and the concrete (maternal).

Gelfant, Blanche H. "Faulkner and Keats: The Ideality of Art in 'The
Bear.'" *Southern Literary Journal*, 2 (fall 1969): 43-65.

Studies the allusive role of "Urn" in Faulkner's "The Bear."

Hamilton, James W. "Object Loss, Dreaming, and Creativity: The Poetry
of John Keats." *The Psychoanalytic Study of the Child*, 24 (1969): 488-531.

This psychoanalytic study asserts that Keats's failure to
mourn the deaths of his parents resulted in a "regressive
fusion with the lost object," attained through dreaming states.
It uses "Psyche," "Urn," and "Nightingale," among other
works, to demonstrate Keats's reliance upon dreams.

Harris, R. W. "The Mansion of the Mind: John Keats." In *Romanticism and
the Social Order, 1780-1830.* n.p.: Barnes and Noble, 1969, pp. 312-327.

Defends romantic poetry from the charge that it is purely
sensuous, lacking in philosophical, social, and political concern.
Examines "Urn" and "Nightingale" to show that Keats is
coping with the paradox of attractive beauty and needful
knowledge.

Heath-Stubbs, John Francis Alexander. *The Ode*. London: Oxford
University Press, 1969.

The stanza form of Keats's odes suggests to Heath-Stubbs the Italian canzone. "Nightingale" reminds him of *A Midsummer Night's Dream* in imagery and ending.

Jabbar, Abdul. "Keats's View of Poetry." *DA,* 30A (1970), 3907 (Case Western Reserve).

Completed in 1969. Uses "Psyche" as evidence that Keats adopted a virtually religious view of poetry.

Jones, James Land. "Keats and the Last Romantics: Hopkins and Yeats." *DA,* 30A (1969), 2530 (Tulane).

Interprets "Nightingale" and the beauty-truth identification in terms of a view of romanticism achieved by combining the theories of René Wellek and Ernst Cassirer.

Jones, John. *John Keats's Dream of Truth.* London: Chatto and Windus, 1969.

Jones bases his approach to the odes and Keats's other works on what he calls "the end-stopped 'feel.'" This refers to Keats's use of "feel" as a noun to replace "feeling." This shift reflects Keats's emphasis on feeling and its ability to reveal truth. In this context, the odes all concern generally the passing of time.

Kauvar, Gerald B. "How Well Can the Fancy Cheat?" In *The Other Poetry of Keats.* Rutherford: Farleigh Dickinson University Press, 1969, pp.64-91.

The chapter on "Nightingale" explains the figurative language in the ode by finding parallels in thought and phraseology in Keats's other poems and in his letters.

Kenny, Blair G. "Keats' 'Ode on a Grecian Urn.'" *Explicator,* 27 (May 1969): #69.

Treats "Urn" as the expression of an experience rather than an abstract creed. The ode illustrates Keats's "Negative Capability," his tendency to free his imagination to identify with things around him.

Lemon, Lee. "Keats's 'Ode on a Grecian Urn.'" In *Approaches to Literature.* New York: Oxford University Press, 1969, pp. 29-65.

A classroom text on the art of literary criticism. The chapter on "Urn" gives five brief essays on the ode, introduced by an explanation of the kind of criticism to be employed. The essays paraphrase the poem, discuss the textual problem of lines 49-50 (arguing for no quotation marks), relate the last two lines to Keats's letters, analyze the figurative language in the poem, and argue that the ode has a two-part structure, stanzas one through four being subjective and stanza five objective.

Myers, Robert Manson. "The Romantic Triumph: The Warp and the Wolf." In *The Overwrought Urn: A Potpourri of Parodies of Critics Who Triumphantly Present the Real Meaning of Authors from Jane Austen to J. D. Salinger.* Ed. Charles Kaplan. New York: Pegasus, 1969, pp. 27-29.

This parody of literary criticism discusses briefly Keats's "Ode on a Greasy Urn" and the "Ode to Madame Nightingale."

Newton, J. M. "A Speculation About Landscape." *Cambridge Quarterly,* 4 (summer 1969): 273-282.

Argues here that Milton's treatment of landscape is superior to Keats's since Milton's reflects more of the active soul of the poet struggling for meaning while Keats's merely celebrates nature passively for its own sake. The assessment of Keats is based mainly on passages from "Autumn," though "Psyche" and "Melancholy" are used as well, along with "The Eve of St. Agnes" and "Endymion."

Pereira, E. "John Keats: The Major Odes of 1819." *Unisa English Studies,* 4 (November 1969): 49-63.

Explicates "Nightingale," "Urn," and "Autumn." At the end, the reader of "Nightingale" knows that the poet has experienced a vision, not just a dream. In "Urn," Keats recognizes that, while art cannot substitute for life, it can afford glimpses into life's hidden meanings. "Autumn" comes nearest to a resolution of the need for permanence and the awareness of flux.

Rose, Alan. "The Impersonal Premise in Wordsworth, Keats, Yeats, and Eliot." *DA,* 30A (1969), 2547 (Brandeis).

Discusses the odes as evidence that Keats developed a belief that poetry should be impersonal.

Wycherley, H. Alan. "Keats: The Terminal Disease and Some Major Poems." *American Notes and Queries,* 7 (April 1969): 118-119.

Connects the symptoms of tuberculosis with the imagery of "Nightingale," "Melancholy," and "Urn."

1970

Abu-Shawareb, Hassan Muhammad Hassan. "Keats's Prescription for Man's Salvation: Theory and Practice." *DA*, 31A (1971), 5347 (South Carolina).

> Completed in 1970. Interprets "Nightingale" and "Melancholy" in terms of Keats's concept of Soul-Making.

Bunn, James H. "Keats's 'Ode to Psyche' and the Transformation of Mental Landscape." *English Literary History*, 37 (1970): 581-594.

> Argues that "Psyche" presents the process by which Keats's mind receives the empathic power of animating objects of its perception. In "Nightingale" and "Urn" Keats projected his animating power back into the objects of his contemplation, but in "Psyche" his mind itself opens into a mental landscape.

Cohn, Robert Greer. "Keats and Mallarmé." *Comparative Literature Studies*, 7 (June 1970): 195-203.

> This essay on the influence of Keats on Mallarmé contends that the atmosphere of "L'Apres-midi d'un Faune" came largely from Keats's odes. It points out other Keatsian influences on Mallarmé as well.

Das, B. "Process and Reality in the Odes of Keats." *Indian Journal of English Studies*, 11 (1970): 17-33.

> Views the theme of the odes as the dilemma of process and permanence. Process, or becoming, is joyful but always ends in sadness at passing joy. Permanence, on the other hand, has stability but a lesser intensity of joy. Keats achieved a realistic solution in "Autumn," which accepts both passion and permanence.

Dawson, Leven Magruder. "Mutability and Irony in the Poetry of John Keats." *DA*, 31A (1970), 2872 (Rice).

> Demonstrates through "Urn" that irony is characteristic of Keats's greatest poetry and provides an ironic interpretation of the view of mutability in "Autumn."

Ende, Stuart Alan. "Vision and Consciousness in Keats's Poetry."*DA*, 31A (1971), 6601 (Cornell).

Completed in 1970. Sees "Psyche" as a proclamation of freedom from Miltonic views of a removed earthly paradise.

Evans, William Richard. "Mythology As Religion in Keats' Poetry." *DA*, 32A (1971), 426 (Columbia).

Completed in 1970. Discusses "Urn" as a religious poem. Keats rejected Christianity and created his personal religion of creativity and love based on what he knew of ancient Greek culture. "Urn" concerns the religious ritual of sacrifice, an act which elevates man in his own eyes and in the sight of the gods. The psychology of sacrifice is explained in terms of Jung's concept of the Self.

Fleissner, Robert F. "Frost's Response to Keats's Risibility." *Ball State University Forum*, 11 (1970): 40-43.

In his short essay comparing Keats's "Why Did I Laugh Tonight?" with Frost's "The Demiurge Laugh," Fleissner discusses briefly lines 49-50 of "Urn." They reflect, he argues, the neoplatonic Augustinian position that abstractions can be understood through a realization of God. Thus, limited by a necessarily imperfect perception of God, man *on earth* can know only the stated equation, "beauty is truth"; he cannot fully understand why that equation is valid.

Gittings, Robert. *The Odes of Keats and Their Earliest Known Manuscripts.* Kent, Ohio: Kent State University Press, 1970.

Discusses generally the ideas in the odes along with the state of Keats's affairs when he wrote them. Reproduces their earliest manuscripts and presents transcriptions of them. In addition, provides for each ode detailed information about the manuscript reproduced, its description, and its composition.

Jerome, Judson. "Dreaming of Death." *Writer's Digest*, 50 (May 1970): 14-19.

Sees the main difference between the speaker in "Nightingale" and the poet to be self-awareness. Because man is conscious of his actions and environment, he is weighed down by the awareness of his own mortality. That is what makes him want to be like the bird but what keeps him from being able to do so.

Lindenberger, Herbert. "Keats's 'To Autumn' and Our Knowledge of a Poem." *College English,* 32 (November 1970): 123-134.

Examines some of the contexts out of which the critics of "To Autumn" have written (including biography, the other odes, Keats's critical ideas, and various ideologies) and shows that there is a value system, or "rhetorical purpose," behind each context controlling its conclusions which is a development of the historical and professional situation of the critic. Nonetheless, Lindenberger argues, such criticism is preferable to what E. D. Hirsch calls "interpretation" because "interpretation," the act of deciding upon the signification of the words, phrases, and sentences in the work, is forced to omit those aspects of poets which it has not the vocabulary to deal with.

Lott, James. "Keats's 'To Autumn': The Poetic Consciousness and the Awareness of Process." *Studies in Romanticism,* 9 (1970): 71-81.

Argues that Keats dramatically employs a perceiver in "Autumn" who, for the first two stanzas, responds wholly to the images of autumn and, in the last stanza, finally becomes aware of the mutability of those things. Thus, the structure of the ode is dramatic.

Meredith, George. *The Letters of George Meredith.* Ed. C. L. Cline. Oxford: Clarendon, 1970.

See 1861.

Mincoff, Marco. "Beauty Is Truth—Once More." *Modern Language Review,* 65 (1970): 267-271.

Views lines 49-50 of "Urn," not as central to the poem, but as a kind of afterthought or reverie which captures the atmosphere of the shifting emotional responses which form the real value of the poem.

Patterson, Charles Ivey. *The Daemonic in the Poetry of John Keats.* Urbana: University of Illinois Press, 1970.

Discusses the importance of the concept of the demonic state for Keats's poetry. From Lempriere's *Classical Dictionary* and *Palmerin of England*, Keats was familiar with the notion of the existence of a set of beings intermediary between gods and men. These demons exist in a state of high intensity beyond morality and can lead men through a trance state to a heightened awareness of beauty and joy. Traces this demonic state through "Urn," "Psyche," "Nightingale," and "Melancholy," but views "Autumn" as anti-demonic in its maintenance of a single state of consciousness.

Quennell, Peter. *Romantic England: Writing and Painting 1717-1851.* New York: Macmillan, 1970.

Interprets lines 51-59 of "Nightingale" briefly as expressing a Freudian death-wish based on a distrust of life stemming from Keats's unstable childhood.

Small, Thomas Edward. "John Keats's Cosmos: Images of Space and Time in the Poetry." *DA,* 31A (1971), 3565 (California-Berkeley).

Completed in 1970. Treats Keats's great poems of 1819 as a culmination of his effort "to express a vision of the cosmos, an order of space and time."

1971

Brisman, Leslie. "'More Glorious to Return': Miltonic Repetition." *Yearbook of English Studies,* 1 (1971): 78-87.

This essay establishes Milton as the source of influence for Keats's use of repetition. It mentions that the effect of the repetition of religious rites in "Psyche" parallels that of Eve's evening song to Adam in *Paradise Lost*. Brisman avoids naming specific influences for specific lines.

Chatterjee, Bhabatosh. "The Great Odes and 'Bright Star.'" In *John Keats: His Mind and Work*. Calcutta: Orient Longman, 1971, pp. 362-416.

Treats the odes as meditative variations on the theme of the contrast between flux and stability. "Psyche" shows that the richness of the human soul has been discovered late in history. "Nightingale" seeks for salvation in the projection of one's self into an intenser plane. "Urn" explores the possibility of communication between the eternal and the temporal worlds. "Melancholy" presents sadness as a constant product of the

ephemerality of joy and beauty. "Autumn" presents the season
in both its aspects, as a time of ripe abundance and as a time
preceding the death of winter.

D'Avanzo, Mario. "Keats's 'Ode on Melancholy,' the Cave of Spleen, and
Belinda." *Humanities Association Bulletin* (Canada), 22 (fall 1971): 9-11.

Posits Keats's debt in "Melancholy" to Pope's depiction of
the Cave of Spleen in "The Rape of the Lock," Canto IV.

Dickstein, Morris. "The Fierce Dispute: The Odes." In *Keats and His Poetry:
A Study in Development.* Chicago: University of Chicago Press, 1971, pp.
189-231.

Connects the ideas and feelings expressed in the odes with
those expressed in Keats's earlier poetry to establish a line of
development. "Psyche" is a poem of process in which the
speaker discovers his worship for the imagination. "Nightingale" achieves a balanced view of the ability of the imagination
to transcend life's ills. And "Urn" is a more objective statement
of the lessons learned in "Nightingale."

Dodd, William Nigel. "Keats's 'Ode to a Nightingale' and 'Ode on a
Grecian Urn': Two Principles of Organization." *Lingue e Stile,* 6 (August
1971): 241-261.

Sees both "Nightingale" and "Urn" as concerning the possibilities of attaining a more intense existence without the
normal drawbacks of human limitation. "Nightingale" is pat-
terned in two movements, one ascending and one descending.
In "Urn," however, the central symbol reveals its character
gradually and accumulatively as it is viewed from each succes-
sive perspective—seven in all.

Dube, Gunakar. "Autumn in Frost and Keats: A Study of Themes and
Patterns." *Literary Criterion,* 9 (summer 1971): 84-88.

Contrasts and compares "Autumn" with Frost's "My November Guest" and "October." Finds Keats idealistic and Frost
realistic.

Eggenschwiler, David. "Nightingales and Byzantine Birds, Something
Less Than Kind." *English Language Notes,* 8 (March 1971): 186-191.

Contrasts Keats's bird in "Nightingale" with Yeats's in

"Sailing to Byzantium." A major difference is that Keats's bird has never been human and therefore sings in oblivion to man's condition. Yeats's, however, is a man turned bird; albeit artificial, it has knowledge which Keats's cannot.

Eggers, J. Philip. "Memory in Mankind: Keats's Historical Imagination." *PMLA*, 86 (October 1971): 990-997.

Discusses the odes within the context of the romantic reunion of poetry with history which counteracted the previous notion that poetry imitated a universal ideal while history recorded an actual event. Traces a historical consciousness through the odes.

Ford, Newell F. "Holy Living and Holy Dying in Keats's Poetry." *Keats-Shelley Journal*, 20 (1971): 37-61.

Argues that Keats's poems expressed increasingly after 1818 a concern with death in terms of religious ritual. Incense, prayer, choir, priest, embalming, requiem, and anthem all are found. Discusses the odes, among other poems, in this light.

"From Corpses to Copses: John Keats and the Enjoyment of Life." *Times Literary Supplement*, April 2, 1971, pp. 365-366.

Reviews in passing Dorothy Hewlett's introduction to *Keats at Wentworth Place*, Timothy Hilton's *Keats and His World*, Robert Gittings' *The Odes of Keats and Their Earliest Known Manuscripts*, and Miriam Allott's *The Poems of John Keats*. The author adopts the Arnoldian stance that Keats's poetry was basically (and perhaps overly) sensuous. In this line, he claims that the lady in stanza two of "Melancholy" is the poet's human mistress.

Gittings, Robert. *Times Literary Supplement*, April 9, 1971, p. 422.

Replies to the *TLS* article of April 2, 1971. Argues that the lady in stanza two of "Melancholy" is a personification of melancholy, not a human mistress.

Glenn, Priscilla Ray. "The Development of Keats's Mythic Understanding of the Function of the Poet.'" *DA*, 32A (1972), 3950 (North Texas State).

Completed in 1971. Demonstrates that the odes contain the major themes of Keats's mature myth of the poet: identity, soul-making, visionary quest, the imagination, and the linking of beauty and truth.

Hilton, Timothy. *Keats and His World*. London: Thames and Hudson, 1971.

Heavily illustrated book on Keats's life and works. Treats the odes as "the summit of Keats's poetic achievement, and perhaps the greatest short poems in Romantic literature." "Nightingale," "Urn," and "Melancholy" are discussed generally.

Holstein, Michael Edward. "Poet, Hero, and Persona: A Study of the Personal and Poetic Identities of John Keats." *DA*, 33A (1973), 3586 (Minnesota).

Completed in 1971. Argues that in the odes Keats generated the poetic identity of a priest of the humanized imagination whose meditations gave birth to the poems.

Hulseberg, Richard Arnold. "The Validation of the Self in Wordsworth and Keats." *DA*, 32A (1972), 5791 (Illinois-Urbana-Champaign).

Completed in 1971. Treats "Nightingale" and "Urn" as examples of second generation romantic poems which illustrate the romantic need to validate and sanctify beliefs through writing poems out of personal experience.

Itzkowitz, Martin E. "Freneau's 'Indian Burying Ground' and Keats' 'Grecian Urn.'" *Early American Literature*, 6 (winter 1971/72): 258-262.

Contrasts the romantic hope of "Urn" with the neoclassical skepticism of Freneau's "Indian Burying Ground."

McCall, Dan. "'The Self-Same Song That Found a Path': Keats and *The Great Gatsby*." *American Literature*, 42 (January 1971): 521-530.

Argues that the influence of "Nightingale" can be seen in Jay Gatsby's desire for mystical union with the beautiful.

Messier, Marta Haake. "From Sleep to Poetry: The Order of the Poems in Keats's 'Lamia' Volume." *DA*, 32A (1972), 4572 (Illinois-Urbana-Champaign).

Completed in 1971. Sees "Nightingale," "Urn," and "Psyche" as analyses of love-melancholy and attempts at constructing a vision. "Autumn" and "Melancholy" stress the dangers and futility of such attempts.

Miller, Bruce E. "Form and Substance in 'Grecian Urn.'" *Keats-Shelley Journal*, 20 (1971): 62-70.

Reads "Urn" as an expression of the idea found in Keats's letter to Bailey of March 13, 1818, concerning the real and the semireal. The melodist and the lovers, in his view, are semireal, the townfolk are real, and the phenomena they represent are seen to interdepend through the greeting of the spirit which is necessary to make semireal things wholly exist and through the ennobling effect of the greeted semireal upon the real.

Primeau, Ronald René. "Keats's Chaucer: Realism and Romanticism in the English Tradition." *DA*, 32A (1972), 4575 (Illinois-Urbana-Champaign).

Completed in 1971. Stresses the influence of Chaucer's *Troilus and Criseyde* on the odes.

Reid, Stephen A. "Keats's Depressive Poetry." *Psychoanalytic Review*, 58 (fall 1971): 395-418.

Discusses the odes as reflective of what Melanie Klein, the British psychoanalyst, calls "the depressive position," which devolves from the first year and a half of life when the infant learns through the frustrations of nursing to have both positive and negative feelings for the same object.

Riley, Sister Maria A. "John Keats, Liturgist of the Poetic Act: An Analysis of Keats's Use of Religious Imagery and Phraseology As a Vehicle for his Poetic Theory." *DA*, 32A (1972), 6449 (Florida State).

Completed in 1971. Focuses on the religious imagery in "Psyche" as expressions of the external reality Keats adopted to shape his internal reality of the imagination.

Sinson, Janice C. "The Odes." In *John Keats and the* Anatomy of Melancholy. London: Keats-Shelley Memorial Association, 1971, pp. 21-30.

Demonstrates Keats's indebtedness to Burton's *Anatomy of Melancholy* for many of the words and images of "Nightingale" and for the basic idea of "Urn"—eros versus agape.

Speirs, John. *Poetry Towards Novel*. London: Faber and Faber, 1971.

Considers "Urn," "Nightingale," "Melancholy," and "Autumn" as examples of the poetic imaginativeness and introspection which characterized early nineteenth-century poets and laid the groundwork for the psychological characterization of the nineteenth-century novel.

Toliver, Harold E. "Keats's Pastoral Alchemy as Therapy." In *Pastoral Forms and Attitudes*. Berkeley: University of California Press, 1971, pp. 260-273.

Considers "Autumn," "Psyche," "Urn," and "Nightingale" with regard to Keats's pastoral dilemma: can the transcendence which can be attained through the pastoral be reconciled with the suffering of mankind?

Vendler, Helen. Rev. of *The Odes of Keats and Their Earliest Known Manuscripts*, by Robert Gittings. *Studies in Romanticism*, 10 (winter 1971): 65-69.

Agrees with Gittings that the last two lines of "Urn" are spoken by the urn, but disputes his contention that "She" in l. 21 of "Melancholy" refers to the goddess of Melancholy. Argues, contrary to Gittings, that there are no signs of decay or disappearance in "Autumn," and questions whether the song of the nightingale typifies the beauty of Nature in "Nightingale." Insists that the odes fulfill more than the technical perfection Gittings claimed; they give complete expression to a "Philosophy" of "agonized questioning" and fulfill Keats's philosophy of negative capability.

Waldoff, Leon. "From Abandonment to Skepticism in Keats." *Essays in Criticism*, 21 (1971): 152-158.

Traces a pattern in Keats's poetry which begins in "Endymion" and is resolved in the odes. This psychological pattern runs from hope in a dream, to abandonment of hope because of its impossibility, to despair, and finally to a skepticism of dream. The dream is a dream of permanence, and it is ultimately resolved in the odes, which arrive at an acceptance of impermanence.

Whitridge, Arnold. "The English Language: A Musical Instrument and a Workaday Tool." *Bulletin of the New York Public Library*, 75 (February 1971): 90-100.

Uses a passage from "Nightingale" to illustrate the possibilities of rhyme in English.

1972

Barfoot, C. C. "A Partial Grammar of Autumn." *Dutch Quarterly Review of Anglo-American Letters,* 2 (1972): 73-81.

Analyzes the relationship of the grammatical structure of "Autumn" to the subject matter of the poem.

Benoit, Raymond. "In Dear Detail By Ideal Light: 'Ode on a Grecian Urn.'" *Costerus,* 3 (1972): 1-7.

Associates the world of the vase which the speaker tries to capture in "Urn" with the pre-Platonic notion of a one-to-one correspondence between appearance and actuality. However, Keats recognizes in the poem that this mode of perception is ultimately unattainable for post-Platonic man.

Brown, Thomas H. "The Quest of Dante Gabriel Rossetti in 'The Blessed Damozel.'" *Victorian Poetry,* 10 (autumn 1972): 273-277.

Demonstrates the Keatsian mood of Rossetti's "The Blessed Damozel" which derives from "Nightingale."

Corrington, John W. "Cassier's [sic] Curse, Keats's Urn, and the Poem Before the Poem." *Forum* (Houston), 10 (1972): 10-14.

Views "Urn" as a resolution of Cassirer's curse, which notes the ultimate inadequacy of any symbol to express complete meaning. Demonstrates in cinematic terms the ode's attainment of the knowledge that the imagination can, through art, realize experience adequately.

Cumings, Alan J. "The Ritual of Ecstasy in the Poetry of John Keats." *DA,* 33A (1973), 3637 (Wisconsin).

Completed in 1972. Argues that Keats's great works embody a ritual in which the poet begins to create a realm of imaginative and sensuous pleasures to escape the pain of realizing ephemerality. This creating process is blissful, but the bliss vanishes when the vision is complete. In the odes, Keats finally makes himself protagonist in this ritual. He seeks to deny the ritual in "Psyche" and "Nightingale" by arresting

it, alternates another kind of beauty in "Urn," and inverts it altogether in "Melancholy." "Autumn" escapes the ritual yet
preserves the recognition of mutability. It is an expression of
continuous ecstasy.

Dunham, Larry Dean. "The Pleasure-Pain Motif in the Poetry of John
Keats." *DA*, 34A (1974), 1275 (Missouri-Columbia).

Completed in 1972. Uses "Melancholy" to show how Keats
treated the pleasure-pain motif with juxtaposition, which occurs when two emotions are present in the poet's mind and he
is aware of their existence and contradictory nature.

Fass, Barbara. "A Biographical Approach to Keats's 'Ode to Psyche.'"
Humanities Association Bulletin, 23 (winter 1972): 23-29.

Argues that Keats chose Psyche to worship in his ode because she had no significant literary tradition which he could
be censured for ignorance of.

French, A. L. "Purposive Imitation: A Skirmish With Literary Theory."
Essays in Criticism, 22 (April 1972): 109-130.

Explores the question of whether bad writing can be
justified by its context. Suggests that such defenses of bad
writing are made more frequently than they are justified.
Takes as an example, among others, the section of "Nightingale" in which the speaker first proclaims his intent to flee this
world, "where men sit and hear each other groan." Charges
that the picture of real life is too flat and not vivid enough to
pave the way for the degree of escape that follows. And attacks
the anticipated defense that the point of the poem is that the
escape was insufficiently motivated. That defense does not
excuse the lapse in descriptive powers in the poem.

Glick, Robert Alan. "Imagery of Light and Darkness in Three Romantic
Poets: Novalis, Keats, and Wordsworth." *DA*, 33A (1973), 6310
(Indiana).

Completed in 1972. Views "Nightingale" as a completely
dualistic poem. The images of light and darkness, representing
the real and the ideal, are never resolved because, although the
real world is hostile, complete submersion into the ideal would
mean annihilation of self.

Gradman, Barry Alan. "Dying Into Life: Metamorphosis In Keats's Poetry."*DA*, 33A (1973), 3583 (Brandeis).

> Completed in 1972. Traces a metamorphosis motif in Keats's work which embodies a dissatisfaction with present state, followed by a metamorphosis characterized by a lapse from normal consciousness, and resulting in a new state of being or a renewed consciousness. From "Nightingale" on, Keats concentrated more on the last stage.

Haley, Bruce E. "The Infinite Will: Shakespeare's *Troilus* and the 'Ode to a Nightingale.'" *Keats-Shelley Journal*, 21-22 (1972-73): 18-23.

> Posits the influence of Shakespeare's *Troilus and Cressida* (III.ii) on "Nightingale."

Hepburn, Ronald W. "Poetry and 'Concrete Imagination': Problems of Truth and Illusion." *British Journal of Aesthetics*, 12 (winter 1972): 3-18.

> Sees the urn as a product of the concrete imagination expressing "a universal human ideal." In the course of the poem, however, the implications of what the urn symbolizes come into question.

Hollingsworth, Keith. "The Nightingale Ode and Sophocles." *Keats-Shelley Journal*, 21-22 (1972-73): 23-27.

> Believes "Nightingale" to have been influenced by *Oedipus At Colonus*, perhaps in Latin translation.

Kestner, Joseph A. "Keats: The Solace of Space." *Illinois Quarterly*, 35 (November 1972): 59-64.

> Argues that the song of the bird in "Nightingale" must be perceived in time and that the vase in "Urn" must be perceived in space. "Nightingale" presents a despairing encounter and "Urn" a triumphant one, since the space-perception of the urn allows a transcendent permanence and the time-perception of the nightingale's song only reminds of mutability.

Kobler, J. F. "Lena Grove: Faulkner's 'Still Unravish'd Bride of Quietness.'" *Arizona Quarterly*, 28 (winter 1972): 339-354.

> Sees Lena Grove in Faulkner's *Light in August* as the thematic equivalent of Keats's "Grecian Urn" and the ode as having numerous other parallels throughout the novel.

O'Keeffe, Timothy. "Ironic Allusion in the Poetry of Wilfred Owen." *Ariel,* 3 (October 1972): 72-81.

>   Claims briefly that Owen echoes the odes, and especially "Melancholy," in his poem *"Apologia Pro Poemate Meo"* for ironic effect.

Pinsker, Sanford. "The Unlearning of Ike McCaslin: An Ironic Reading of William Faulkner's 'The Bear.'" *Topic,* 23 (spring 1972): 35-51.

>   This essay on Faulkner's "The Bear" discusses Ike Mc-Caslin's grasp of "Urn."

Pulleyn, Mary Margaret Buck. "Keats's View of Death." *DA,* 33A (1972), 324 (Minnesota).

>   Argues that all the odes concern mutability and death. "Urn" proposes the imagination as a means of transcending mortal limitations. "Nightingale" courts oblivion as a wished-for escape when hope of transcendence fails. "Melancholy" rejects oblivion in favor of the intensities of experience. And "Autumn" expresses acceptance of the death process.

Robinson, Jeffrey Cane. "Keats and the Waking Dream." *DA,* 32A (1972), 7001 (Brandeis).

>   Treats the odes as various manifestations of reverie, in which thoughts pass through the consciousness with no pull toward resolution.

Sallé, Jean-Claude. "'Forlorn' in Milton and Keats." *Notes and Queries,* 217 (August 1972): 293.

>   Suggests that "forlorn" in "Nightingale" may echo *Paradise Lost,* IX, 908-910.

----------. "The Pious Frauds of Art: A Reading of the 'Ode on a Grecian Urn.'" *Studies in Romanticism,* 11 (spring 1972): 79-93.

>   Views "Urn" as retrospective of Keats's thought, especially that found in his letter to Bailey, November 22, 1817. In the ode, Keats comes to modify his position on the value of beauty in the light of what he has learned about human suffering. Art cannot be a means of permanent transcendence, but it can have a consolatory value.

Stephenson, William. "Applications of Communications Theory: II—Interpretations of Keats' 'Ode on a Grecian Urn.'" *Psychological Record,* 22 (spring 1972): 177-192.

An attempt to demonstrate the objective substructure of humanistic studies. Uses Q-methodology on "Urn," categorizing a sample of opinions on that poem into levels of insight. Suggests that such a tool might be used to measure the effectiveness of humanities courses in developing the individual, but prefers to validify the study of literature for its quality of "communication-pleasure."

Stillinger, Jack. Rev. of *The Odes of Keats and Their Earliest Known Manuscripts,* by Robert Gittings. *Journal of English and Germanic Philology,* 71 (April 1972): 263-267.

Corrects Gittings in the following matters: 1) the Morgan MS of "Psyche" is not the one Keats gave Reynolds; 2) George Keats's transcript of "Urn" is not its earliest known manuscript—Charles Brown's is; 3) it was Keats, not his publishers, who changed "fan" to "roof" in line 10 of "Psyche"; and 4) the two stanzas of "Melancholy" in the Robert H. Taylor collection at Princeton are first drafts.

Thompson, Leslie M. "Ritual Sacrifice and Time in 'Ode on a Grecian Urn.'" *Keats-Shelley Journal,* 21-22 (1972-73): 27-29.

Argues that the sacrifice scene in "Urn" is in harmony with a major theme of the whole poem: man's desire to get outside the flow of time and mutability and into a world of lasting beauty. A primitive sacrifice was an attempt to deny or annul time by establishing a cycle of renewal.

Walker, Carol Kyros. "The Longest Resonance: A Comparative Study of Keats and Stevens." *DA,* 33A (1973), 5695 (Illinois-Urbana-Champaign).

Completed in 1972. Treats "Nightingale" as a precursor to Stevens' "Sunday Morning" in its comment on mortality and its conclusions on the relationship between permanence and change and between art and nature.

Wesling, Donald. "The Dialectical Criticism of Poetry: An Instance from Keats." *Mosaic,* 5 (1972): 81-96.

Approaches "Nightingale" as an artifact which supports the Marxist view of the pattern of history. Analyzes the poem as a Hegelian dialectic, pitting its classical literary form and images against its technical innovations and synaesthesia, resulting in an unresolved synthesis. In this view, Keats was in opposition to nineteenth-century bourgeois ideas.

Yeats, William Butler. *Memoirs: Autobiography—First Draft; Journal.* Ed. Denis Donoghue. London: Macmillan, 1972.

See 1909.

Zak, William Frank. "Keats and the Ideal of Disinterestedness: Aesthetic Distance and Control in the Major Poetry." *DA,* 33A (1973), 5208 (Michigan).

Completed in 1972. Emphasizes that the disinterested activity of the visionary imagination was a standard for Keats, using the odes as late expressions of what for him was a lifetime concern.

1973

Anderson, Erland Gregory. "Harmonious Madness: A Study of Musical Metaphors in the Poetry of Coleridge, Shelley, and Keats." *DA,* 34A (1974), 4185 (Washington).

Completed in 1973. Points out how Keats used musical metaphors in the odes to reveal the various perspectives of visionary experience.

Antonelli, Edward Anthony. "The Pain of Truth: Keats' Struggle to Verify the Imaginative Experience." *DA,* 34A (1973), 2545 (Washington).

Attempts to trace the "inner drama of Keats's creative mind" in its search for the validity of imaginative experience. The odes point to a growing disenchantment with visionary revelation.

Bernstein, Gene Morrison. "Keats's 'Ode on a Grecian Urn': Individuation and the Mandala." *Massachusetts Studies in English,* 4 (spring 1973): 24-30.

Treats "Urn" as a reconciliation of a longing for the atemporal and divine with an acceptance of the temporal and mortal through the projection of a mandala, the urn itself. The projection is a manifestation of Jung's concept of individuation, the process of continual becoming which fuses the conscious with the unconscious.

Booth, James. "Keats: 'Ode on a Grecian Urn.'" *Critical Survey*, 6 (summer 1973): 59-64.

Argues that "Urn" presents a painful contrast of the beauty of the world with its transience and imperfection. The poem contemplates an escape from the pain into the perfect world of art but rejects complete escape in the end, while still affirming the ability of art to offer some comfort.

Brisman, Leslie. "Silence and Keats." In *Milton's Poetry of Choice and Its Romantic Heirs*. Ithaca, New York: Cornell University Press, 1973, pp. 93-110.

Analyzes the odes, among Keats's other poems, as the kind of poetry of choice Milton wrote in "Lycidas." Conceives them as embodying a stilled moment of apprehension of alternatives just prior to making a choice about an appropriate response to death.

Brockbank, J. P. "'Ode on a Grecian Urn': Reflections on a Masterpiece." *Delta: The Cambridge Literary Magazine*, 51 (spring 1973): 3-19.

Explicates "Urn" with an eye to the momentum of the words and to the harmonic timbre Keats creates among them by repeating similar sounds and meanings.

Brown, E. Carole. "The Matrix of the Dream: Poetry and Love in the Major Poems of Keats." *DA*, 34A (1973), 719 (New York-Buffalo).

Discusses "Psyche" as one of Keats's dream vision poems, which usually dealt with creativity and love.

Chavis, Geraldine Giebel. "Dreams As Motif in John Keats' Works." *DA*, 34A (1974), 6631 (Syracuse).

Completed in 1973. Focuses on "Psyche" and "Nightingale" as expressing ambivalence toward the idyllic dreams of Keats's earlier writings.

Clatanoff, Doris Ann Risch. "Poetry and Music: Coleridge, Shelley, and

Keats and the Musical Milieu of Their Day." *DA,* 34A (1973), 2551 (Nebraska-Lincoln).

Argues that "Nightingale" and "Urn" compare to the sonata form and "Autumn" parallels a fugue.

Cognard, Anne Maria MacLeod. "The Classical Affinity of Spenser and Keats: A Study of Time and Value." *DA,* 34A (1974), 5903 (Texas Christian).

Completed in 1973. Analyzes "Urn" to show Keats's affinity with Spenser on the matter of time. Both poets embraced process and recognized time as a means of creating value.

Demmin, Julia Laker. "Myth and Mythmaking in Keats and Arnold." *DA,* 34A (1974), 7701 (Illinois-Urbana-Champaign).

Completed in 1973. Views "Urn" and Arnold's "Empedocles on Etna" as myths of moderate desire and "Nightingale," "Autumn," "Resignation," and "The Scholar-Gipsy" as myths of process.

Hartman, Geoffrey H. "Poem and Ideology: A Study of Keats's 'To Autumn.'" In *Literary Theory and Structure: Essays in Honor of William K. Wimsatt.* Ed. Frank Brady, John Palmer, and Martin Price. New Haven: Yale University Press, 1973, pp. 305-330.

Argues that in contrast to most of the other odes "Autumn" belongs in the English or Hesperian (Western) mode of sublime poem rather than to the Eastern or epiphanic kind. The epiphanic tradition requires the presence or possible presence of a god and uses language of religious rapture. "Autumn," however, is characterized by pictorial description and everyday immediacy.

Lams, Victor J. "Ruth, Milton, and Keats's 'Ode to a Nightingale.'" *Modern Language Quarterly,* 34 (1973): 417-435.

Argues that since Keats's "soul-making" theory grew out of Milton's theology, "Nightingale," which is a departure from that theory, is in part a reaction against Milton. Keats rejected Milton's theology of possible transcendence but adapted his energy for his own purposes.

Lawson, Margaret Ledford. "Sensation in the Poetry of Keats." *DA,* 34A (1973), 2569 (North Carolina-Chapel Hill).

Demonstrates that Keats exalted sensation in his early poetry but that later it came into conflict with his rational faculties, through which he began to perceive life's tragic qualities. The odes explore man's limitations and possibilities.

Low, Donald A. "Byron and the 'Grecian Urn.'" *Times Literary Supplement,* October 26, 1973, p. 1314.

Argues in a letter that "Urn" was influenced by the opening of Canto II of "Childe Harold's Pilgrimage," especially regarding the urn, the sacrifice, and Socrates's saying.

May, Charles E. "Hardy's 'Darkling Thrush': The 'Nightingale' Grown Old." *Victorian Poetry,* 11 (1973): 62-65.

Argues that in "The Darkling Thrush" Hardy consciously played off the romantic view of nature in "Nightingale" to achieve an ironic rejection of it.

Ogden, James. "Henry Alford and Keats's Reputation." *Keats-Shelley Memorial Bulletin,* 24 (1973): 8-11.

Reports that Henry Alford, in his essay on Keats appearing in *Dearden's Miscellany,* 4 (August 1840): 611-618, cites "Nightingale" as the best of Keats's shorter works and especially praises the seventh stanza.

Plambeck, Vernon Lewis. "Realism in Keats: A Study of Four Odes and Their Relationship to the Earlier Poems." Diss. University of Nebraska 1973.

Written under Bernice Slote. Undertakes to do two things in regard to "Indolence," "Melancholy," "Urn," and "Nightingale": 1) to show that they do not propose escape as a desirable alternative to facing the real world with all its sorrows; and 2) to show their relationship to Keats's other poetry. Uses Keats's other poetry to support his argument that Keats embraced reality in these odes.

Snyder, Elliott Leslie. "The New Criticism and the Poetry of John Keats." *DA,* 34A (1973), 2580 (Connecticut).

Analyzes the New Criticism of "Nightingale," as a lyric, and "Melancholy," as a rhetorical poem, and concludes that New Criticism tends to reduce these works to one Ur-poem made up of ideas expressed elsewhere in Keats's letters and other poems.

Sperry, Stuart M. *Keats the Poet.* Princeton, New Jersey: Princeton University Press, 1973.

> In his chapters on the odes, Sperry discusses "Psyche," "Nightingale," "Urn," "Melancholy," and "Indolence" as a sequence mainly in terms of the conflict between mythical oneness and historical indeterminacy. In this conflict, the primitive ability to perceive and integrate is contrasted with the modern inability to arrive at final determinations. He sees "Autumn" as a reconciliation of the concept of autumn as a personified abstraction with the concept of it as a seasonal interval. The result is an awareness of process.

Spicer, Harold. "'To Burst Joy's Grape Against a Palate Fine': Negative Capability in Keats's Odes." *Indiana English Journal,* 7 (1973): 41-45.

> Uses the odes to explain Keats's theory of negative capability. Each of the odes embodies a desire to leave the present state of identity and enter into an intense perception of beauty.

Stone, William B. "Ike McCaslin and the Grecian Urn." *Studies in Short Fiction,* 10 (winter 1973): 93-94.

> Discusses "Urn" in reference to Faulkner's "The Bear."

Thekla, Sister. *The Disinterested Heart: The Philosophy of John Keats.* Newport Pagnell: Greek Orthodox Monastery of the Assumption, 1973.

> Treats various recurrent themes or ideas in Keats's poetry— beauty, death, ambition, passion, sleep, et al.— in the context of a Christian view of transcendent reality. Discusses the odes briefly along with other poems and passages from the letters as illustrations of Keats's philosophy.

Thomas, C. T. "The Metrical Structure of Keats's Odes of 1819." In *Literary Studies: Homage to Dr. A. Sivaramasubramonia Aiyer.* Ed. K.P.K. Menon, M. Manuel, and K. Ayyappa Paniker. Trivandrum, India: St. Joseph's Press for the Dr. A. Sivaramasubramonia Aiyer Memorial Committee, 1973, pp. 163-172.

> Argues that Keats developed the ode stanza form out of his dissatisfaction with the sonnet. The eighteenth-century ode was also a major force in the development of Keats's ode form.

Tintner, Adeline R. "Keats and James and *The Princess Casamassima.*" *Nineteenth Century Fiction,* 28 (1973): 179-193.

> Uses James's reference to "Nightingale" in Chapter 22 of *The Princess Casamassima* as a springboard to a study of the Keatsian material in the novel. Finds allusions to "Nightingale" and "Urn," as well as to other of Keats's poems, throughout the book and argues for parallels between Hyacinth and Keats.

Vendler, Helen. "The Experiential Beginnings of Keats's Odes." *Studies in Romanticism,* 12 (summer 1973): 591-606.

> Argues that Keats did not compose the stanzas of the odes in the order in which we have them. Instead, behind each of the odes lies a primary experience which acted as a guiding catalyst for the other stanzas. In "Autumn" it was the experience of the stubble-fields; in "Urn" a feeling of sorrow and sexual frustration; in "Nightingale" a longing for death; and in "Melancholy" an angry rejection by Keats's lover.

Wilkes, John Edwin, III. "Aeolian Visitations and the Harp Defrauded: Essays on Donne, Blake, Wordsworth, Keats, Flaubert, Heine and James Wright." *DA,* 35A (1974), 1129 (California-Santa Cruz).

> Completed in 1973. Reads the odes in terms of the romantic question of how long self-generated and self-contained worlds can be sustained.

Yakushigawa, Koichi. "What the Urn Said." *Doshisha Literature,* 27 (November 1973): 28-50.

> Placing "Urn" in the context of "Nightingale"'s abstractness and "Autumn"'s concreteness, Yakushigawa views "Urn" as the building up and eventual bursting of an ecstatic oxymoron involving the vitality of time and the beauty of timelessness. When the oxymoron finally yields, the poet faces the world of time.

1974

Bell, Arthur H. "'The Depth of Things': Keats and Human Space." *Keats-Shelley Journal,* 23 (1974): 77-94.

> This essay on Keats's use of space in several of his works

discusses the contrast between the emptiness of the speaker
and the fullness of the bird as it acts in "Nightingale."

Cooke, Michael G. "De Quincey, Coleridge, and the Formal Uses of Intoxication." *Yale French Studies,* 50 (1974): 26-40.

   Although Cooke deals primarily with the use of intoxication
   in the poetry of De Quincey and Coleridge, he also includes a
   consideration of Keats's "Nightingale" in light of his understanding of the nature of intoxication, i. e., that intoxication
   reflects the dual inadequacy of the person to life and life to the
   person.

Daalder, Joost. "W. H. Auden's 'The Shield of Achilles' and Its Sources."
Journal of the Australasian Universities Language and Literature Association, 42
(November 1974): 186-198.

   Argues Auden alluded to Keats in "The Shield of Achilles" to
   express the modern situation of not being able to compose a
   romantic poem on a work of art.

D'Avanzo, Mario L. " 'Ode on a Grecian Urn' and *The Excursion." Keats-
Shelley Journal,* 23 (1974): 95-105.

   Discusses the influences of Wordsworth's *The Excursion* on
   the thought, language, and tone of "Urn."

Doggett, Frank. "Romanticism's Singing Bird." *Studies in English Literature,*
14 (autumn 1974): 547-561.

   Discusses "Nightingale" as the best example of the romantic
   poetic convention of the singing bird.

Korenman, Joan S. "Faulkner's Grecian Urn." *Southern Literary Journal,* 7
(fall 1974): 3-23.

   Suggests that Faulkner was attracted to "Urn" by its attitude
   toward time and change. Both Faulkner and Keats express an
   ambivalence toward the conflict between the beauty of stasis
   and the necessity of change.

Malagi, R. A. "Versions of Melancholy: Keats's 'Ode on Melancholy' and
Milton's 'Il Penseroso.'" *Journal of Karnatak University Humanities,* 18
(1974): 69-83.

   Reads both "Il Penseroso" and "Melancholy" as juvenile

works expressing a common quest for a life-mission. Milton's achievement is superior, however, because it can be seen as part of the pattern of development of his Christian humanism. Keats's ode, unsupported by a lifetime of work and thought, remains a floundering attempt at attaining immortality through wisdom born of sorrow.

Mansell, Darrel. "Keats's Urn: 'On' and on." *Language and Style,* 7 (1974): 235-244.

Interprets "Urn" as an imaginative reaction to the urn rather than as an attempt to depict the urn in poetry, as in ekphrasis. Thus, line 49 has a circular meaning: an attribute of an object is an attribute of a statement, and an attribute of a statement is an attribute of an object. This means that the urn is beautiful because the poet says it is and that the poet says the urn is beautiful because it is beautiful. This kind of reasoning reinforces the unravished circularity of the urn; it will yield no meaning of its own, but the meaning that can be created by responding to it is nonetheless valid.

Matthey, Francois. "Balance and Complexity." in *The Evolution of Keats's Structural Imagery.* Bern: Francke, 1974, pp. 197-244.

Keats moved from the traditional romantic structure of descent/ascent in his poetry, as in "Endymion," to a pyramid structure of ascent and descent most effectively employed in the odes. Matthey examines the rhyme scheme of Keats's early odes and the poems just preceding them to show the development of the "sonnet stanza." Then he discusses the imagery of each of the odes to show Keats's use of pyramid structure in each.

Miers, Paul David. "Keats's Myth of Consciousness: A Phenomenology of Mind and Nature." *DA,* 35A (1975), 6149 (Missouri-Columbia).

Completed in 1974. Presents the odes as "a dialogue of consciousness in which the mind pursues its own transcendent ground."

Primeau, Ronald. "Chaucer's 'Troilus and Criseyde' and the Rhythm of Experience in Keats's 'What Can I Do to Drive Away.'" *Keats-Shelley Journal,* 23 (1974): 106-118.

Argues here that Keats's poems to Fanny of 1819 derived

from his reading of "Troilus and Criseyde," and that they are closely related thematically to the odes. Approached through "Troilus and Criseyde" and the Fanny poems, the odes are interpreted as expressing a rejection of escape from life and a realization of the necessary connection between sweetness and pain.

Ricks, Christopher. *Keats and Embarrassment*. Oxford: Clarendon Press, 1974.

Deals with embarrassment as a moral concern in the nineteenth century as seen in Keats's poetry. It conceives of embarrassment as a situation in which one is startled or arrested by the inability to choose an appropriate behavior. At various places in his book, Ricks considers briefly the speaker's abandonment of his own role for the bird's in "Nightingale," the blushful quality of the Hippocrene in the same poem, the series of questions about the meaning of the figures in "Urn," and the joy/sorrow paradox in "Melancholy."

Smallwood, R. L. "The Occasion of Keats's 'Ode to a Nightingale.'" *Durham University Journal*, 67 (1974): 49-56.

Argues for the accuracy of Brown's account of the composition of "Nightingale" and goes on to give a reading of the poem based on the divergences from the facts of that account within the poem, especially emphasizing the importance of the shift from day to night in the poem.

Stillinger, Jack. *The Texts of Keats's Poems*. Cambridge: Harvard University Press, 1974.

Treats each of the odes, along with the rest of Keats's poems, in his fourth chapter: "The Histories of the Texts." Discusses the dates of composition, gives the details of publication, cites page references in Garrod and Allott (who serve as his standard texts), indicates locations of holograph and transcript copies, mentions the availability of facsimiles in printed sources, discusses the relationships among manuscripts and early printed versions, suggests the copy text for a definitive edition, and notes the sources for Garrod's and Allott's texts and points out their mistakes.

Tate, Priscilla Weston. *From Innocence Through Experience: Keats's Myth of the*

Poet. Salzburg: Institut Fur Englische Sprache und Literatur, Universitat Salzburg, 1974.

Conceives of Keats's personal myth of the poet as related to his idea on soul-making, beauty/truth, the imagination, identity, and the visionary nature of the poet's quest. Discusses the odes in this context, using Blake's vocabulary of Innocence, Experience, and Higher Innocence.

Welch, Thomas M. "The Central Imagery of Keats's Poetry." *DA,* 35A (1975), 6114 (Kansas).

Completed in 1974. Traces Keats's psychomachia in the terms of Freud and Burrow. The odes depict the debilitating effects of attempted regression to the preconscious state.

Woodman, R. C. "Satan in the 'Vale of Soul-Making': A Survey from Blake to Ginsburg." *Humanities Association Review,* 25 (spring 1974): 108-121.

Discusses the development of the idea that God is created in the mind of man. First treats Keats's "Psyche" as exemplary of this initial idea, then traces its development through a satanic stage (because man's nature came to be seen as evil, the gods it creates must be demons) to a nihilistic stage (rejecting evil as a basis for morality but finding nothing to take its place).

1975

Argulewicz, Emma Francello. "Progressive Dark Imagery in Keats and the Ode 'To Autumn.'" *DA,* 36A (1975), 1515 (New York-Binghamton).

Views "Autumn" as a serious poem of ideas. The imagery portraying the darker side of existence achieves a resolution and acceptance in this ode which it had not attained in previous poems.

Bloom, Harold. "In the Shadow of Milton." In *A Map of Misreading.* New York: Oxford University Press, 1975, pp. 144-159.

A development of *Anxiety of Influence,* this book analyzes several poets' influence by Milton in terms of a system combining Isaac Luria's Kabbalistic theosophical speculation and Sigmund Freud's psychological theory. Views "Psyche" as a process of depreciation through internalization of Wordsworth's and Milton's earliness and a recognition of belatedness as Keats's true muse.

Brisman, Leslie. "Keats, Milton, and What One May 'Very Naturally Suppose.'" *Milton and the Romantics*, 1 (November 1975): 4-7.

Interprets "Psyche" and "Lamia" to demonstrate that Keats, unlike Milton, sought to express a mythology of continuity with nature.

Gradman, Barry. *"Measure for Measure* and Keats's 'Nightingale' Ode." *English Language Notes*, 12 (March 1975): 177-182.

Based on the fact that Keats's copy of Shakespeare is heavily underscored and marked in parts of *Measure for Measure*, Gradman finds evidence of influence of the play on "Nightingale." Specifically, the speeches of the Duke and Claudio (III.i) have echoes in stanzas III and VI of "Nightingale." The Duke's despair can be found in stanza III of "Nightingale," and the recoil at the effect of death as expressed by Claudio's answer is found in the last lines of stanza VI.

Grennan, Eamon. "Keats's *Contemptus Mundi:* A Shakespearean Influence on the 'Ode to a Nightingale.'" *Modern Language Quarterly*, 36 (September 1975): 272-292.

Argues that "Nightingale" was influenced by *Measure for Measure*, especially by the speeches of Claudio in III.i. Stanzas III and VI of "Nightingale" are most heavily influenced.

Harding, Eugene J. "Possible Pun in Keats's 'Ode to a Nightingale.'" *Keats-Shelley Journal*, 24 (1975): 15-16.

Suggests a pun on the word *tread* in "Nightingale" based on the meaning "to copulate" and the theories of Thomas Malthus.

Johnston, Priscilla Winthrop. "Keats and Tennyson: Two Modes in Nineteenth-Century Classical Myth." *DAI*, 37A (July 1976), 332 (Brown).

Completed in 1975. Examines the uses of classical mythology for Keats and Tennyson, especially as it helped them express their shared idea of vision as divinely controlled. The odes express a variety of hypotheses on this subject.

Jones, James Land. *Adam's Dream: Mythic Consciousness in Keats and Yeats.* Athens: University of Georgia Press, 1975.

Examines the poetry of Keats and Yeats in this book as reflecting a mythic consciousness. By mythic Jones basically means tending to unify the elements of existence (fuse subject and object, if you will), interweaving the notions of past, present, and future into a more simultaneous concept of time. He discusses each of the odes from this standpoint, examining "Nightingale" in detail to show its fusion of joy and pain.

Kunitz, Stanley. "The Modernity of Keats." In *A Kind of Order, a Kind of Folly.* Boston: Little, Brown, 1975, pp. 59-73.

Gives a brief consideration of the odes in this general essay on Keats prepared as a lecture. Discusses "Nightingale" as an advance over Keats's early verse and a development of Renaissance poetry; treats "Urn" as a paradox of irreconciliation between the timeless and temporal; and praises "Autumn" as music poetry, citing it as the consummation of Keats's art.

Pearce, Donald. "Thoughts on the Autumn Ode of Keats." *Ariel,* 6 (July 1975): 3-19.

Argues that "Autumn" was an experiment in which Keats tried to use a purer, more natural English by avoiding Miltonic inversions and words with origins in the romance languages. Relates the nature of this experiment to the theme of the poem by linking Milton with the use of a philosophical system. "Autumn" argues, in form and content, that the correct apprehension of nature is direct, without a system or external set of values and perceptive of the fruit of the object perceived.

Posey, Horace G. "Keats's 'Ode on Melancholy': Analogue of the Imagination." *Concerning Poetry* (West Washington State College), 8 (1975): 61-69.

Argues that "Melancholy" concerns the creative act, which stems from the beauty apprehended through the intensity of a melancholy mood.

Schall, Keith Linwood. "John Keats: The Aesthetics of Apprehension." *DA,* 37A (1977), 5801 (Nevada-Reno).

Completed in 1975. Analyzes the thematic and aesthetic

continuity of the odes. The odes are unified by a common concern with poetics and with beauty.

Shokoff, James. "Soul-Making in 'Ode on a Grecian Urn.'" *Keats-Shelley Journal,* 24 (1975): 102-107.

Interprets "Urn" in light of Keats's "soul-making" letter to George and Georgiana Keats, February-May 1819.

Solomon, Harry M. "Shaftesbury's *Characteristics* and the Conclusion of 'Ode on a Grecian Urn.'" *Keats-Shelley Journal,* 24 (1975): 89-101.

Argues that the source for lines 49-50 and the inspiration for "Urn" in general was Anthony Ashley Cooper, Third Earl of Shaftesbury's *Characteristics of Men, Manners, Opinions, Times.* the essay "Sensus Communis," which states "beauty is Truth." Traces the sequence of Keats's reading in that work.

Ward, Arthur Douglas. "Death and Eroticism in the Poetry of Keats and Tennyson." *DAI,* 37A (July 1976), 344 (California-Berkeley).

Completed in 1975. Argues that Tennyson's poetry expressing an ambivalent attitude toward, and sometimes a fusion of, death and sexuality is more satisfyingly comprehensive than Keats's. In "Autumn," Keats limited his interests to those of the species, while Tennyson was concerned with the individual human soul.

1976

Black, Michael. "The Musical Analogy." *English,* 25 (summer 1976): 111-134.

Conducts an analysis of the opening of "Melancholy" by pursuing an analogy between poetry and music, describing the kinds of notes appropriate to the words and the relationships between them.

Brown, Homer. "Creations and Destroyings: Keats's Protestant Hymn, the 'Ode to Psyche.'" *Diacritics,* 6 (winter 1976): 48-56.

Explores Keats's method of supplementing and substituting for ideas and attitudes held by other men and other cultures— primarily Milton and Wordsworth. "Psyche" poses a replacement for Milton's religion while avoiding Wordsworth's deification of man's inner experience.

Brown, Robert Wayne. "Transcendence and Reality: Imagery, Experience, and 'Soul-Making' in John Keats's 'Eve of St. Agnes' 'La Belle Dame,' and Five Great Odes." *DA*, 37A (1977), 4362 (Nebraska-Lincoln).

   Completed in 1976. Conceives of the odes as expressing the notion of possible transcendence found in Keats's Soul-Making philosophy.

Cluysenaar, Anne. *Aspects of Literary Stylistics: A Discussion of Dominant Structures in Verse and Prose.* New York: St. Martin's Press, 1976.

   Analyzes metrical similarities between the opening of "Nightingale" and a passage from the "To be or not to be" soliloquy in *Hamlet.* Suggests that such a correlation amounts to an allusion and that the reader should therefore be alert to thematic comparisons.

Coomar, Devinder Mohan. "Silence, Language and the Poetry of Criticism in Romantic Expression: Blake, Keats, Foscolo, and Tagore." *DA*, 37A (1976), 3601 (California-Riverside).

   Discusses "Urn" in order to establish the existence of a concept of meta-poetry in which silence is used to express both the "terror of the nightmare world of history" and the ineffable experience of man's divine potentialities.

Einstadter, Marcel. "The Concept of Time in Rabbinic Thought and Romantic Literature." *DAI*, 37A (August 1976), 1046 (Fordham).

   Examines "Urn" as an attempt to solve the problem of the passing of time. "Urn" expresses the futility of the human condition under time's tyranny and poses an alternative dream of the arrest of time. Rabbinic thought resolves this dilemma through the concept of an afterlife in *Talmud Torah.*

Ende, Stuart A. "Identification and Identity: The 'Ode to Psyche' and the 'Ode to a Nightingale.'" In *Keats and the Sublime.* New Haven: Yale University Press, 1976, pp. 119-144.

   Considers "Psyche," "Nightingale," and, briefly, "Autumn" in the Freudian terms of a subject-object dialogue. In "Nightingale," the speaker longs to submerge himself in the sublimity of the bird, but a love of his native elements and a fear of losing them prevents his doing so. In "Psyche," a circular structure is set up in which the speaker loses himself to the vision of "Psyche" and is able to assimilate it as his own. Similarly, in "Autumn" the speaker suspends himself between the sublimity of the season and the death implicit in its existence.

Fitch, Patrick Roland. "The Dialectical Function of the Imagination in the Poetry of Wordsworth, Keats, and Yeats." *DA*, 37A (1976), 1561 (Tulsa).

> Analyzes the odes as essentially dialogues between the voice of mortality and the voice of immortality. The ode stanza enabled Keats to harmonize the two. The basis for this study is Hegelian dialectic.

Fraustino, Daniel Victor. "Negative Capability and the Poetry of John Keats." *DA*, 37A (1977), 5141 (New York-Binghamton).

> Completed in 1976. Examines the odes as shaped by the concept of Negative Capability. "Nightingale" refuses to go outside the experience presented to resolve its complexity, and "Melancholy" affirms life's dialectics, leaving that complexity intact.

Gradman, Barry. "*King Lear* and the Image of Ruth in Keats's Nightingale Ode." *Keats-Shelley Journal*, 25 (1976): 15-22.

> Argues that when Keats included the image of Ruth in stanza seven of "Nightingale" he was thinking unconsciously of Cordelia in *King Lear*, IV, iv, 1-20, where she appears weeping in the cornfields of France. Such a conflation of characters accounts for the dissimilarity of Keats's Ruth and the Bible's.

Hall, Elizabeth. "Keats and Bowles." *Notes and Queries*, OS 221 (March 1976): 112.

> Suggests that William Lisle Bowles's poem "Old Time's Holiday" has parallels for the scythe and the lifted hair of "Autumn."

Hunter, Eva. "'Cold Pastoral': A Reading of Keats's 'Ode on a Grecian Urn.'" *Unisa English Studies*, 14 (1976): 57-59.

Defends the last stanza of "Urn." The urn is "Cold" because "to arrest flux is to deny existence." Moreover, art is subordinate to life because living beings impart to art works their value and essence. The last line and a half expresses Keats's concept of existence as a "vale of soul-making" where the inability to attain the ideal is a necessity.

Mandel, Siegfried. "The Nightingale in the Loom of Life." *Mosaic*, Vol. 9, No. 3 (spring 1976): 117-134.

Surveys literary treatments of the nightingale from ancient Greece to the present day. Keats's ode is an abandonment to an experience; the speaker explores the sensations of the bird, but experiences them in a more self-conscious and complex way.

Pinsky, Robert, III. "III. The Romantic Persistence: 'Romantic': 'Ode to a Nightingale.'" In *The Situation of Poetry: Contemporary Poetry and Its Traditions*. Princeton: Princeton University Press, 1976, pp. 47-61.

Explicates "Nightingale" as a prototype of the conflict characteristic of modern poetry "between the idea of experience as unreflective, a flow of absolutely particular moments, and the reality of language as reflective, an arrangement of perfectly abstract categories." The speaker is not envious of the bird because he would have to die to achieve its unreflectiveness. The ending suggests that poetry may be able to capture both reflective sequence and unreflective timelessness.

Pison, Thomas. "A Phenomenological Approach to Keats's 'To Autumn.'" In *Phenomenology, Structuralism, Semiology*. Ed. Harry R. Garvin. Lewisburg, Pennsylvania: Bucknell University Press, 1976, pp. 37-47. This is *Bucknell Review*, 22 (April 1976): 37-47.

Traces the development of thought in "Autumn" from the viewpoint of Martin Heidegger, who emphasizes the temporal nature of existence and posits the human value of developing a future; to that of Gaston Bachelard, who sees life as essentially characterized by a man-space relationship; and, finally, to that of Hans-Georg Gadamer, who insists on the importance of being able to leave the past behind in order to move into the future.

Primeau, Ronald. "Countee Cullen and Keats's 'Vale of Soul-Making.'" *Papers on Language and Literature*, 12 (winter 1976): 73-86.

Traces various ways in which Countee Cullen was influenced by the odes and the soul-making philosophy.

Reibetanz, John. "'The Whitsun Weddings': Larkin's reinterpretation of Time and Form in Keats." *Contemporary Literature*, 17 (autumn 1976): 529-540.

Demonstrates the way in which the formal aspects of Larkin's "The Whitsun Weddings" are a conscious response to "Urn." Where Keats's stanza forms reinforce the timelessness of his ode, Larkin's revisions of those same basic forms reflect the temporality of his work.

Robinson, Jeffrey. "Dante's *Paradiso* and Keats's 'Ode to a Nightingale.'" *Keats-Shelley Journal*, 25 (1976): 13-15.

Argues that, though there is no evidence Keats ever opened his last two volumes of *The Divine Comedy*, "Nightingale" was influenced by the "Paradiso," xxxiii, 55-60 and 85-88. Suggests that Keats took the idea of an unwilling separation from a vision from Dante as well as the phrase "sole self," and points toward an interpretation of the ode which has the poet enter into a larger frame of perception at the end, rather than return to "ordinary reality."

Ryan, Robert M. *Keats: The Religious Sense*. Princeton: Princeton University Press, 1976.

Argues that Keats resolved the problem of suffering in the world for himself with his theory of soul-making, and subsequently found an inner peace which is revealed in "Autumn."

Sams, Larry Marshall. "Isaac McCaslin and Keats's 'Ode on a Grecian Urn.'" *Southern Review* (LSU), 12 (summer 1976): 632-639.

Traces Faulkner's use of "Urn" for developing and reinforcing the theme of the contrast between "evanescence and eternality" in the Isaac McCaslin sections of *Go Down Moses* ("The Old People," "The Bear," and "Delta Autumn").

Simpson, David. "Keats's Lady, Metaphor, and the Rhetoric of Neurosis." *Studies in Romanticism*, 15 (spring 1976): 265-288.

Simpson introduces his essay on "La Belle Dame Sans Merci" with a parallel approach to "Urn." When measured by the traditional persona structure, "Urn" can be seen to have a poet operating behind the speaker, judging that speaker with a compassionate irony. However, since the original urn is unknown, presumably the speaker, his reactions to the urn, and the urn itself are all creations of the poet. This draws the poet more deeply into the poem, and "Urn" becomes a forum for the poet's reflection on himself in the same way that a person might analyze his own dreams in Freudian psychology.

Wilson, Harry B. "Psychological Projection in Six Romantic Poems, English and American." *DAI*, 37A (December 1976), 3631 (California-Davis).

Interprets "Nightingale" as a poem of "psychological projection," in which the speaker, in a state of personal crisis, expresses his own emotional and mental state using objects drawn from nature. In "Nightingale," the speaker expresses "his desires to escape the burden of consciousness, to write poetry with ease, and to achieve immortality."

Worthington, Anne Poole. "The Triadic Archetype in Keats' Poetry." *DA*, 38A (1977), 3525 (Maryland).

Completed in 1976. Considers "Psyche" and "Autumn" in terms of the triadic archetypal concept of innocence, experience, and the need to reconcile them. These two odes especially display a conscious desire for reconcilement.

1977

Biswas, Pratap. "Keats's Cold Pastoral." *University of Toronto Quarterly*, Vol. 47, No. 2 (winter 1977-78): 95-111.

Demonstrates the pattern of "ecstatic absorption" and then "disenchanted recoil" common to both "Nightingale" and "Urn," and goes on to argue "Urn"'s insistence on the superiority of reality over dreams. In the first three stanzas the speaker becomes increasingly absorbed in the joy of the scenes on the urn, but in the fourth stanza he comes to realize that there is a harsh reality underlying them all. Thus, in the final stanza he realizes that pastoral enchantment is a deception and claims that real beauty resides in truth. The urn is a friend to man because it teaches him this lesson.

Cavanaugh, Hilayne E. "Faulkner, Stasis, and Keats's 'Ode on a Grecian Urn.'" *DA,* 38A (1977), 2783 (Nebraska-Lincoln).

Examines Faulkner's use of "Urn" as a reflection expressing his notion that art should arrest the motion of life for future contemplation. Traces imagery of or allusions to "Urn" in *A Green Bough, Mosquitos, As I Lay Dying, Light in August, Requiem for a Nun, The Hamlet, The Mansion, Flags in the Dust, Sanctuary,* and *Go Down, Moses.*

Corballis, R. P. "Keats and Ben Jonson." *Notes and Queries,* NS Vol. 24, No. 4 (July-August 1977): 330.

The opening of "Nightingale" was influenced by Ben Jonson's *Sejanus,* III, 595-598.

Cosgrove, Brian. "'The Winter's Tale' and the Limits of Criticism." *Studies,* 66 (summer/autumn 1977): 176-187.

Suggests briefly in passing that *The Winter's Tale* shares an affinity with "Autumn" in its acceptance of process.

Culler, Jonathan. "Apostrophe." *Diacritics,* Vol. 7, No. 4 (winter 1977): 59-69.

Claims the apostrophe as the highest development of the romantic lyric, since it establishes for the speaker an "I-thou" relationship with the universe, thus achieving for him visionary powers and reconciling subject with object. Uses "Nightingale" briefly as an example of the fragility of this harmonious relationship for romantic poets.

Feidel, Jan. "The Poetry of Keats and Baudelaire." *DA,* 38A (1977), 2759 (Rutgers).

In arguing that Keats more than Poe served as Baudelaire's poetic model, this invokes "Urn" to show Keats's influence on "La Beauté" in matters of the power of the imagination.

Ghiselin, Brewster. "Art and Psychiatry: Characterization As Therapy, Therapy As Characterization." *Michigan Quarterly Review,* Vol. 16, No. 1 (winter 1977): 12-22.

Compares writers to psychiatrists: the psychiatrist tries to arrive at a workable character for his patient in much the same way that the writer tries to arrive at a workable character for a figure in his writing. The psychiatrist is intellectual, however, and the writer is intuitive.

Uses the last two lines of "Urn" as a brief example of a synthesis of both the authorial and psychiatric methods.

Green, Eugene, and Rosemary M. Green. "Keats's Use of Names in 'Endymion' and in the Odes." *Studies in Romanticism*, 16 (1977): 15-34.

Demonstrates Keats's extensive use of names in "Endymion" and argues that they perform personal, thematic, and stylistic functions. Then traces Keats's use of names through the odes, arguing that his technique was advanced by the development of epithets which support the temporal/eternal theme.

Hagstrum, Jean H. "Eros and Psyche: Some Versions of Romantic Love and Delicacy." *Critical Inquiry*, Vol. 3, No. 3 (spring 1977): 521-542.

Qualifies Keats's claim that Psyche was the "latest born" of the gods by tracing her representation in literature and, especially, the plastic arts back to the fourth century B.C. Shows Shelley to reflect Psyche's traditional hermaphroditic or unisexual qualities through his interest in incest. No direct analysis of "Psyche."

Hankiss, Elemér. "On the Structure of Beauty." *Angol Filologiai Tanulmanyok (Hungarian Studies in English)*, 11 (1977): 57-64.

Uses various kinds of paradoxical tensions in "Urn" (moving/unmoving, temporary/timeless, concrete/abstract, valuable/valueless, audible/inaudible, real/apparent, existent/nonexistent) to prove that paradox is the foundation of beauty.

Kinnaird, John. "Hazlitt, Keats, and the Poetics of Intersubjectivity." *Criticism*, 19 (winter 1977): 1-16.

Argues that Hazlitt's conception of poetry as "intersubjective" is germinal to an understanding of romantic poetry. Hazlitt defined poetry as the movement of imagination and passion confronting an object and event. In the act of the imaginative perception of an object, the poet, heightened by passion, was capable of transcending his own personality and expressing a universal vision, regardless of how particular his object. Gives a brief discussion of "Psyche," "Urn," and "Nightingale" as embodiments of this principle.

Martin, William Joseph. "John Keats and the Aesthetics of the Imagination." *DAI,* 38A (September 1977), 1413 (Notre Dame).

The odes refuse to take refuge from life's sorrows in flights of the imagination, as Keats's earlier poetry had done, and yet they still celebrate life's beauty in the face of its harshness.

Rayan, Krishna. "The Grecian Urn Re-Read." *Mosaic,* Vol. 11, No. 1 (fall 1977): 15-20.

Argues that "Urn" asserts the superiority of the silent suggestiveness of the plastic arts over the time-limited and concrete expression of poetry.

Ross, Donald, Jr. "Structural Elements in Keats's Sonnets and Odes." *Cahiers de Lexicologie,* Vol. 31, No. 2 (1977): 95-117.

Applies the computer program "Eyeball" in a stylistic analysis of Keats's sonnets and odes. Concludes, contrary to Bate, that Keats did not develop the ode stanza from the sonnet form. Notes the stylistic similarity between the odes and the sonnets, especially those of 1818. Contains twenty-two graphs and six charts.

Stape, John H. "Myth, Allusion, and Symbol in E. M. Forster's 'The Other Side of the Hedge.'" *Studies in Short Fiction,* Vol. 14, No. 4 (fall 1977): 375-378.

Points out allusions to "Nightingale" in the conclusion of E. M. Forster's short story "The Other Side of the Hedge."

Stephenson, William C. "The Performing Narrator in Keats's Poetry." *Keats-Shelley Journal,* 26 (1977): 51-71.

Argues that the narrator in Keats's poetry typically moves from a sense of timelessness and spacelessness (*kairos*) to a time-bound world (*chronos*). In "Psyche," "Urn," and "Nightingale," the narrator first surrenders to a vision of concord and then is reminded of its limitations.

Vaillancourt, André Philippe. "John Keats' Dissolving Imagination: Its

Paradisal and Demonic Dimensions." *DAI*, 38A (June 1978), 7352 (Wisconsin-Madison).

Completed in 1977. Traces images of fading, melting, dissolving, fainting, withering, and decaying through Keats's poetry. The odes "explore the idea that dissolution means corruption as well as refinement."

Waldoff, Leon. "The Theme of Mutability in the 'Ode to Psyche.'" *PMLA*, 92 (May 1977): 410-419.

Suggests a reading of "Psyche" which connects the poem with the other odes in a unified sequence. Sees two strains in the poem. In the first, the poet views the goddess as mortal since her "life" depends upon being recognized and worshipped. The poet sets up a psychological defense against mutability by insuring the goddess' immortality within his own mind. In the second strain, the poet adopts Psyche as a presiding spirit (perhaps because of the early loss of his mother) who will guide him in his struggle through the vale of soul-making. Thus, the poem ends with the poet's eager anticipation of success in the struggle to achieve a kind of reassuring permanence, limited to his mind though it may be, against mutability.

1978

Brown, Keith. "A Short *Course of the Belles Lettres* for Keatsians?" *English*, 27 (spring 1978): 27-32.

Puts the last two lines of "Urn" in the context of Abbot Batteux's *A Course of the Belle Lettres*. The beauty/truth equation means that highest truth can only be found in works of art. The last line and a half can validly be interpreted in various ways.

Candido, Joseph. "*A Midsummer Night's Dream* and 'Ode to a Nightingale': A Further Instance of Keats's Indebtedness." *American Notes and Queries*, Vol. 16, No. 10 (June 1978): 154-155.

Stanza five of "Nightingale" was influenced by *A Midsummer Night's Dream*, II.ii.248-254. Other lines in the ode derive from the play, too.

Freeman, Donald C. "Keats's 'To Autumn': Poetry As Process and Pattern." *Language and Style*, Vol. 11, No. 1 (winter 1978): 3-17.

Demonstrates "To Autumn'"s syntax to be mimetic of its subject matter. Using transformational grammar as a basis, argues that Keats turns Autumn, normally a subject, into an agent, and then merges Autumn with her creations to become a subject of the imagination.

Harris, Irene Strickler. "The Influence of Shakespeare on the Odes of Keats." *DAI*, 38A (June 1978), 7345 (Boston University).

"...correlates images in the odes and in the works of Shakespeare, Keats's markings of the plays, and associations with Shakespeare in Keats's letters." Finds in the odes a pattern of conversion, reconsideration, intensification, rejection, objectification, and atonement with Shakespeare.

Hill, James L. "The Function of the Poem in Keats's 'Ode to [sic] a Grecian Urn' and Wordsworth's 'Resolution and Independence.'" *The Centennial Review*, Vol. 22, No. 4 (fall 1978): 424-444.

"Urn" turns private experience into public artifact, the temporal into the spatial, and "the actuality of process into the appearance of permanence." Similarly, "Resolution and Independence" transforms the leech-gatherer from a "becoming" (a man resulting from the shaping forces of his history) into a "being" (an object of meditation for Wordsworth).

Hirsch, E. D., Jr. "The Well-Read Urn: A Thought Experiment." In *History as a Tool in Critical Interpretation*. Ed. Thomas F. Rugh and Erin R. Silva. Provo: Brigham Young University Press, 1978, pp. 47-50.

One of a collection of essays dealing with the theme of the first Brigham Young University Symposium on the Humanities: "Does history constitute a legitimate critical tool for the art or literary critic?" Hirsch argues that, for all practical purposes, polysemy in interpretation only exists where historical facts are few or uncertain. Uses as an example the assertion that if a letter by Keats were discovered explaining the meaning of the last two lines of "Urn," real debate over their meaning would cease.

Kappel, Andrew J. "The Immortality of the Natural: Keats' 'Ode to a

Nightingale.'" *Journal of English Literary History*, 45 (summer 1978): 270-279; 282-284.

Accounts for the bird's immortality and for the figure of Ruth in stanza seven of "Nightingale" by pointing out that the speaker of the ode is striving for an ontological shift from human awareness of death to natural ignorance of it (and hence to a feeling of immortality). The Biblical Ruth, as a character who was willing to move into a new territory, supports the speaker's desire to change ontologies. "Autumn" is an advance over the other odes because it quietly courts the possibility of a different ontology instead of struggling to assert that a change had taken place and then collapsing in failure.

McGee, Harold James. "Keats and the Progress of Taste." *DAI*, 40A (July 1979), 272 (Yale).

Completed in 1978. Delineates Keats's progression from the idea of beauty to the idea of sublimity. The odes present an alienation from traditional beauty but do not fully develop a sublime vision.

Nemoianu, Virgil. "The Dialectics of Movement of Keats's 'To Autumn.'" *PMLA*, 93 (March 1978): 205-214.

Outlines various patterns of movement in "Autumn"—temporal, spatial, seasonal, diurnal, metrical, et al.—and demonstrates his thesis that valid interpretations of the ode should view the poem as concerning the functioning of Nature and should devolve from a synthesis of the implications of these patterns.

Rhodes, Jack Wright. "Trends in the Criticism of Keats's Odes." *DA*, 39A (May 1979), 6782 (South Carolina).

Completed in 1978. Attempts "to establish the trends in the responses to the odes" from the time of their publication to 1979, examine the causes of these trends, and trace their interrelationships. Includes an extensive annotated bibliography.

Sherwin, Paul. "Dying Into Life: Keats's Struggle with Milton in 'Hyperion.'" *PMLA*, 93 (1978): 383-395.

Asserts that stanzas 5-7 of "Nightingale" are a conscious dialogue with "Lycidas."

Sinha, V. N. "The Imagery and Language of Keats' Odes." *Language Forum Monographs—III.* New Delhi: Bahri Publications, 1978.

   Devotes a chapter to each of the major odes, emphasizing the synaesthetic quality of the imagery. The "Conclusion" analyzes the image patterns among the odes.

Swinden, Patrick. "John Keats' 'To Autumn.'" *Critical Quarterly,* Vol. 20, No. 4 (1978): 57-60.

   Poses the question: why, in a poem about autumn, did Keats omit any mention of falling leaves, one of the season's main characteristics? Answer: falling leaves are too suggestive of death for a poem emphasizing the regenerative fulfillment of autumn.

Taylor, Mark. "Keats' 'Ode to a Nightingale.'" *Explicator,* Vol. 36, No. 3 (spring 1978): 24-26.

   Argues that the "emperor and clown" of "Nightingale" were inspired by Alexander the Great and Yorick in the grave-digger's speech in *Hamlet,* V.i.

Verghese, P. C. "A Worshipper of Beauty." *Commonwealth Quarterly,* Vol. 2, No. 7 (1978): 124-127.

   Uses "Urn" as evidence that Keats worshipped spiritual beauty.

Wolfson, Susan Jean. "The Interrogative Present: Speaker as Questioner in Wordsworth and Keats." *DA,* 40A (July 1979), 281 (California-Berkeley).

   Completed in 1978. Views questioning for Keats as "the central activity of the imagination." Treats the odes as "experiments with poetic modes of inquiry."

Wooster, Margaret Irene. "Against Closure: Keats and the Suspense of Writing." *DAI,* 39A (July 1978): 302 (SUNY-Buffalo).

   Demonstrates two voices in Romantic poetry, a sublime and classical voice of stability and closure, and a skeptical and sub-lunary voice of authorial interruption. These two voices alternate most freely in the odes.

1979

Bouchard, Charles Joseph. "Shakespeare's Influence on Keats: The Aesthetics of Dream-Poetry." *DAI*, 40A (July 1979), 263-264 (Queen's University at Kingston, Canada).

Demonstrates, through the odes, that Keats believed the soul remembers universal truths in the creative act as in a dream and that Keats therefore tried to keep "tendentious concerns" out of his poems.

Chavkin, Allan. "Keats's Open Endings." *Research Studies* (Washington State University), Vol. 47, No. 2 (June 1979): 108-115.

Argues that, unlike Wordsworth who found consolation for man's mutability in nature, Keats was alienated by his awareness of the unrealistic nature of transcendence. Shows this alienation at the ends of "Melancholy" and "Autumn." Gives a stanza-by-stanza reading of "Nightingale" demonstrating Keats's alienation throughout.

Jarrett, David. "A Source for Keats's Magic Casements." *Notes and Queries*, NS Vol. 26, No. 3 (June 1979): 232-235.

Anne Radcliffe's *The Mysteries of Udolpho*, Book III, Chapter vii, supplies the casements, the yearning for death as an escape, the lonely and exiled heroine, the southern pastoral setting, the midnight music, and the moonlit sea for Keats's "Urn."

McGann, Jerome. "Keats and the Criticism." *MLN*, Vol. 94, No. 5 (December 1979): 988-1032.

Echoing the Bakhtin School, McGann urges historical awareness in literary criticism, especially a knowledge of publication facts. "Urn"'s first appearance in *The Annals of the Fine Arts* validates the study of the original sources of the vase in the poem and leads to a concrete interpretation of the ode. "Autumn"'s publication in the 1820 volume indicates Keats's unpolitical intentions in the poem and suggests the interpretation that the world of art is more powerful than the forces of science or politics.

Ober, William B. "Drowsed With the Fume of Poppies: Opium and John Keats." In *Boswell's Clap and Other Essays: Medical Analyses of Literary Men's Afflictions*. Carbondale: Southern Illinois University Press, 1979, pp. 118-136.

A physician traces Keats's on-and-off involvement with opium throughout his life and examines "Nightingale" in detail as a response to an opium experience. The trance-like state, the depersonalization, the obtunded sensory perceptions and mental processes, the hallucination, the spatial distortion, the solipsism and narcissism, and the final disorientation are characteristic of drugged states.

Patterson, Annabel M. "'How to load and...bend': Syntax and Interpretation in Keats's 'To Autumn,'" *PMLA,* Vol. 94, No. 3 (May 1979): 449-458.

Criticizes the contradictory syntactical analyses of "Autumn" done by Freeman and Hartman, claiming that they found semantic structures to reflect their preconceived interpretations of the poem. Gives a syntactically-supported interpretation of "Autumn" as a "betrayed georgic": man cannot depend for nurture upon nature, which is carelessly indifferent to his needs.

Sharp, Ronald A. *Keats, Skepticism, and the Religion of Beauty.* Athens: University of Georgia Press, 1979, pp. 58-64; 151-157.

This book seeks to establish that Keats's toughmindedness and tender-heartedness were not in conflict. Keats was a religious skeptic who developed a system of consolation for life's woes based on aestheticism. For Keats, however, beauty did not have a transcendent power; rather, it served the purely human end of making life worth living. In "Melancholy" Keats affirms an earthly religion of the beauty of melancholy, which affirms life's value without ignoring its troubles. In "Urn" Keats points out the function of art to supply a sense of beauty among the pains of existence, not beyond them.

----------. "'A Recourse Somewhat Human': Keats's Religion of Beauty." *Kenyon Review,* NS Vol. 1, No. 3 (summer 1979): 22-49.

Argues that Keats developed a humanistic religious view based on man's need to bear his earthly sorrows. Emphasizes the religious elements of "Melancholy," which suggests that the beauty of melancholy gives it a religious consolatory significance. Also asserts the holiness of the last two lines of "Urn," which offer beauty and truth as ways of coping with life's ills.

Woodman, Ross G. "Milton's Urania and Her Romantic Descendents." *University of Toronto Quarterly*, Vol. 48, No. 3 (spring 1979): 189-208.

> Establishes parallels between Keats's Queen-Moon in "Nightingale" and Milton's Urania of *Paradise Lost*. The Queen-Moon is superior to the nightingale in Keats's poem just as the vision of Urania is superior to that of the unregenerate "Pegasean wing" (*PL*, VII, 18-21).

1980

Barry, Peter. "The Enactment Fallacy." *Essays in Criticism*, Vol. 30, No. 2 (April 1980): 95-104.

> Cites as a fallacy the concept that in a good poem most elements of sound relate directly to meaning. Uses "Autumn" as an example and contradicts Leavis' contention in *Revaluation* that "keep/Steady in ll. 19-20 enacts formally the balancing movement of the gleaner.

Canfield, J. Douglas. "Faulkner's Grecian Urn and Ike McCaslin's Empty Legacies." *Arizona Quarterly*, Vol. 36, No. 4 (winter 1980): 359-384.

> Analyzes the importance of "Urn" in "Go Down, Moses" and other Faulkner works. Argues that urns for Faulkner represent the emptiness and impossibility of the dream of permanence and transcendence. Faulkner uses Keats's poetry as an expression of "the language of desire."

LaCassagnère, Christian. "The 'Ode to a Nightingale' and Keats's Tragic Myth." *Durham University Journal*, Vol. 72, No. 2 (June 1980): 169-175.

> Finds a tripartite attempt in "Nightingale" to attain an ecstatic "fellowship with essence." The speaker seeks to merge with the bird, which has already merged with the forest. Death (unconsciousness) dissolves the ecstasy, leaving the speaker isolated. "Autumn" plays out the same pattern, but embraces death at the end as an experience of beauty.

Manning, Peter J. "Keats's and Wordsworth's Nightingale." *English Language Notes*, Vol. 17, No. 3 (March 1980): 189-192.

> Shows the significance of Wordsworth's "O Nightingale! thou surely art" for Keats's "Nightingale."

Mellor, Anne K. "Keats and the Vale of Soul-Making." In *English Romantic Irony*. Cambridge: Harvard University Press, 1980, pp. 77-108.

> Finds Friedrich von Schlegel's romantic irony in Keats's concept of soul-making, which finds value in accepting both life's pains and its pleasures, its realism and idealism. The odes serve as "almost perfect examples of romantic irony." In "Psyche," naive pastoralism is replaced by self-conscious sentimentality. In "Nightingale," the desire for imaginative flight is counterbalanced by a realization of life's harsh realities. In "Urn," the deathless realm of art plays against unavoidable human pain and mortality. "Melancholy" asserts the value of the consciousness of loss itself. And "Autumn" arrives at a celebration of the process of experiencing life in all its aspects, both fruitful and dying.

Sato, Toshihiko. "Keats's 'Ode on a Grecian Urn.'" *Explicator*, Vol. 38, No. 3 (spring 1980): 2-4.

> Accounts for the gap between stanzas IV and V of "Urn" by arguing that in that space the speaker transcends the conventional maxim *"ars longa, vita brevis."* The ode does not merely express that idea; it triumphs over it through the consoling power of beauty.

Stempel, Daniel. "Disappearing into the Text: Dithyramb and Nome in Keats's Odes." *Hawaii Review*, 10 (spring/fall 1980): 167-172.

> Associates "Nightingale" with a dithyramb (a hymn to Dionysius characterized by music, Will, and time) and "Urn" with a nome (a hymn to Apollo characterized by sculpture, dream, and eternity).

Teunissen, John J., and Evelyn J. Hinz. "'Ode on a Grecian Urn': Keats's 'Laocoön.'" *English Studies in Canada*, Vol. 6, No. 2 (summer 1980): 176-201.

> Argues that "Urn," like Lessing's *Lacoön*, demonstrates the differing objectives of the poetic and the plastic arts. Keats ironically points up the limitations of the urn: unlike poetry, it cannot criticize its subject, relate a narrative, or present more than one point of view.

Vendler, Helen. "Stevens and Keats' 'To Autumn.'" In *Wallace Stevens: A*

Celebration. Ed. Frank Doggett and Robert Buttel. Princeton: Princeton University Press, 1980, pp. 171-195.

Demonstrates the influence of "Autumn" throughout the poetry of Wallace Stevens. Traces Stevens' development of "Autumn"'s presentational qualities into a more modern form.

Yost, George. "Keats's Poignancy and the Fine Excess." *South Atlantic Bulletin,* Vol. 45, No. 4 (November 1980): 15-22.

In the process of demonstrating "Isabella"'s joining of poignancy and delicacy with "a fine excess," this points out the delicacy in "Psyche" and poignancy in "Nightingale," "Urn," "Melancholy," and "Autumn."

AUTHOR INDEX

SUBJECT INDEX